LEARNING TOGETHER

*How to Foster Creativity,
Self-Fulfillment, and
Social Awareness in
Today's Students and Teachers*

by
Elizabeth Monroe Drews

PRENTICE-HALL, INC.
ENGLEWOOD CLIFFS, NEW JERSEY

D1218451

To my students

LEARNING TOGETHER: How to Foster Creativity,
Self-Fulfillment, and Social Awareness in Today's Students and Teachers
by Elizabeth Monroe Drews

ISBN: 0-13-527036-7
Library of Congress Catalog Card Number: 70-172679

Printed in the United States of America *T*

Prentice-Hall International, Inc., London
Prentice-Hall of Australia, Pty. Ltd., North Sydney
Prentice-Hall of Canada, Ltd., Toronto
Prentice-Hall of India Private Ltd., New Delhi
Prentice-Hall of Japan, Inc., Tokyo

Table of Contents

Foreword

This book, in a sense, is a personal statement to my fellow teachers and fellow students. It comes out of studying, teaching, and writing about learning and education from the Depression of the thirties to that of the early seventies. These are my reflections on what I have experienced—projected, I hope, on the plane of a larger understanding.

This is not a textbook, but a book for the general reader. The few footnotes serve only to indicate the source in case you may want to explore further. The bibliography may be used in the same way. Of course, no one, myself included, can possibly read every printed source. This is particularly true of a topic as broad as learning, which ideally comprises all human activities. For the purpose of learning is the same as that of life itself: It is to help both teacher and student become more fully human.

When friends ask me how long I spent on the book, I could say two years or ten. But more literally, I have spent my entire life on it. Ever since the age of eleven I have thought about teaching, as well as reading and learning. You could call these my addictions. In this book, therefore, I am offering both the fruit of my experience and the philosophy which it has produced. Learning together is not only the intimate personal relationship which Buber emphasizes between child and teacher, between comrades, friends and lovers, but also the relationship of each and every one of us to the universe—our reaching toward the universal mind, our glimpses of cosmic consciousness, those flashes of insight when we are most truly in tune and can most vividly sense the altogetherness of everything. As the world enters upon a new age, so too does education. It is becoming, it must embrace, the whole of life. If things are in the saddle and ride mankind—as Emerson warned us more than a century ago, and as millions are feeling today—our lives do not have to be like that. We can get out from under, move away, take a new look, start again.

All of us now can choose for ourselves how we want to learn—an opportunity people have never had before. Prior to the mid-nineteenth century, most human beings received most of their education from their experience of life. Formal instruction, literacy, access to books and to such schools as existed, were restricted to a few. Nowadays, in what are called the developed countries, attendance in school for a prescribed number of years is required of all children. But there has been increasing criticism in recent years of what Paul Goodman has labeled "compulsory mis-education." Many of us feel that the most meaningful portion of our education is what we acquire for ourselves through our own perceptions and interests, whether inside or outside of formal institutions and structures. Since the purpose in education is to become more fully human, any school (even the best) can be only a partial contributor to this goal. We learn this best in our relationships with others and at any time of day and in all seasons.

In the broadest sense I am indebted to everyone whose life has touched mine—to my family, my neighbors, my friends, and the hundreds of people I have met and responded to as I have traveled. Even conventions become bearable if I meet someone who wants to share ideas. Many of my best teachers have been much younger than I and these experiences have convinced me that we learn best about the young by learning with them and from them, not by standing back and taking notes. We also learn best when we "hang loose" and stay out of the straitjackets of preconception and *a priori* theory. Beyond all these debts to direct experiencing is what I owe to the books I read and the people who write them. A major part of my sustenance is provided by the printed word. Agreeing with Thoreau that "books must be read as deliberately and reservedly as they were written," I can understand why Alexander carried the *Iliad* in a precious casket on his expeditions and Whitman carried Emerson's essays to work each day in his lunch pail. I have dined royally on peanut butter sandwiches with Abraham Maslow as well as with Emerson and Thoreau.

It is my firm conviction that each of us controls his own life; and if you or I let someone take over and make us into talking puppets, it is our decision to give up the ghost. And if we agree with Tillich that "we are never so human as at the moment of decision," then we must extend our humanness to being responsible. If I chose to accept the humanistic psychologists as my mentors (when the pressure from the university psychology departments was to embrace behaviorism or Freudianism), then it is I, not those departments, who must be accountable for my view of human nature and the learning process. I am what I know, not what I was taught. If one or two books, such as Maslow's *Motivation and Personality* and Fromm's *Art of Loving,* could crowd out the influence of dozens of assigned texts, then I must recognize the power of people and ideas to convert and the capacity that each of us has for self-direction. As Thoreau says, we can literally date "a new era in [our lives] from the reading of a book!"

My explorations and experiences with creativity, self-realization and social sensitivity were always guided by the very people I studied under and studied with. These were often one and the same—my mentors, my co-workers, and my students. And none was hesitant about setting me straight when I was misguided or out-of-phase with reality.

Among my early teachers I remember with still vibrant enthusiasm, Laura Judy in the eighth grade, Leo Goodman in Oregon City High School, Elizabeth Montgomery and Maude Kerns at the University of Oregon, Irving Anderson at the University of Michigan, and many, many others. Among friends and co-workers I owe an untold amount to Annemarie and George Roeper at the Roeper City and Country School (who enlarged my understanding of child development); to Richard Schiefelbusch, Director of the Child Research Bureau at the University of Kansas (who helped to clarify my point of view by his skill in dialectics); to Douglas Knowlton, a superb filmmaker, and Arthur Hitchcock (then Executive Director of the APGA), who believed in what I was doing, for helping to make the *Being and Becoming* film series possible; to Arlis Thornblade Stewart, Robert Trezise, Charlotte Whitney, and many others whose devotion and imagination helped to create the *Four Worlds Textbook;* to Forrest Averill, Lansing Superintendent of Schools, whose integrity and good will made working in the schools a pleasure; to Mike Grost, Sue Montgomery, and Fariyal Sheriff and countless other young friends and co-workers who not only expanded my mind but also warmed my heart; to my brother, Bill Monroe, and his friend, Roger Bishop, for that delightful—and all too brief—interlude, Fernwood, and Dorris Lee who encouraged us; to my dozens—even hundreds—of wonderful students in Lansing and Portland and points in between and beyond; to my daughter, Karen, for her wisdom and tolerance; to Leslie Lipson who helped me see the project "steadily and see it whole"; to Gladys Carr my editor, who understood what I was trying to say long before I mastered the language in which I finally said it.*

*All of these and many others will be found in various places in the book, but in relating actual events I have often concealed identities by using fictitious names.

LEARNING
TOGETHER

1 • Introduction

In one of the myths of ancient Greece, the city of Thebes was terrorized by the Sphinx. This monster asked all passersby a riddle, and killed them when they failed to answer it correctly. There were many who died until one day Oedipus solved the riddle, whereupon the Sphinx destroyed itself. Using a creative intelligence, Oedipus saved his own life and set others free.

This is a book basically about creativity, the most distinctively human of all our attributes. Creativity is the union of independence, spontaneity, and originality. In different forms and varying degrees, it is present in each and every person and reveals itself in the special style that is our own. All of us have potentialities extending far beyond what we have realized and including many of which we are totally unaware. In fact, we go through life using only a fraction of the abilities we possess. Much of the frustration, the unhappiness, the alienation of our contemporary culture arises because so few of our latent capacities find adequate expression.

In our midst there are also some highly creative persons who are endowed with exceptional gifts. The rarest of all are those whom we call geniuses. We never know how or where these will develop. In fact, in any one of us there may well be a genius trying to emerge.

Some years ago, when I was Director of Psychological Services in a Midwestern city of medium size, I studied children in the public schools and tried to understand more about their capacities. Among them I found in every one of the twelve age groups (of two thousand each) at least ten youngsters with I.Q.s approaching 180. Most of these were also outstanding in the various ways we had developed at that time of identifying creativity—in spheres which ranged beyond the cognitive to the aesthetic and the social. And there was also one clear genius whose talents exceeded all known scales of measurement. My point is simply this: If in that single city there were 120 children of truly exceptional qualities, similarly gifted individuals are to be found in every other community, urban or rural, large or small. The problem, then, is how to liberate and develop their talents, along with the intellectual abilities of everyone else, for individual and social betterment.

At present, however, most creative potentialities of most people are not developed, but stifled. This is due partly to a failure to recognize individual creativity where it exists and partly to the constraints of a social system which is not designed to encourage the spontaneous or welcome the original. We were born, as Wordsworth said, "trailing clouds of glory"; but these have been swept away by socialization and education, as if they were untidy cobwebs rather than the sensitive membranes from which growth might proceed.

Our children are taught to don masks before they recognize their own faces. They are made to put their tender, pliable forms into prefabricated shells—the cultural roles prescribed for age, sex, and class. All too soon the open faces and fluid selves are disfigured as were the bound feet of the women of Manchu China. They are crushed to meet a social expectancy. Those who fail to escape the constraints of masks and sheaths can look only ahead, not up or down, right or left.

But for all—at any time in life—there can be an unmasking. The sheaths can fall away. The pallid, sun-starved forms can be set free. The hard "cake of custom," that shell which confines and constricts us, can be pried open. We can be reborn into the world. In this new state, we will be vulnerable, defenseless, naked, but we will be free. Thus we can open our arms to others without restraint. We can become brother or sister to all humanity.

In this book, I shall raise several questions which touch on this general theme and shall try to suggest some answers. What can we do to develop our creative gifts and use them for the common good? How can each of us continue to grow individually and, at the same time, socially—in a constructive community with our fellow beings? What is there in our present thought patterns and practices and institutions which dams our energies and diverts them so often along harmful directions? How can education be humanized so that learning becomes a joyous experience in which the student eagerly wants to participate? What has been happening in America to lead so many people to question the values of the established system and the wisdom of its controlling authorities? How can we find our way to higher values than those we generally practise?

In the course of discussing these questions, I shall tell about some students whom I have known, of how they felt and thought; about the family patterns of the 1950's and 60's, and especially the role of the mothers; of the orthodox school system and the types of teachers who staff it; and of the protests which the young have expressed in recent years— whether loud, soft, or silent, violent or peaceful, visionary or concrete, down-to-earth or up-in-the-clouds.

Plato described the lot of his fellow humans as similar to that of prisoners in a cave watching on a wall the shadows of objects behind them whose true shapes and colors they could not see. Education he conceived to be, as the word signifies, a "leading out" towards the light where truth might be found. But the process, he warned, can be painful because we are not accustomed to see things as they really are. How can we help people leave the cave, and discover not only pain but the true community? How can they find their mentors and friends and lovers—how can they find joy? How can they find themselves? The East has given us an answer here, by as Lao-tse suggests "letting be."

II • The Case of Don Saxon

In America today a new pattern for youth is emerging—a new breed of child and perhaps of man. Parents are pleased, appalled, or waiting watchfully, depending upon their own values and the behavior of their own progeny. The most striking examples among this next generation will, unless the future is radically different from the past, have the most telling effects on society.

One blazing comet among today's youth is Don Saxon. Although (or because?) he was brilliant, he found himself in such revolt that he could not stay in orbit and follow the prescriptive education of the school. At age seventeen, he was a drop-out and "failure."

When I first knew Don well he was fourteen, blond, and softly handsome, with the good height and the square turn to his shoulders which only a decade or two ago would have been the almost certain mark of the high school athlete. But there the resemblance stopped. He was just a shade too slender; his eyes and mouth gave his face the wrong expression. Instead of open and hearty, he was gentle and troubled

—some would call him sullen. His hair curled below his ears, softly but undeniably, and touched his collar. There was no beard, but one suspected that this might be the case only because the beard was not yet ready to grace the face rather than that the boy would turn a razor against this extrusion.

With its aura of beat-hippie-artist, Don's physical appearance deflected the eye and the mind of almost any of his elders, and in certain adults called forth an impregnable barrier of prejudice and hostility. His true glory—running wild over all the earth and inhabiting books in particular—was his mind. He was gifted in the mold of a young Shelley. With his gentle yet full-bodied voice, he expressed—in the unvarnished and often abrasive argot of the 60's—thoughts not unlike those of naturalistic philosophers since the days of Socrates.

As his friend and psychologist I was quite overwhelmed by the range of his knowledge and the clarity of his thought, and using the technician-instrumental culture of the time, my Special Services department had labeled him as "having superior intelligence" and recorded his eighth-grade reading skills as better than those of many college graduates. But his teachers failed him, so that he did not graduate from high school with his class. This account is an appeal to a higher court, where hopefully the judge and jury will be more sensitively attuned to humanity as well as to the current culture.

Don was the youngest child of a large, chaotic, fatherless, Roman Catholic family. He was born in Kentucky, but moved to the Midwest with his family when he was two. At this time his parents were permanently separated, leaving the mother alone with four girls and three boys. Don's exceptional memory reaches back to his days in Kentucky when "we used to go up and down the railroad tracks and collect iron for a penny a pound and bones for two cents a pound. You made maybe twenty-five cents a day—but I guess that's all we had to do." Since then his family has remained in Lansing, Michigan, although one could not say that they have become settled. As a ninth-grader, Don casually remarked, "I think I've lived in about twelve different houses in this town."

When Don described his family, they emerged as bizarre as J. D. Salinger's Glass family. His brothers and sisters range from ages seventeen to thirty, but "Nobody in my family is married. I wish they would get married so I could go over to their houses and eat." His observations led him to report, "My brothers aren't superior, but my sisters are, as a rule, pretty intelligent." He described them as follows:

> Recently my sister, 27 years old, had what is popularly known as a nervous breakdown and spent some time in a California state hospital. The others? One is a nun, another is considered insane, the other one likes to think, but is so politically oriented she can't think. That's the trouble with our family; we go off—we're zealots.

Don described his mother as "a character" and "nurturant." Apparently she is an intelligent and whimsical woman who has fleeting interests in the arts, is always reading and has a supportive but nonrestrictive relationship with him. When asked what values or aspirations his mother had encouraged, Don somewhat sardonically replied, "Grow up, learn something, get rich, and support me."

Don has always enjoyed an extraordinary amount of personal freedom. As a young child he "used to run out and play in the traffic; that was my game. The only object was to run across the street as many times as you could before the next car. I was hit by a car; it really wasn't too intelligent." He occasionally regrets his lack of paternal guidance and said, "I never had a father to restrain me, so I would just run amuck." As a ninth-grader he flirted with the dangerous and illegal—minor shoplifting, moving automobiles, and other delinquent offenses. During the tenth grade, however, he referred himself to the Guidance Clinic, and seemed to find some support and solace. That year, as he reported, he felt he was developing a "practical conscience."

Because Don's family moved so often within the city, he

changed schools frequently. Aware of his superiority from
the beginning, he did not feel that such shifts impaired his
intellectual development.

> The first grade, we had a spelling bee. Oh, I was great! Oh, I mean
> I was astounding! I was taking on fourth-graders and whomping
> them into the ground. Only finally I got stuck on "friend."
> "Friend' in the first grade. What the heck! I could spell hippo-
> potamus when I was four—but now I can't.

Don was reading, in fact, before he began school: "I wasn't
reading Plato and any of that stuff, but prayer books, the
Bible, and stuff. And I was reading 'General Electric' on the
refrigerator."

HOW DON FAILED—THE SCHOOL'S CASE

The records in our Lansing special services office showed
that Don had attended at least four elementary schools in the
city, and at the time he began speaking for himself, had
already spent two years in East Junior High School. Notes in
his file were scattered; often, they appeared to have been
made on the back of an envelope while one of the psychologists stood outside the principal's office or used the nurse's
telephone.

The information in Don's psychological file begins when
he was in the first grade. At this time his perplexed teacher
had reported that he seemed to be able to read everything in
the room; she, therefore, made out a referral to request that a
psychologist look into so abnormal a situation. A later telephone conversation, however, jotted in pencil on the margin
of this referral, indicated that the school no longer wanted a
psychological study. It seemed that, as a result of conferring
with each other, the first-grade teachers had decided that
Don could not have learned to read the "right" way, and that
he should therefore learn again by starting out with the rest
of the class in the pre-primers.

Evidently Don did learn to read again without suffering

too much personal torment or causing unnecessary anguish to his young classmates and his teacher. But, by the third grade he had moved to another school where he met a "professional" teacher, Miss Pfuffel, who was anguish, concern, and stern duty personified. She saw herself as the guardian of children —from their environment, from each other, and from themselves, and she frequently called a psychologist or the secretary in Special Services to share her wisdom. Don fascinated and tormented her. "It wasn't what he said, but how he looked at me—as if he were some superior being, a Supreme Court judge, or an ancient prophet, instead of a blond little boy."

Her observations, however, were kept well within the usual boundaries, and her reports rarely reflected her interest in spiritualism and migration of souls—which she had confessed to a psychologist in an unguarded moment. Instead, notes from her frequent calls indicated that

> Donnie obviously comes from the wrong kind of family, and I
> will try not to expect too much from him. His mother does not
> come to PTA, and no one answers the phone at their home during
> the day. She probably isn't interested in her son's work. He lives
> on the southeast edge of our district in one of the old row houses
> where the population, including the Mexican migrants, comes and
> goes.

Miss Pfuffel read the school's records (the CA-39) on Don carefully and talked to his first-grade teacher at the primary grade teachers' orientation meeting just after Labor Day. She found that he could apparently read when he entered school, but that this was dismissed as "some kind of memory feat" and thus Don was taught to read like everyone else. His first-grade teacher reported that she had been right in her judgment about his reading, for he read "Dick and Jane" slowly and haltingly just like all the other beginners. When he read so rapidly out of the newspaper, it was really "just a clever trick."

The only consistent misdemeanor reported was that Don

brought "junk" and old dog-eared books to school. Whenever his "treasures" were taken away, he would sulk and refuse to do anything. As Miss Pfuffel commented,

> The "junk" was not too clean and the old books were gray with age and frayed at the corners. Probably mice and rats have been gnawing at them. There was a water-soaked and mildewed one about the pilgrims, *Pilgrim's Progress* or something. I asked Don if he'd like to report on that at Thanksgiving and he didn't answer at all, didn't even seem to hear me although I asked him twice.

Despite Miss Pfuffel's doubts she was professional and fair-minded about all of her children, including Don. By the end of the year she indicated that

> Don has surprised us. He is cleaner and he smells better than his neighbors from Detroit Street and he does read better than we thought an eight-year-old could. The librarian has had a hard time keeping him out of the books that are assigned to the upper grades and the school nurse said he gave her a very complete lecture on the physiology and bone structure of the body the other day.

(Miss Pfuffel's parenthetical remark to the psychologist was that "he probably knows a lot more about a lot of things than he should.")

She tried hard to keep him with his class and to make him a good group member. Often he seemed to resist, but never with any determined show of will or temper. As Miss Pfuffel reported it,

> I have tried to keep him with the class in reading, although by the second day he was in school last fall he informed me that he had read all of the third-grade reader, *Streets and Roads*. In fact, he has done fairly well in reading this year, but he does lose his place more often than he should. I think he looks out of the window during reading class, but I just never seem to be able to catch him at it.

"In arithmetic," she commented, "he can always get the right answers to story problems without writing them out." This added to Miss Pfuffel's worries:

> Sometimes I have to remind him several times that what counts is whether or not he puts his numbers down right, not whether he can work the problem in his head—after all, he might be cheating. He objects to doing the practice pages in multiplication and was almost impertinent one day when he told me that doing 75 problems all alike was a better job for a machine than for him. I simply told him that he, like everyone else, has to do all the work or he will have to spend another year in the third grade and he wouldn't like that, would he.

Miss Pfuffel continued to reminisce:

> Don sings and draws surprisingly well and just before Christmas he wrote a play in what he called "free verse." I told him that we had better stick to the play we had found in a book in the library and I pointed out he might have made his lines rhyme better. For some reason his eyes filled with tears and he didn't say another word. His family is a strange one and Donnie seems to be getting more sullen and stubborn as he gets older.

Although his marks were high, the fourth-grade reports on Don were almost uniformly negative in terms of attitude and behavior. According to his teacher, "Don mutters and he drags his feet; but he does his work and, although I often make him copy it over, he does it well." This teacher was only one year from retirement. As the psychologist saw it, her natural patience had long since frayed, leaving her nerves exposed and dangling. By accident or design, Don touched her at the quick far more often than other children until she responded in the only way she knew. "Clamping down," was what she said. "I simply made up my mind not to let him get away with anything."

The principal in this school, Mrs. Bergstrom, found herself part of a problem that finally erupted between teacher and boy. It seems Don had come to Mrs. Bergstrom, sobbing and disconsolate. His teacher had written at the top of his latest literary production, "a stupid paper," and had given him a failing mark on his original essay. The principal examined the smudged and crumpled sheaf of pages that might easily become a *cause célèbre*, their title being "I Want to Be a Beachcomber." The assignment had been to write an essay on a career choice.

Mrs. Bergstrom commented to Don's teacher: "Well, maybe that's what he wants to be when he grows up."

The latter countered with, "Oh, no, I know he wants to be an electronic engineer."

Then in desperation, the principal said: "Maybe he was just trying to be creative."

To this the teacher replied: "Well, when I *want* him to be creative, I'll tell him when he *can* be."

By fifth grade Don had moved again and had evidently decided, according to the reports, to do only "so much and no more." However, as a result of a "search for talent" testing program, he had been chosen, despite his occasional poor attitudes, to participate in a special-interest group for gifted children. Special Services administered the program, and I was particularly interested in helping the group of children known as "low-achieving gifted."

In Don's school the gifted group of nine boys and girls met in the library twice a week with a special teacher, Mrs. Jones, and Don quickly became the star. Mrs. Jones wrote simple poetry and shared it with the children. These were lower-class and lower-middle-class youngsters, most of whom had never been introduced to poetic efforts beyond the adman's jingles on TV. Mrs. Jones' report noted,

> Soon they were excited explorers in the realm of verse and Don became the Captain Cook of this new region. He read poetry and wrote not only more free verse but tried out the rhymed and stylized forms, using as models everything from the "Song of Solomon" and Elizabethan lyrics to the ballad forms used by his English ancestors in Kentucky.

> The excitement was contagious and one day in an overflow of
> enthusiasm, Dolores remarked that she understood poets had to
> get a license. Billy joined in quickly, saying that he too had heard
> it and that probably they got them in New York City. [Green-
> wich Village?] But Don with his superior wisdom about poetry
> and the world corrected them all: "I am sure they go to Washing-
> ton, D.C., for their licenses. You know in Washington there's a
> bureau for everything and I'm sure if you would check on it
> you'd find a Bureau of Poetry."

Mrs. Jones indicated that she had simply smiled and had
not interrupted the free flow of discovery dialogue until it
had run out on its own accord—at which time she told the
youngsters in a matter-of-fact tone the difference between
literal and figurative speech.

Between the fifth and sixth grades Don's family moved
again. But this time there was no surcease offered by an
interest group for gifted children, nor was there a librarian
who would allow browsing before and after school. Evidently
spurred by the activities the special-interest group had offered, Don brought a vast store of artifacts to school. The
principal, Miss DeHaan, reported that she saw nothing wrong
with this. After reading Mrs. Jones' report on his poetic
tendencies, she had decided that the boy needed such things
to look at, dream about, write about, and talk about. She
herself had tried writing verse when she was young and knew
that budding poets needed to be given a little leeway. As Miss
DeHaan recalled, Don had brought not only well-aged and
much-read books, but also an abalone shell that one of his
sisters had found for him in California, a bird's nest in which
a family of cardinals had resided outside his bedroom window that spring, and a dry cell battery—ready for any possible inventive turn of mind. Miss DeHaan was soon torn
between sympathy for the boy and her professional urge to
support his teacher.

Mr. Hewitt, Don's sixth-grade teacher, was new to the
classroom, straight out of the Army with the testy discipline
still in his voice. The children were lined up, marched in, and

seated in rows. The blackboards were washed clean and woe to any youngster who marred them with tic-tac-toe at recess. Each eraser sat in place as if numbered, paralleled by its companion chalk, preferably full-size and squeak-proof.

In this ordered world Don proved to be an instant irritant. It wasn't that he was openly defiant—as Miss DeHaan saw it—it was just that he had a style of living and walking and sitting that was as pliable and fluid as the Army style was rigid and fixed. Don's feet were in the aisle. He sat with his neck against the seat top rather than his hips neatly right-angled. Unpedigreed books were read at forbidden times. And there was always that dreadful mess with Don called "a collection" and which he proceeded to use to explain points to the class that Mr. Hewitt didn't want made. Finally, in true sergeant style, Mr. Hewitt exploded with an order to Don: "Take that junk home and never bring it back again!"

Miss DeHaan continued to reconstruct the story for the psychologist whom Mr. Hewitt had requested:

> Don was very sensitive as poets have always been. He took his treasures home, but he must have vowed revenge. On the fall term achievement tests this boy, who read the Bible in the King James version before he went to school, managed to test at dull normal in intelligence and to qualify for the remedial section as a result of his poor showing on the reading test.

Miss DeHaan tried (rather unsuccessfully) to disguise her admiration for the boy. She continued to weave together remembered incidents and comments from both Don and Mr. Hewitt. Not only did Don rebel in grand style, but his anger continued to smolder. He taught himself the Morse code and soon had instructed the entire class. Messages filled the air, but their origin was always out of the teacher's range of vision. Mr. Hewitt, evidently a true slow learner (but never so designated by *his* principal), failed to master the code.

The school records on Don became increasingly negative. At this time Mr. Hewitt had referred Don to Special Services as a candidate for special education, claiming that the enclosed test scores showed him to be dull normal. He asked that Don be considered for any available program: mentally retarded, emotionally disturbed, or Boys' Vocational School. However, when the school psychologist administered an adult Wechsler, Don was found "highly gifted." The college interne psychologist who went to the school was not as unbiased as Miss DeHaan. Frankly charmed by Don, he angrily said that the one in need of institutional care was Mr. Hewitt. The young man (then half-way through his university doctoral program) and the twelve-year-old became telephone friends for the rest of the year.

In junior high school, Don found nothing to interest him until the ninth grade. And perhaps, as adolescents often do, because he wanted to become a personality in his own right and to outgrow the look of a tow-headed choir boy, he became outspoken and sullen by turns. In eighth-grade English class he refused to learn the date of O. Henry's birth. When asked to select a special project, his choice of topic was a critical comparison of Freud and Ibsen, using their views on the nature of man as the dimension for evaluation. The teacher, a former remedial instructor, did not know who Ibsen was. In angry despair, Don exploded with such searing expletives that, even in second- and third-hand form, the message that raced through the teacher's room and the corridors nearly resulted in his expulsion. Fortunately he had made his major point in middle English, and the teacher had forgotten her Chaucer.

His grades were "Gentleman's C" or lower and his attitude was described almost equally as aggressive or withdrawn. "Does not do his school work" became an habitually recorded offense; his time was spent in other ways. Only occasionally could Don find someone to talk with about his reading, his music, and his poetry. In the eighth grade a young student teacher showed interest in him and they talked about books they were both reading. Don became her devoted disciple, to the point that she was warned by her supervisor "not to make friends with the students."

The ninth grade began as another year of borderline-failure. Only in Mrs. McDowell's social studies class, taught seminar-style for a selected group of the most able ninth graders, did he find a challenge. There, the teacher used Socratic questioning, a style which Don embraced as if to the manner born. Mrs. McDowell saw him as the super-star in a galaxy of stars. His oral vocabulary increased exponentially, and whenever a teacher dropped her defenses and asked a broadside question, he could make a good clean point with a cutting edge. Questions he asked of fellow students, of teachers and administrators, would have done credit to Socrates himself: *"Is that action for the good of man?" "What is the purpose of these acts?" "What is the nature of man?" "And what his relationship to the cosmos?"*

Again, attacks on Don in the teacher's room reverberated with, "Who does he think he is, anyhow?" "Poor White Trash, I'd say." "He has a sister who's in an institution, you know." "I predict he will never graduate from high school—such impertinence!!" "Always reading—doesn't he have a mind of his own?" "Mrs. McDowell lets her kids get away with murder." Only Mrs. McDowell and Don's counselor supported the boy in these informal kangaroo courts.

The daily war of nerves continued with the exception of that single hour of solace and joy when Mrs. McDowell talked of what she read and believed, and of how the world went around—and the students responded in kind. Mrs. McDowell saw Don coming to class with pockets bulging with paperbacks and heard him defend causes and opinions with a zealot's ardor. This was his world. She had told him that she was completing her doctorate, and Don resolved that he, too, would pursue higher learning.

The following summer, wanting to avoid the fates of his brothers and sisters, he decided to take his emotional life in hand and referred himself to the Child Guidance Clinic. That fall, when he entered senior high school, he made friends with a young school counselor. Together the two plotted for Don's entry to a small college on an early admission basis. There was one near Chicago that accepted gifted high school students, but the problem was money.

Don could not meet the rigid requirements or tolerate the mass instruction in the high school. Throughout the year the counselor made efforts to help him escape, and as Don saw it, "save himself." But despite Herculean efforts to move the outside world, Don could not bring himself to compromise, let alone cooperate. Gradually, his situation worsened.

His counselor was told that through the Greensleeves Folk Singers, Don had made friends with Hal Vener, a university literature major and the son of the Dean of Social Science at Midwest University. Whenever possible, he would go home with Hal, sit in the Vener living room, studying and reading. He consumed everything in sight including copies of *The Nation, New Republic, I. F. Stone's Weekly, The American Scholar, Daedalus, Atlantic, Harper's, Trans-action.* One day he heard Dr. Vener refer to social class, and suddenly Don thought he might do the term assignment for twelfth-grade social problems after all. He said that his class was discussing social status and that each student was supposed to write a paper on it, but that the only book suggested beyond the text was Vance Packard's *The Status Seekers.* What would Dean Vener suggest? The Dean pulled a copy of Max Weber's *The Theory of Social and Economic Organization* from his shelves and told Don this was the classic and no one should discuss social class without knowing what Weber had to say.

Don borrowed that book and a few others and literally buried himself for days while he read with fascination. He wrote a detailed and insightful critique of Weber, contending that such a universalistic theory could not be said to fit families like Don's and other old American rural families that had known more affluent times. Weber's was an Industrial Age theory and just did not fit those people who had never joined the age. However, Don did agree that Weber was right about "the social fiction"* and the bureaucratic game.

Don was proud of the paper—the best work he had ever done, truly scholarly, every annotation correct, the assumptions carefully stated. But his social studies teacher was the football coach who was having a busy season. When Don got up to give the preliminary report on his paper and mentioned Max Weber, the teacher bluntly said: "It all sounds Leftist to me. I never heard of him, but he must be a Communist." Don was so taken aback that he could not continue. For the first time in years he let his emotions show. Tears filled his eyes, his voice broke, and he slumped into his seat—defeated. The tragedy was that he did not bother to turn in the final draft of the paper and failed the course for which he had studied hundreds of hours.

Since this was his senior year and his grade-point average was in delicate balance, that final failure meant there were no more chances, no more appeals. He had received official warning from the principal's office that any grade below "D" during the senior year would mean that he could not graduate. Dispirited to the point of considering suicide, Don did not return to school the next week and contacted his counselor only by telephone. There was no reasoning with him— he was through.

---

*Ernest Becker uses this term in discussing the view of Weber, Veblen and others that people give credence to myths about society which the realities often contradict. *Beyond Alienation*, New York; Braziller, 1967, p. 127 ff.

III • How the School Failed — Don's Case

During the time that Don was in the ninth grade, teachers and counselors in the public schools helped to develop a new humanities program for gifted students with funds from a government grant which I had received. The plan was to give the students an opportunity to discuss such questions as: "Who am I? What is the world all about? How can I make a contribution?"

We developed an open-ended anthology, entitled *The Four Worlds*, which attempted to encompass some major aspects of nature and of human existence. These worlds were the natural, aesthetic, technological, and human. They presented to each student the great issues of the times, and could be reshaped as the student desired. In addition I produced ten half-hour style-of-life films, called the "Being and Becoming" series, designed to introduce the students to the daily lives and belief systems of artists and philosophers, scientists and public figures. In each of the four junior high schools, classes in this program were given to ninth graders.*

Don was enrolled at that time in Mrs. McDowell's class at East Junior High. On a number of occasions throughout the year he was observed in the classroom and his comments were captured on recordings made of discussions. Not surprisingly he was one of those students who eagerly came forward to explore theories of motivation, and creativity, as well as visions of the future with the psychologists from Special Services and the research personnel from the university. He and some of his friends asked if they could have a copy of the Rokeach "dogmatism" and "ethnocentrism" scales to study, because they planned to devise scales of their own. Having read Milton Rokeach's *The Open and Closed Mind,* they were generally interested in the literature on the authoritarian personality.

Don was excited about the readings and films, and made many suggestions for improving them. Due to the quality of his contributions and his unusually high test scores in aesthetic and theoretical values and in critical thinking, he was one of the 45 who were chosen for a series of depth interviews that I was conducting in my research studies of the Creative Intellectual Style. In the following pages, which are based on those interviews, Don does much of the talking.

Although he remembers himself as "basically uncooperative," Don did excel in school.

> All the time I got A's. Nothing happened until fifth grade, then I started thinking, "What good is it doing me—working so hard to get good grades when they don't even count?" so I stopped. Laid off until the ninth grade.

Later he indicated that he then intended to raise his grade-point average in order to gain admittance to college. How-

---

*This program is described in Chapter XXI. For the full report see Elizabeth Monroe Drews, *The Creative Intellectual Style in Gifted Adolescents, Being and Becoming: A Cosmic Approach to Counseling and Curriculum;* Vol. II (East Lansing: Michigan State University, College of Education, 1965).

ever, at no time was Don enthusiastic about joining the ranks of honor students. "What really gets me is those honor assemblies," he exclaimed. "All those stupid people. That, that really fractures me. There are people I know who can't even spell or read or write, and they have something like a 3.917."

Don read and thought seriously and at length about the ideas he encountered. His concern was with qualities of mind and character rather than specific information. By the end of the ninth grade his reading ventures would have done credit to the best of college students:

> I read Plato, Sophocles, Aristophanes, and Aristotle. I usually read about a series of four things. Right now I am reading *The Origin of Species,* the *Communist Manifesto, Utilitarianism* and something else. . . . We have a lot of books in the house. I read a Bertrand Russell book—as I read his things I began to see that you should respect truth above everything else—I was knocked out when someone stole the book. That man really speaks his mind.

Don's adventures of the mind extended beyond contemplation; he not only examined various issues but also spent a great deal of time developing logical arguments, either for or against a particular idea. "I've taken on a new interest in critical analysis," he once remarked. His critical eye relentlessly observed the social order and found little to praise. "Through the years, it has been my experience . . . that most people are not rational at all."

Don was sensitively aware of, and responsive to, ideas of many kinds:

> I once belonged to the Catholic Church. I went for reasons unknown, but mostly because of family commitments. I began to read things, see, and I began to see the picture a little better. I read something by Thomas Aquinas—something that's as biased as it can be—on the belief in God, and I read a lot of other things. I'm not an atheist; I'm more unitarian than anything else. I believe that I'm right and that they are probably wrong. But if they want to believe, that's all right with me. I don't go along with these guys who shout that they don't believe in God. People be-

> lieve in God because it answers a lot of unanswerable questions
> for them.
>
> I believe that God was something that people made up when they
> were too tired or too confused to find out what really happened.
> Now with Darwin it was different. He was a worker. He would go
> back, find, trace, and work to find out if he could get a logical
> basis for belief. But these people just, well, believe.

Although he disavowed all inclinations toward altruism,
Don felt there is much to be valued in many kinds of people.
For example: "A lot of people who are classified as insane
and retarded have a great capacity for feeling." He continued:

> There are obvious wrongs being done to minority groups. People
> don't have a right to kill other people or make jokes out of other
> people. I don't even want to talk about it. It's not a question of
> minority groups. It is a matter of wrongs being done to people.

Like most gifted adolescents, Don has a consuming interest
in education. In all of our contacts with him he talked
fluently about the content of education, the teachers, the
teaching process, and the grading system. From his observations he concluded that schools may be a poor way to get an
education. "The most meaningful thing I've heard is that
education may occur least often in the classroom . . . the
least valuable thing is formal education." He has even
thought about teaching children himself—in ways that he
"would have liked to have been taught."

On books:

> All parts of education should complement each other. Textbooks
> should be written well: Literature should go along with history;
> social science should be concerned with chemistry. Everything
> should go together. Most texts are stupidly written. History
> books should include more of the contemporary world. Science
> books should be revised every year—science is the most greatly
> changing field there is.

On teachers:

> We need a new crop. What we need is people who vibrate knowl-
> edge . . . teacher philosophers. People who create things! Capital
> E–Empathy; capital T–Truth; capital L–Love. The teachers
> should believe in something and vibrate this. They should be so
> damned interested in what they are teaching that it catches on.
> You can't be phony about it.
>
> The most important consideration is what we do with our minds.
> A mind can be beautiful. Socrates had a beautiful mind and so
> did Rousseau. I often feel much closer to them than to some
> teachers I have had. Those men were great, but they were hum-
> ble. And they were ready to die for their ideals. Socrates did.
> Now *they* were educators, but I wish teachers would understand
> that people aren't good educators just because they are postgrad-
> uates from Columbia–the ones who think they're God. I don't
> dig them. There's a quality in man, and I guess that quality is
> humility, and not enough teachers have it.
>
> Teachers should try to talk to kids in such a manner that the
> kid'll feel free to communicate. The most stupid thing is when
> teachers say, "If you don't understand something, come up and
> ask me." You don't tell someone to feel free. They either are or
> they aren't.

On grades:

> A lot of things are wrong with education–I'm going to blast you
> education people. You don't learn as much as you could by the
> present system. I'm so anti-grading that I can hardly talk about it.
> It classifies students–it doesn't make them feel as equal learners.
> It makes them feel as equal achievers to the stupid standards
> which don't indicate high levels of learning, only teacher satisfac-
> tion.
>
> The solution I believe requires a more intense study than is going
> on now–if we change the grading system it shouldn't be gradual
> because a lot of people are being hurt. A lot of people don't de-
> sire to please the teacher.
>
> In education you should compete with yourself. You should say,
> "I'm going to know 18,000 more things about this subject at the

end of the course than I do now." What about casting away all
standards and saying, "Here's a group of people—teach them."

Don tends to despair of human beings and their powers to
help themselves. He seems to see too much and see too
clearly. Great though his compassion is, it is generally reserved for individuals he knows and likes. At the end of the
ninth grade he commented, "People are so *glaaah*, I . . . I . . .
I can't even express my opinion of them. I just have no
affection for them at all." This extreme position was somewhat modified during the years I knew him, but he remained
an idealist who searched the philosophers for answers to the
perennial questions: "What is the good life? What is friendship?" Both, he thought, could be improved by "Empathy.
It's very complex. Euripides said, 'True happiness lies in the
enjoyment of one's self and the companionship of a few
select friends!' John Donne said, 'Friendships should be re-
ciprocal, or else bad imbalances occur.' " Don continued:

> The world that makes sense is the one you put together yourself.
> That's why Euripides and Thoreau can be your best friends. You
> have to make a place for them in your mind and you are glad to
> ask them in. All you need is a little imagination.

Don felt that "The great tragedy of our time is that people
don't get to do what they want to do." Earlier he had
observed, "When you're young you can't do anything because you have to lead a scheduled life. Only during July and
August can you lead your own life." He sees at least one
version of his ideal existence as a Thoreau-like withdrawal
from the demoralization of social institutions: "I'd like to go
up into Canada and live. Get myself a cabin back in the
nowheres, way out in the empties."

Forced as he was to stay and face it all, he tended to be
the silent antagonist and to resist rules and teachers' directions. Having mastered the fine art of passive resistance, he
had a beautiful rationale to support it:

> I think you can learn more (consume more) getting worse grades, because when you get better grades you just take in a little bit of everything rather than delve into the most pertinent points.

In his early interviews, there were times when this sense of independence reached heights of defiance.

> It has been my experience that people weren't worth the time of day. They're greedy. You give them something good and they turn it into something evil. There's just one person you can rely on in this world and that is number one.

Later on, I found him somewhat more hopeful about the society that he still termed "decadent." He felt that youth, at least, might find a way. But the young must remain independent and apart from the adults who were already lost souls: "When I get to be President, I'm going down to the high schools. That's where I'm going to get ideas. Young people are a lot more creative, and they think a lot more than these old factory workers. That's what I'll do." And yet he would probably not turn to the teen cult to seek direction:

> I don't have the gang spirit . . . [it's] so nauseating. There's nothing complex about it. It's all the same—no difference between any of them. I can't see it.

The larger society remains a negative force, protecting itself and never freeing the individual:

> It's not out to do any good, if you ask me. Ever since the beginning of earth, societies have come and gone. They started out bad and they ended up worse. Other societies have taken over and continued oppression. That's the way it happens. A society has never really helped anything; it's always been an individual.

In almost all respects, Don was the intuitive artist—endlessly self-aware and perpetually floundering as he tried to find direction, yet with the observer's eye out for beauty of phrase or accuracy of characterization. He identified with Holden Caulfield in *The Catcher in the Rye*–a book which he saw as a work of art:

> He reminds me a lot of me. The last page, that's what does it. He tells me what street I'm supposed to go to and he says, "I'll show you after I get out of here." That's really a great ending–that really smashed me.

Don had also carefully considered and defined beauty:

> Anything that is natural is beautiful, and anything that is unnatural is ugly. This doesn't exclude man-made things; if things are made with some kind of idea in mind, then they become natural. The thing that really knocks me out are things that have stayed the same for years–like rock formations. The Grand Canyon would knock me out if it weren't cluttered with beer cans. Just one beer can spoils it all!

He tended to follow his intuitions and to be caught by passions. Although he had written some poetry, he was not really won over to the art form until the summer before he entered senior high school: "I started to read Keats and I have been reading that guy like crazy this summer. I was telling myself I was going to learn to type and to learn German, but all I've been doing is reading."

Don feels that beauty is a great and often unmet need:

> People respond to beauty nowadays a lot more because they have to contend with so many ugly things like war, politics, strikes, riots, like that. They freshen when they see something that isn't ugly, but then they go back to their homes and forget all about the beauty they've seen. That's the way people are.

And he reflected on some of the larger issues:

> Painting, poetry, music–they all come from the same source. I love them all, but I don't like someone to interfere. Teachers can break the spell and there is no art without magic. They can almost make you hate poetry because they don't understand it. It can get so lifeless that you feel you'll have a death on your hands

any minute. Instead of trying to understand, they want to dissect it or smooth it out and make it rhyme. Her friends couldn't even leave Emily Dickinson's poems alone. But true artists just seem to know what is right. They have to break rules. They play it by ear and they play it by eye. If I ever prayed, I'd ask for my ear to never, never turn to tin.

Teachers can't teach you to see and hear, but they can encourage you to look. I'll always look or listen to something that someone loves. There is always a reason. Loving isn't ever automatic, but teaching often is.

Again and again, Don would refer to what he would do "when I am President." But almost in the next breath he seemed to remember the perfidy of human beings and that they were not worth the effort: "I wouldn't want to do this to myself. I'm content to be a decadent American—it's a crummy thing to say. People I try to help resent me to such an extent that I just don't try anymore." Such thoughts brought him at times to visions of mass destruction followed by suicide: "It would be a spectacular." In his first interview, he spoke of a daydream—of waiting for a crowd of people to appear as he stood on a ledge, armed with six grenades that he had stolen from an armory. "Then I would just dive on the pile, you know." Such comments were much more frequent in our early encounters with him, before his self-referral to the guidance clinic and the arduous task of trying to get himself in hand.

Although his despair was intense and quite evident in all of our contacts with him, it was often short-lived. His capacity for joy, his desire for omnipotence, and his need to use his superabundant resources, would return him to visions of self-fulfillment and a sense of destiny:

I like to think that everything I do . . . contributes to the world, to the cultural scene. . . . All men are brothers. We had better know that and know it well before it's too late. As John Donne said, "No man is an island, entire of itself; every man is a piece of the continent, a part of the main; if a clod be washed away by the sea, Europe is the less, as well as if a promontory were, as well as if a manor of thy friend's or of thine own were; any man's death diminishes me, because I am involved in mankind; and therefore never send to know for whom the bell tolls; it tolls for thee."

There is always a terrible dilemma. It's important to do what you want to do. Things are usually worthless unless they are made by someone who cares. An artist has to love his work, a musician has to be a captive of his music, a teacher should be transported by joy. That's what caring is all about—joy. One person can't change the world, and no one group of people can change the world, but they can make a difference. They can change their environment to fit their own specifications.

His modesty was not pronounced. In the first interview he proclaimed, "Ever since I was a young lad, I had this superiority complex." A year later he continued to talk about the fact that he liked to be different. He admired people who have purpose and who "stand by their convictions."

His interests seemed to know no bounds. Asked what he wanted to do with his life, he replied:

It's a mixture of umpteen desires. I would like to write; I would like to be a folk singer; I would like to be a Lit teacher; I would like to be a psychologist; I would like to be a psycho-analyst; I would like to be a wrestling coach; I would like to be a farmer; I would like to be a postman. No, I don't want to do everything. I don't want to work in a factory.

IV • Achievement for What?

America is said to be proud of her machines that think—and afraid of her men and women who do. Hearing this remark, a very gifted student who customarily made low grades, observed, "Of course, thinking is all right if you think like a machine and learn only what the school tells you to—no more, no less—and do the kind of work that is required by the system." In such an atmosphere, this student said, the creativity of genius or of distinctive moral leadership probably would not fare well.

If what this girl reported was true, one would expect that in the America of the late twentieth century the Miltons would be more apt to be mute and inglorious than to become foreign secretaries. Thus the girl who early shows the disposition to think for herself, the boy who devises a new kind of music, the child who comments on the moral fiber of the society may be in trouble almost immediately. They are not apt to achieve in the ways that society prescribes (or is the word proscribes?) for the young, that is, to do well in school or to be a success in the Establishment. Janice failed a test in

tenth-grade biology when she defined the subject by saying:
"Biology is like beauty; it needs no definition." The Beatles
were indifferent students, and definitely low achievers by the
traditional standards of musicianship, until they developed a
form of music which has been judged "unique and memor-
able."

Yet, even though there are prescriptions for the most
approved patterns of success, America has remained in some
ways a pluralistic society. The very force of the youth revolution since 1964 speaks to the fact that freedom to veer to
the right or to the left was allowed—at least up to a point.
The Bill of Rights was written by a group of men who felt
the American Constitution should contain an affirmation of
the basic rights of all individuals (minorities included) in
relation to the power of the government and whatever majority or minority supports it.

As we shall see, at least three channels of achievement have
been available to the gifted young, and only in one of these
does the flow occasionally have to escape underground to
maintain its force. It is by the standards of these routes that
success in life must be judged.

Of course nothing is quite this simple. Primitive men
were generally limited to achievement as hunters and fishers
and to putting their souls in the hands of the local witch-
doctor. But as civilization became diversified and options
increased, individuals could choose vastly different courses.

After World War II and particularly after the Russians
launched their first Sputnik in 1957, there occurred what
John Gardner called, "A Great Hunt for Educated Talent."
Along with this came efforts to teach more and newer subject
matter, to teach it better, and to delve into the whole
problem of achievement and motivation. Some members of
the public and certain politicians asked repeatedly: "Why are
we behind Russia?" "Why aren't our schools turning out
great scientists?" "Why don't American school children work
as hard as students in Russia and China?"

The search for such understandings moved over a broad

spectrum during the decades of the 50's and 60's. During that time I was doing research on intellectual giftedness and creative potential, asking about the meaning of achievement and motivation and why some young people did well in school and others, equally able, did not.* There were all kinds of "instant answers" to such questions. American children, some critics said, had been raised and educated in ways that were too loose and permissive. John Dewey and later Benjamin Spock were excoriated. McGuffey's readers were revisited. Homework was reinstated. And along with the continuing interest in Freud, sex came to be held as the explanation for everything.

Coming right to this point one day, I asked a class of superior high school students why girls received better grades than boys. The girls had the answer: "We're expected to do good in school, while the boys have to make good in life." In this straightforward way, two kinds of achievement were defined—school success and success in life. The former, I was told, was measured by grades and test scores, while the latter was just what everyone said it was: making money, having status, wielding power.

The teachers and the test makers defined and provided ratings for the former, or such was the impression I gained from reading the burgeoning research on school achievement. The talisman of this kind of success, more often than not, was school marks, and they proved to be rather reliable. It is

*I spent the first twenty years of my professional life working with and developing programs for those who had difficulty learning—children with reading problems, slow learners, and the emotionally disturbed. Both in my master's thesis and in my doctoral dissertation, I searched for the cause of reading disability and learning problems and the earliest programs I developed were designed to remedy these situations. Also, I studied how the classroom climate and personal interactions affected the self-concepts of children who found learning difficult. Along with these interests, I had an equally great desire (often unrequited) to know more about those children who were at the other end of the scale—the "more of" youngsters: Those who were creative and zestful rather than alienated and unhappy; those who found learning a joy rather than a hard grind. From 1959 through 1966, the U.S. Office of Education awarded me a series of grants, six in all, to study these creative and intellectually gifted young people.

true that inconsistencies were apparent when the grading process was examined closely. But a general truth emerged which was more important than the exceptions: Students who received high marks in one class normally received them in others. And those who were good high school students usually became good college students.

During this period the success-in-life gambit was an even more popular area of study. Sociologists developed rating scales to calibrate an individual's ascent or descent, terming these processes "upward mobility" and "downward mobility." The assumption of such calibrators seemed to be that "what is, is right" and "if it exists, measure it." A minority of social scientists from several disciplines raised their eyebrows and wrote *The Power Elite, The Affluent Society, The New Industrial State, The Technological Society, The Unprepared Society, The Accidental Century,* and *Post-Historic Man.** These concerned philosophers, as well as the statisticians of the *status quo*, seemed to recognize that a condition existed in America which was called success, and which, according to one's point of view, could be evaluated and measured, or described and criticized.

From reading the analyses of both calibrators and critics, I concluded that there was some overlap between being a good student and being a success in life. But more important than doing well in school was whether an individual had been graduated and from what school—The Old School Tie Syndrome. Some of the calibrators took note of the total number of years of education, and a few reverted to the pre-industrial revolution concept of the eliteness of one's family. The latter, in turn, was often based on length of residence in the United States and/or in the local community. Coming from an old family, especially if it were a wealthy one, gave one points at the outset.

More often than not these old families were WASP or the

*These books were written, respectively, oy: C. Wright Mills, John K. Galbraith (2), Jacques Ellul, Donald Michael, Michael Harrington, Roderick Seidenberg.

next best thing, northwestern European. Many of them were or had been landowners and some had been slave-holders.

Mass education and the triumph of rote learning are only a century old. Before the standard of school grades, and earlier than the criteria of inherited status or money earned, there had been other routes to success. These were by creative innovation—intellectual and/or spiritual, or thrust of power—political and/or economic. The first innovators to be recognized in popular history were generally social philosophers or saintly sages (Socrates, Gautama, or Jesus) or military conquerors and rulers (Alexander or Caesar). "Think right and act right" was the thesis of the former group; "might makes right," the maxim of the latter. In those days—in fact, throughout history prior to the nineteenth century—achievement in terms of mastering the abstractions in the copybooks was little valued. Literate societies, it is true, always had their armies of clerks, the studious and well-disciplined people who are strictly programmed to follow a routine. But such "scribes" were relegated to the same category as the Pharisees. They were hired to keep the accounts and record the deeds of the Pharoahs.

The philosopher, the saint, and the self-actualizing genius represent quite another manner of being than the political potentate or the conscientious clerk. Typically they follow separate routes to success and enter at different ports of arrival. But if the schools expect students to do their assignments rather than to think and create, and if their society expects them to be successful adults rather than creative and thoughtful, how is it possible for a sage or genius to emerge? Perhaps this is why Einstein and Tolstoy disliked school so intensely; why Jane Addams and Marie Curie, although they tolerated it, considered themselves self-taught in their major interests. All were motivated by concerns far afield from "getting good grades" or "becoming the president of the company."

How many of our young have capacities comparable to those of a Leo Tolstoy or a Marie Curie is not known, but their numbers, in my view, are far greater than is generally acknowledged. Unfortunately, few find ways to emerge, and only a few of those who do are recognized or encouraged. Until very recently a majority of gifted youth have rather resolutely kept their originality within acceptable bounds.

The kinds of achievement to which I have been referring—that of the philosopher or artist, of the power-monger, or the industrious clerk—do not apply only to earlier history. The equivalents of these three groups are present in each new class of students entering high school every year. This I found amply confirmed in the studies of gifted high school students which I began in the early 50's. Later when I was searching for terms to describe the groups, I asked some of the most gifted young people what kinds of students they commonly observed. Developing these ideas, my daughter and I selected names for the types, and also worked out descriptions for each. The types were called: Creative Intellectual, Studious, Social Leader.*

The Social Leaders among the able students appeared well adjusted in the most conventional definitions of the term. Outwardly they were adapted to the school and the society. They accepted the current definition of success. Some remained at a stage of materialistic self-interest, being avid for status and power and willing to use any means to achieve their ends. Those young people who chose the designation of Social Leader felt this characterization not only apt but also desirable.

*In 1959 I began my study with four categories, namely: Creative Intellectuals, Studious, Social Leaders, and Rebels; however, so few high school students were willing to identify themselves as Rebels at that time that no analysis could be made of the findings on this type. I commented briefly on the characteristics of the four types, including the Rebels in an essay published in 1963: "The Four Faces of Able Adolescents," *Saturday Review,* Vol. 46: (January, 1963), pp. 68-71, and provided the full data in a report written for the U.S. Office of Education: *The Creative Intellectual Style in Gifted Adolescents;* Motivation to Learn, Attitudes, Interests, and Values, Vol. I (East Lansing: Michigan State University, College of Education, 1964).

Most had moved ahead in their character development to the point where they had become reliable and responsible. This was the group who selected as a self description the type of young person I called Studious. While motivated by a desire to please others, particularly their parents and teachers, they also had a conscience. The third pattern which a considerable number of high school students selected as an appropriate self-definition was the one I called Creative Intellectual. These were students who had already taken the first arduous and little rewarded steps on the route toward becoming a "truth seeker."

Students, of course, are not pure types. In common with all individuals, they are clusters of tendencies among which some are dominant or characteristic. When asked, they can tell you who and what they are.

Some of the more gifted of the Studious drifted, perhaps unknowingly, into creative intellectual habits when given minimal encouragement. Very rarely, however, is anyone both Social Leader and Creative Intellectual. In most cases, the conformity which seeks achievement in the American tradition and the nonconformity of the Creative Intellectual were mutually exclusive qualities.

In the study of the new humanities program in which Don Saxon participated, we had not only allowed ninth graders to choose their own topics of research—but had encouraged them to become their best possible selves and to reflect on the larger issues as they read about the world. The year (1963-64) after the experiment had been completed we found that some 36 percent called themselves Creative Intellectuals. By contrast, in a study conducted in the same schools three years earlier (1960-61),* only about one-fifth of a group of college-bound tenth graders so described themselves.

In this earlier study of high school students (designed to find and study all gifted tenth, eleventh, and twelfth graders

*Elizabeth Monroe Drews, *The Creative Intellectual Style in Gifted Adolescents*, Vol. I, *op. cit.*

in the city) 60 percent chose Studious as their most appropriate self-description by contrast with the 20 percent who
chose the description of Social Leader or Creative Intellectual. There were approximately 400 students in this sample,
all with IQ's of 120 or above. In contrast to these more gifted
students, most adolescents (*i.e.*, those whose intellectual abilities tested in the average range) chose the social leader
description as best representing their attitudes, interests, and
values. For this sample we selected a random group of about
200 eleventh graders, one out of every five.

Of these three categories the Creative Intellectuals not
only tested higher in intelligence than any of the other types
of able adolescents, but also were better informed. Their
mean scores on achievement tests were higher than those of
the other two groups. Nevertheless the schools often designated them as low achievers, and it was a fact that they
received low grades in relation to their ability. They tested
high on creativity measures (*i.e.*, had scores similar to those
of successful artists, writers, and scientists) but were rated by
their teachers as less creative than their social leader classmates whose attitudes and interests resembled those of bank-
ers or undertakers.

This phenomenon of low ratings by their teachers has been
observed in many of the studies made of eminent and creative adults. Perhaps it can be best explained by the fact that
so many of these young people resist the usual school routines. They prefer to order their own days rather than to
move to the stimulus of the warning bell; they want to
choose what they are going to read and make up their own
minds about its meaning. As far as "success in life" is concerned, it seems fairly obvious that there are more individuals
in American society who receive recognition and approval for
holding important executive posts and making money—many
make very large amounts—than there are Creative Intellectuals who become renowned as scientists, artists, social revolutionaries, or saints.

In comparing kinds of Creative Intellectuals with one another scientists, of course, have received more recognition than artists. This has been true ever since Newton's genius blazed across the heavens of the West, opening them as a public playground for satellites and spaceships. Until that time this area had been the well-guarded premises of the Church and the storied residence of the venerable Jehovah. Not only do scientists receive more of society's accolades and higher salary checks, but studies of creativity have focused mainly on *male* scientists rather than on women.

As we have seen, when Creative Intellectuals as a group are compared with Social Leaders, the situation is quite different. For example far more people know the names of athletes (the stars of the gridiron and the diamond) than of Nobel prize winners. In the arts a Leonard Bernstein is a rarity, although during the 60's the young have managed to produce a rather substantial number of composers and/or performers —perhaps a sign of where their values lie. Among the Creative Intellectuals, social reformers and altruists are the least apt to be celebrated, the most often condemned.

Martin Luther King reputedly was spied on and was eventually assassinated, and Ralph Nader has escaped character assassination only by his impeccable habits. Both King and Nader have had great capacity to attract disciples. King's influence was worldwide and of almost Gandhi-esque proportions. And while in his early thirties Nader was already attracting large crowds as a speaker on college campuses. Perhaps as the adherents of what Rollo May calls the Myth of Caring* increase, or become more visible, there will be more tolerance of such humane views and greater recognition of their positive contributions to the human cause. But then, again, perhaps being a "social reformer" and a "success in society" are contradictions in terms. To achieve their kind of success, which means winning converts, reformers often have to wait until the generation that follows their own.

Similarly, society discredits or barely rewards many other

*Rollo May, *Love and Will* (New York: W. W. Norton, 1969), p. 306.

patterns of being and becoming. Although there may be less overt hostility toward them, most who earnestly search for truth and beauty are not readily accepted. The kind of innovation which affects what goes on inside our heads or which changes the way we see the world is suspect. Technological changes which result in faster cars and planes are another matter. These provide excitement and thrills at the visceral level; they speed up the process of buying and selling; and they make it possible for the pleasure spots of the world to be almost immediately accessible to the well-heeled.

Pleasure and success, expediency and opportunism—the values classically held to be at the bottom of the growth scale and still so considered by mental health experts, thoughtful theologians, and "third force" psychologists—have been thrust to the top of the American achievement ladder. Fun and games (the pleasure ethic), which are on the lowest rung of the Hindu hierarchy, have become, along with success, the ultimate aim as the admen play it. Thus the "highest" values for the businessman or the bureaucrat are hedonism and materialism. Eloise and Abelard are replaced by the high-priced call girl and her expense-account executive.

Academics are also infected by the virus that has sickened the society. Characteristically they have worked for the Pentagon not the ghetto poor; studied the elite, not the masses; the "affluent," not the "good society"; the "president of the company," not the "good person"; and power, not love. Only in the late 60's did groups of radical dissidents emerge in the professional associations and the universities.

Humanistic and existential philosophers elevate to the apex of their hierarchies the ideals of altruistic and empathic love, the quest for truth, and the search for beauty. But while Creative Intellectuals are habitually discounted in our society, the discount rate is the highest for those who follow the way of humanitarian-altruism. Those who lead their lives according to such values are dismissed as misfits, as we have seen, unless they somehow manage to bypass the many shoals in the Great Society. Only a very few in the humanitarian-altruistic realm—an Eleanor Roosevelt or a Mahatma Ghandi —receive honor and acclaim, and this usually late in their lives. Other Creative Intellectuals who are dedicated to the common good also encounter problems. After all their concerns are philosophical, complex, intuitive, in the head and heart.

Working in science, the Creative Intellectuals tend to be generalists—unacceptable in an age of specialists. They are ecologists and moralists who often lash out at an apathetic citizenry and a corrupt, or at least frighteningly careless, government. They want to look at man whole rather than to partition him and study the segments. And instead of merely studying how he behaves, they ask whether his behavior is good. Among the social philosophers there are many who also become angry prophets and self-appointed censors. In the mid-60's, Jules Henry wrote that probably over 50 percent of American scientific talent had been "put out to pasture on the rank grasses of death ... [these with] engineers and technicians constitute the well-fed, comfortably housed culture of death ... an elite of death."

Those who create in the arts also find the cult of absurdity rides high, as does the fashion of nihilism. Art is seldom used as a criticism of life or as a way to discover the greatness of the past, the best that was thought and said, in order to build a better future. The West tends not only to exile beauty, as Camus said, but also to derogate goodness. And, as noted earlier, altruistic love fares even worse in the market place (business and academic). Again and again, in the honors sections which I taught from 1957 to 1966 at Michigan State University, students commented, as they began to read Erich Fromm's *Art of Loving* and Viktor Frankl's *Man's Search for Meaning*, and study Carl Rogers' client-centered philosophy and Abraham Maslow's concepts of human excellence, that they had never before heard a professor say anything good about a human being.

When human beings are seen in this piecemeal fashion, it becomes more understandable why machines are often thought more precious than people and why the exponents of the rights of the under classes have characteristically encountered so much trouble. The War on Poverty—a gesture toward altruism—was starved to make way for the War in Vietnam—a show of might. Slum clearance projects often provide more profits for realtors and the construction industry than good living conditions for ghetto residents. Such great humanitarians as Florence Nightingale and Jane Addams, who showed compassion for the most miserable soldier or the most unlikely immigrant, had to overcome obstacle after obstacle. But their truly magnificent accomplishments, and even their names, are omitted from the texts that pass for history. Among the comparatively few Creative Intellectuals who have been recognized, chance was probably as important a factor as character, ability, and perseverance.

In the American high school of the 50's and early 60's, as Jules Henry pointed out, there were only two routes to success. One was typically taken by the Studious and the other by the Social Leader, who was usually popular because of his participation in school activities or sports. (Or perhaps he participated because he was popular.) In studies of high and low achievement in school, the student who receives good grades, is considered the high achiever. Thus he is contrasted with someone labeled the underachiever. The latter, possessing relatively the same or even more ability, receives lower grades. A third way of being was explored by Chris in Henry's *Culture Against Man*. As a Creative Intellectual Chris found that he had no one to talk to, no one to encourage him, and no one to supply a haven in the typical high school. Searching for self and for meaning in life, he had given up poker as a way of passing time. Poker, as he explained, does not have an ideology.

In an early piece of research (published originally in 1957) a colleague, John Teahan, and I investigated the qualities and background factors that distinguish high and low achievers. Since school marks were the criteria, the study was straightforward but, as I look back on it now, limited. However, since it was done with proper controls and the appropriate methodology and was written in the required format, it has been reprinted in a number of anthologies in social psychology and educational sociology. By dividing a group of gifted children into high achievers (those with good marks) and low achievers (those with poor grades) and by asking their mothers to take an attitude test on child-rearing practices, we discovered that the mothers of high achievers were more demanding.

However, consistent differences between the low and high achieving students were hard to find. Certain low achievers cared little or nothing about academic learning, and according to their own self descriptions, were more interested in manipulating people and running things. By contrast some of the low achievers were extremely well informed and reported reading more books than the high. I interviewed one low achiever named Allen, a "B-" boy, who told me he was reading forty hours a week as well as going to school. He was not exactly a social skyrocket, probably he should be called a dud—a big, overgrown fall guy. Other students would snatch his lunch away from him, pull his cap down over his eyes, and show their disdain in other unsubtle fashions. Yet he turned out to be an expert in naval history and in many other areas. His mother reported a number of his accomplishments. One evening their dinner guest was a pharmacist, and Allen discussed pharmacology as intelligently as any adult. The summer before, mother and son had visited the United Nations Building. Here Allen, just out of eighth grade, met a couple of visiting diplomats who soon were deep in conversation with him, discussing peacetime uses of atomic energy. When the conversation ended they turned to Allen's mother and commented that he was the best informed person on that subject whom they had met in the United States.

The significant point was that the low achievers included both Creative Intellectuals and Social Leaders—and in about equal numbers. When these two kinds of low achievers, so dramatically unlike, were averaged together, the resulting mélange obscured all differences. "Any non-swimmer," as someone has said, "can drown in a river *averaging* three feet deep."

As we have seen the most typical American route to success has been through position, power, and possessions. Already in school the Social Leaders vied for position and power, and were displaying their possessions. (In the days when cashmere sweaters were counted, one girl owned thirty-seven.) But their major success has to wait for the market-place or the political arena—what they call the "real world." For them, the school was a testing theater but little more. Sociologists generally accepted this interpretation of success and, as noted before, used it to judge achievement. In other words, the socioeconomic status scales that they have devised typically rate preeminence on the basis of occupation and income. And this is what the Social Leaders themselves began to value when they were still quite young. Some went so far as to choose their friends for reasons of influence and social rank. They used as criteria whether or not the clothes were "mod," the cars "posh," and the fathers well-heeled.

When high achievement is branded and packaged in terms of the school's (teacher's) judgment or in those of society's monetary and status rewards, it is not necessarily related to personal feelings of fulfillment. Nor does it give the individual the sense that he has made an original and truly personal contribution. Achievement judged solely by the individual's compliance with someone else's expectancies and standards may be the very opposite of finding the self. Good students know that generally they will not receive high grades if they spend their time learning how to think, discovering what they think, or voicing their own opinions. Instead, they will do "best" if they read what is assigned—and little more—and shape their opinions (and answers on tests) to conform to the teacher's prestated judgments or the textbook's pontifica-tions. Successful men in the marketplace (academic or other) are well aware that "fitting in" to the company is more important than "speaking out." *Who* you know, they affirm, is more important than *what* you know.

In fact unless you know and are seen with the right people and "fit in" with respect to dress, patterns of deference, and even styles of recreation, you are apt to be moved "down" or "out." All too often "speaking out"–if the ideas you express happen to be contrary to company policy or even to the boss' biases–can also mean "losing out." Such subjugation of one's critical intelligence to the imperative of the system can be alienating if the demands continue too long or too relentlessly. One can find oneself through one's work, it is true, but only when this allows for self-expression. Otherwise, there is only the system's prefabricated image: the public school student and the organization man.

There seemed to be no doubt that, given a certain minimum level of ability, character or belief system or philosophy was a most important factor in determining how individuals will achieve and will live their lives. This is much like the point made by Donald Mackinnon and others who have studied creativity: Beyond a certain level of intelligence (120 IQ is often used as a base) creativity and intelligence are not clearly related. It must be remembered, however, that high creativity in a given field is based on unusual abilities to deal with that medium. Outstanding musicians characteristically have high, seemingly innate, talent in music; and, as Frank Barron's findings confirm, gifted writers have very superior verbal intelligence.

At about the time I began to look into this matter of motivation to learn, Robert Peck and Robert Havighurst published their hierarchy of character development. Although the two studies were conducted quite independently, their several levels corresponded well with the types mentioned above.

At the lower level of character development they described expedient and opportunistic behavior. Such descriptions coincided with my finding (1960-61) that students who classified themselves as Social Leaders were often willing to achieve their ends by any means. Many admitted to stealing when young and to cheating on tests in school. They expected to continue this sort of behavior in business. Valuing pleasure, power, and money, a majority of the boys did not "blame anyone for trying to grab all he can get in this world."* By contrast less than a third of the Studious and Creative Intellectuals felt this way. Many Social Leaders argued that they must always be vigilant against the wiles of others—"if you get tricked, you have just yourself to blame."

As a group the Social Leaders tended to conform to teenage mores rather than to those of the teacher. However, they did well enough, and sometimes very well, academically. It is just that their social interests came first. While the Studious were preparing for examinations and the Creative Intellectuals were reading about existentialism, the Social Leaders were probably out electing someone to office or, better yet, getting themselves elected.

This social behavior seemingly does not interfere with getting high grades as much as does intellectual or creative behavior. At least in this early study the Social Leaders consistently received better grades than the Creative Intellectuals. Perhaps this was because many schools value and understand sociability more than intellectuality, or because these Social Leaders were able enough and charming enough to handle all that was required academically. Teachers, at any rate, found them hard to resist.

This was a particularly handsome group, boys and girls alike. Many of the boys were top athletes and mature for their age. As one girl said about them, "They are man-type boys." They tended to be lionized and become the BMOC's (Big Man on Campus) and the Big Sports Heroes. (They didn't go in for fencing or Ping-Pong or chess; however, it was

---

*Quotations come from the instruments used in the study. Each item was analyzed to determine its relative appeal to the three types. Tables presenting this item analysis can be found in *The Creative Intellectual Style in Gifted Adolescents*, Vol. I, *op. cit.*

all right to be the captain or the quarterback on the football team.) The girls were equally attractive, well built, and coordinated. Many became majorettes and cheerleaders. Some came from homes with money, some did not. All of them, however, liked to spend it on themselves. Clothes were a "big thing"—they really mattered.

The Social Leaders generally began dating early. They started attending social functions, and, although a number came from quite average homes, many already had connections at the country club or were making them. A number of years ago I worked as a consultant to the English department of a "gold coast" high school in a large Eastern city. I felt that knowing why you do things often improves the doing, so I had suggested to a young English teacher that he ask the students why they took English. The question fell on unprimed ears—no one knew. A simpler question seemed to be: "Why do you take physical education?" But again there was a lack of response. It would seem that such terms as cooperation and sportsmanship (or: "What are the virtues of physical education?") might be volunteered readily. But still there was dead silence. A few offered such inanities as "you could take showers and get clean"—this, coming from two-bathroom homes! Finally one of the boys in the back of the room put his hand up and laconically volunteered: "Well, ya gotta know how to do somethin' when ya go to the country club."

Their parents were often young and handsome, well educated and well connected. Their basic values were materialistic, rounded out with hedonism; but they tempered their competitiveness with good-humored togetherness. Neither the parents nor the students were visionaries. They rarely gave a second thought to the starving millions in densest India. But they were community-minded—doing "good" for the community and being chairman of the committee that did it had high prestige. This meant working for the crusade of the moment, but not, of course, for an unpopular cause.

The Social Leaders, in fact, had thoroughly acquired the American taste for living in the present. For them the ideal school assignment "requires little study or thought once it is learned." They preferred the "tried and true" to the examined life, the "known" to the "unknown," "facts" to "ideas," the "here and now" to the "far away and long ago" or the "emergent future." They showed little inclination for lifetime learning, or for examining the life process critically. Philosophical discussions were avoided if possible. As they put it: "We can't solve our problems anyway," or "Everything will work out if we will stop interfering."

With no desire for improvement ("Only a fool would change his way of life"), they felt that the rest of the world should conform to our way. Believing that the "way in this nation is best for all," they did not seem squeamish about imposing it on others, even with force. One of those most committed to these beliefs wrote an essay, which said in brief: "What I want to do is run the world, not change it."

As the survey results were studied, the class discussions read through, and the interviews analyzed, it was quite apparent that these students did not want to think deeply or to plan ahead. Most who called themselves Social Leaders indicated strong interest in personal gain (affluence, power) and did not seem to worry about the destruction or exploitation that might be necessary to "feather their own nests." Generally they viewed people either as things to be manipulated or as "bad animals" to be controlled and exploited.

All of this seems to have led them to a glib, off-the-top-of-the-head way of dealing with things. They were masters of the quip and the wisecrack, but not of the epigram. Businessmen of that era actually hoped to develop such talents by participating in "brainstorming" sessions. Here, grown men learned to be "clever," perhaps to "regress in the service of the ego" in the way any free-wheeling second grader might do after a swig of chocolate milk. They came up with such catch phrases as "Low Cal Vitalis for fatheads" and "Chlorophyl aspirin for stinking headaches." As adults these Social Leaders were prime exponents of technical change and marketing, for this was profitable. In fact most would ravage nature for the sake of what they called progress—*i.e.*, their personal bank accounts and the GNP (Gross National Product). Of course, they had less faith in human progress or in man's ability to change himself. Spirituality was often derided. The Social Leader might go to church if this were socially (read "economically") advantageous, but had little belief in or tolerance for religious and philosophical thought or for any formulations that depict humanity as basically good. Choosing to see man as a conniver and a manager, their effort was to be the masters in the game of expediency and opportunism. In short they espoused what is sometimes called the dominant American value system, placing their stress on power, hedonism, and materialism.

At a mid-level of development, Peck and Havighurst described both conforming behavior and what they called an irrational-conscientious style. These descriptions fitted in well with my findings about the attitudes and values of the group I called Studious. These high achievers did all of their assignments and they did them well (although perhaps not always joyfully), but were more proficient in academic than creative performance. They worked hard (studying more hours per week than any other adolescent group) but tended to lack imagination and intellectual initiative. They seemed all too willing to fit into the conventional academic norm of following instructions, taking examinations, and solving the problems set forth by teacher and textbook. Although David Riesman had despaired of the vitality of the Protestant Ethic, these groups seemed to find hard work "a good thing" in and of itself. Nevertheless they were pleasant and agreeable and managed to combine the twentieth-century Social Ethic with the Protestant Ethic of an earlier era. Some fitted in with all the smoothness of Gray Flannel and could truthfully have used as their motto, "I came, I saw, I concurred."

They were attuned to what parents and school (particularly school) expected. They tended to conform to what teachers demanded or even to what they suggested. Since teachers' expectations, behavior, and attitudes were more often than not at odds with the dominant teenage culture, this meant that these students generally put their schoolwork ahead of pleasure. They were not often school leaders, but they did their work and they turned it in on time. They might not be highly creative and original, but many were *highly* productive in terms of such things as the number of problems completed or the number of words in a theme.

Many of these high achievers wanted to know just how to do something and when it must be completed, but they were not so interested in knowing the "why" of facts as were the Creative Intellectuals. They wanted assignments to be explicit. They preferred to use textbooks and workbooks if given a choice, and they were the one group who did extra workbook exercises just for fun. In college they tended to prefer lectures to discussion groups—they sometimes described discussion groups as a sharing of ignorance. They did not want the professor to ramble or digress or tell funny stories; they wanted him to lecture from an outline so they could put their own notes in the same form and then memorize them. Their feeling for logic was good; their sense of organization superb. They wanted "a place for everything and everything in its place." However, this meant that they often rejected learning approaches which lacked an apparent structure and avoided tasks that were oriented to process rather than to product. They sometimes felt that learning for learning's sake might interfere with getting ahead in the world. For them education had to be instrumental.

In this exploratory research on the students who described themselves as Studious, we found that they typically said they read to be well-rounded and to help their grades. Among school-year interests recreation rated lowest (both in relation to all other interests checked and compared to choices made by other groups), while school subjects proved very popular. In their future lives they wanted to be hard-working and conscientious, to help others, and to live by the rules. They liked a schedule that was "set" and a life that was "ordered."

They tended to be deadly serious and sometimes they took themselves that way. However, they were neat and attractive —the girls were often very pretty—and they made fine, up-standing citizens. They would be excellent employees. They might not scintillate at parties but they would shine on their monthly reports. They were punctual and not a little punctilious.

In these studies concerned with the characteristics of gifted students, as I mentioned before, I found the Studious to be the dominant type. Their responses on attitude, interest, and value scales showed them to be primarily concerned with conformity. Their behavior was standard-traditional and far from rebellious. Not only did they follow the Protestant Ethic (in Max Weber's terms) but the "conventional wisdom" (as John Galbraith has characterized it).

At the highest level of development Peck and Havighurst described a group whom they called rational-altruists. In their attitudes and values these closely resembled the students I have called Creative Intellectuals, although my studies gave more emphasis than theirs to the aesthetic dimension and to creativity.

Frequently, as we have seen, these Creative Intellectuals were not only low achievers, but also the most vocal members of the counter-culture. In the fashion of Don Saxon, they often refused to "work up to their ability" in school and showed an unwillingness to "give their all" to the organization. In response many adults have reacted against them. Their sweeping condemnations often included all the young— "law and order" became a political issue. The formula of the backlash was: "Throw out the troublemakers." However, as Richard Flacks, the sociologist, noted, if steps were taken to remove these young people from the colleges—or to keep radicals from enrolling—we would have to bar those who test the highest on intelligence and achievement, who have the best educated parents, and who want to devote their lives to education and social welfare.

V • The Creative Intellectuals

Now and in the future, the improvement of our society depends on persons with the gifts of a Don Saxon. We must do what has been done so seldom—provide the conditions which will enable them to develop most fully. What is more, we must go far beyond our present efforts in our attempts to discover and understand them. By studying those who are most predisposed to creative intellectual growth, we can derive clues for helping them both to find their individual identity and to contribute to their society—which nearly all of them strongly desire to do. We need to know not only how a Don Saxon emerged, but what he might become in a society that encouraged the full realization of his potential.

Always a relatively small group in any society, the Creative Intellectuals, both the mature and the maturing, are particularly sensitive to the world of ideas and of humanistic values, and are acutely aware of the past and the future. They invent and respond to images that present the more noble and effective styles of life and the great blazing hopes of mankind. This same sensitivity also makes them more conscious of society's flaws and at times more prone to despair. Many seem to possess what Paul Tillich called the "courage to be an individual" together with the desire to define and affirm themselves.

Although their elders may not like the definitions, and although they are often unsure what are the best values or directions to choose, they want life, above all, to be worth living. Some are beginning to understand that life must have meaning at its center, that each individual must consciously search for this in his or her own distinctive way—the theme of Hermann Hesse's *Siddhartha*. The most mature have come to recognize a personal responsibility both for their own lives and for those of others; and the wisest know that their ideas of a future self and of an emerging world will give this self and world their form. They realize, moreover, that such images can be fashioned only out of self-awareness and knowledge about human potentialities. Thus all Creative Intellectuals, from the young student to the greatest of the philosophers, have chosen as the ideal direction of growth that route which enables them to discover who and what they are, to grasp more completely the meaning of others, and to sense more clearly the nature and purpose of life itself.

The approach that these would-be movers and changers have taken is intellectual, in the sense that it involves ideas and a willingness to use one's reason in rebuilding a world nearer to the heart's desire. It is also creative in the sense that imagination is given full play, inventing, not copying. Creative Intellectuals interpret the perceptions of the senses through a variety of symbols of which they are the true and original creators—through language, mathematics, form, design, music, and rhythm.

Of all people the gifted youth, and particularly the Creative Intellectuals among the gifted, are the most idiosyncratic and individualistic. While it is true that every human being is unlike all other human beings, those that differ most from their fellows are the Creative Intellectuals. At the same time, however, they want to identify with all mankind. Even without a systematic study of history, they have sensed the lesson that all tribal walls which divide humanity must, like those of ancient Jericho, be leveled. Highly self-conscious and self-critical, they are painfully aware that humanity at large is barely beginning to be human. It is this complementarity—their concern to be unique while simultaneously being kin to all—which distinguishes them.

In fact they demand that people with universal views and sympathies step forth, speak out, and lead. They would agree with John Gardner's dictum:

> Never in our history have we stood in such desperate need of men and women of intelligence, imagination and courage. The challenge is there—greater than any generation has ever faced.

Creative intellectual youth, particularly those with an activist bent, have accepted this challenge. They are not striving to be sophisticated or popular. Often they support religious and racial equality to the point of living it out (to their parent's dismay), and political freedom (to their government's consternation). And generally they show profound opposition to warfare and destruction (including that of nature), to exploitation (of all weaker organisms, whether individuals or groups, people or animals), and to authoritarianism (on the part of those who control them—parents, teachers, and school administrators). Concerned about the integrity of their elders, they search for people to trust, occasionally joining in the cynical chorus "Don't trust anyone over thirty." But as was shown by the enthusiasm among JFK's followers, and by the dedication of the Gene McCarthy youth brigade, Gardner was right as he continued: "Men of integrity, by their very existence, rekindle the belief that as a people we can live above the level of moral squalor."

Among the very brightest of the Creative Intellectuals this concern for the condition of their fellow men can emerge at a very early age. When the prodigy Mike Grost* was nine years old I asked him what the great frontiers of mankind were. He did not answer "space," but replied instead: "the human mind and human relations." At that time he was much involved in his own study of truth-in-packaging, and had concluded that people could safely be told the truth and that there was no other way for manufacturers to present their products. He not only had a faith in the common people, but also a desire to take action in the world and make it better. This desire already extended to political participation. When Senator Barry Goldwater was a Presidential candidate, Mike said he would very much like to campaign against him; but, being so young and so small, he was afraid that people would not take him seriously.

Before he had entered school, Mike had read extensively in mathematics and astronomy. But school was another matter. Here, when he entered kindergarten, he searched valiantly to find something to do with his time. As a nine-year-old he reflected on his mental preoccupations at age five:

> I did interaction studies in the kindergarten of who was talking and how much each one was listened to in our class. I even kept a chart which showed just how many times the different children and the teacher made comments. Some said very little, and I noticed that these had little power in the classroom. They were mainly pushed around by others. I called them pawns. But others were kings and queens—natural leaders. When they spoke, the others paid attention.

Bertrand Russell, an orphan at age three, did not attend school until he entered Cambridge at eighteen. But he had

---

*One of the outstanding experiences of my life was the opportunity to work closely with Mike Grost during my last four years as a professor at Michigan State University (1962-66). He was in and out of my office, came to my university seminars and to informal gatherings at my home, and became a friend of my students, secretaries, and research staff. Around Mike the degree of excitement was always intense. With him there was no alternative but to be involved and to learn at an accelerated rate and frequently at a high pitch. His mother writes about his early years in an intimate and humorous book, *Genius in Residence*, Prentice-Hall, 1970.

free access to the fine library of his grandfather who had been a Liberal Prime Minister of England. Prior to Cambridge Bertrand was tutored privately and had the opportunity to engage in many interchanges with relatives and learned family friends.

Mike, on the other hand, had become unhappy with school by the time he was seven or eight. He found it difficult to occupy his mind fruitfully while others were reading and reciting. By age nine he tested in the top 10 percent in all the usual areas of knowledge when compared with graduating high school seniors. As a result he was allowed to attend honors classes at the university in the morning, while he continued in elementary school in the afternoon. It was at this time that he began his efforts to understand the relationship between science and religion. He analyzed all of his readings in the university honors natural science class, concluding that the selections were biased and unbalanced and that the works of the philosophical-religious scientists were much less often selected than those of the pragmatist-empiricist atheists and agnostics.

Mike said he daydreamed at age nine, not only about a world society with its own language and government, but also about ways of dealing with space, as far out as the eighth dimension. Along with these far-ranging flights of imagination, Mike continued with his critical analysis of the way knowledge had been ordered and the world viewed by the great philosophers. When asked what books he would take with him to a desert island, he replied that he would choose only two books, Russell and Whitehead's *Principia Mathematica* and Thomas Aquinas' *Summa Theologica.* He would not take his much-loved Arthur Conan Doyle stories about Sherlock Holmes since he already knew all these by heart. Asked his reason for choosing the *Principia* and the *Summa,* he declared that he felt there must be some way of bringing about a rapprochement between the two. At this time he had already done his analysis of the readings in the university natural science course.

It was Mike's opinion that St. Thomas had been working in a situation which put him under a great handicap. For example the interpretations of Aristotle upon which he relied were inadequate. As Mike pointed out, "The Dead Sea scrolls had not yet been discovered, and the translations of Aristotle were in many ways inaccurate." Mike also reported that St. Thomas was further hampered in his insights by the fact that the major theological innovations of his time were occurring in England, not in France where he lived. Thus it was Mike's conclusion that he personally could make a great contribution to knowledge by rewriting St. Thomas in terms of twentieth-century insights, particularly those of Russell and Whitehead.

In recent decades American psychologists have made much of the importance of environment in shaping and sharpening a child's motivation to learn. Barren environments, they rightly point out, are detrimental to growth. In the late 60's a plan to provide compensatory education was advanced by the United States Office of Education as a way to avoid the most marked deprivation. But what is truly amazing, yet little studied, is the fact that many eminent persons have emerged from (and apparently have been nurtured by) some very limiting environments.

Helen Keller is a case in point.* As the result of an illness at eighteen months she became blind, deaf, and unable to speak—in legal classification, an idiot. Until she was almost seven years old she was a "living nullity." Understanding none of the meaning of the life that swirled around her, she was encased in darkness and a terrible silence, from which she struck out senselessly like a captive wild animal. Yet once she was exposed to learning and had discovered what it meant to read, within a month she had mastered the process and become a reader. Immediately her thirst for

*The material in this section is based on Helen Keller's *The Story of My Life* (New York: Dell Publishing Co., Inc., original copyright, 1961); Van Wyck Brooks *Heller Keller* (New York: E.P. Dutton & Co., Inc., 1956), and *The Encyclopaedia Britannica,* 1969 edition.

knowledge became unquenchable. When her grasp of Braille was still only elementary, she preferred reading to herself to having someone else read to her. She was independent, perfectionist, and determined.

She wanted to proceed at her own pace and in her own way. Once at the age of eight when someone intervened in what she was doing, she was visibly disturbed. At this point Anne Sullivan, her teacher, asked her what she was thinking about. Helen replied, "I am preparing to assert my independence." She exhibited exuberance and great vitality in all that she did. Knowledge was gathered omnivorously and taken in great gulps. In the Braille library at Perkins Institute, she would wander from bookshelf to bookshelf, sampling at will even if she understood "only one word in ten or two words on an [entire] page." As is so often true with the gifted (and perhaps with almost all children), by some miraculous process the barely understood became almost completely usable.

Helen reported: "Everything I found in books that pleased me I retained in my memory." She speaks of remembering whole sentences, which she could not comprehend at the time. Yet afterward, when she began to talk and write, "these words and sentences would flash out quite naturally, so that my friends wondered at the richness of my vocabulary."*

Anne Sullivan was hailed as one of the world's great teachers. Marie Montessori, likewise a renowned teacher, recognizing the similarity of their approaches, once commented as she pointed to Anne, "I have been called a pioneer, but there is your pioneer!" Both women felt that the unruliness of children was primarily due to mishandling at the outset of their lives. Both believed—and their work bore this out—that it was natural for children to prefer what was right and good for them. As Van Wyck Brooks, Helen's biographer, said of her: "Helen was never happier than when she was serving others."

*Helen Keller, *The Story of My Life, op. cit.*

Within a year or two after learning to read, Helen was well into German, Latin, and Greek. At ten she wrote to the director of the Perkins Institute, Michael Anagnos, a long idiomatic letter in French without any assistance.

In her reading her taste always moved her toward great minds. Asked at twelve what book she would like to take on a long railway journey, she replied, *Paradise Lost*, which she then proceeded to read on the train.

By twelve it was apparent that Helen had discovered in herself the philosophic mind. After studying a map of Greece for some time, she turned to Anne and said, "Such a strange thing has happened. I have been in Athens! I have been far away all this time, and I haven't left the room." Later Helen wrote about this, "I had broken through my limitations . . . Deafness and blindness, then, were of no real account. They were to be relegated to the outer circle of my life." In college she came to recognize that her discovery was the essence of Descartes' axiom, "I think, therefore I am." This was the way she could "bridge over the dark silent void."

Much of what Helen was and what she accomplished lay in her thoughts, her own conceptions of what she wanted to be. Her models were Schiller's Joan of Arc, Socrates who drank hemlock rather than surrender to the established system, and Ulysses, "steadfast to the end." Like Henry James' heroine, Isabel Archer, she "spent half her time in thinking of beauty, and bravery, and magnanimity. She had a fixed determination to regard the world as a place of brightness, of free expansion, of irresistible action."

Ben Hickock, who preferred learning to read out of the yellow pages of the telephone directory to the simpler world of children's books, wanted always to deal with basic issues. One day when he was five, his mother said that, in between bites of his afternoon peanut butter sandwich, he asked her with scarcely muted excitement, "How are imagination and intuition different?" After struggling to answer that question, she reeled back helplessly when he next asked her how AC and DC current differed.

At age seven Rousseau had already read volumes of fiction (the adult, romantic variety) to his father—sometimes the two stayed up all night long—but he had also begun going through the volumes of his grandfather, a minister, and, as he described him, "a man of taste and intellect." The young Jean Jacques read such books as Plutarch's *Lives of Famous Men* to his father as he worked, and the two discussed these ideas. He was, as he recalls in *The Confessions,*

> occupied with thoughts of Rome and Athens, living as it were amongst their great men, myself by birth the citizen of a republic and the son of a father whose patriotism was his strongest passion. I was fired by his example; I believed myself a Greek or a Roman.

Such children show amazing self-confidence when they are extremely young. There were, in their environments, many sources of information and at least some inspiration—but the richness of the environment that is apparent to one is not obvious to all. Charlotte Buhler has shown in her early studies of the behavior of infants that some were much more responsive to their environment than others, and that all behaved differently. There are many varieties—apathetic and somnolent babies, babies that are unhappy, and eager happy ones. Some smile a lot and watch happenings with care; others babble endlessly and begin talking early; still others finger, mouth, and manipulate everything around them. Almost all the gifted babies are more alert than the general run. They begin to talk sooner and many walk earlier, although early talking is a more common sign of giftedness than early walking.

David Wechsler, the psychologist, has said that one way to identify the gifted is to look for those who, when compared with their age-mates, do things very much better and very much faster. They are the "more of" people, who are bigger and better looking. They have even been hailed as more moral (although the group has never been completely exonerated from charges relating to missing library books). In my studies I found that they held more offices, got better grades, and certainly read more books. The Creative Intellectuals tended, in particular, to emphasize the last.

Observing these able young people in the schools, I found that these generalizations held true in a majority of cases. This summation of the stellar qualities of the gifted leads naturally to the question: "How could this happen?" There are a number of possible explanations for this "more of" phenomenon. One might be the capacity for mastering complexity and another, skill in organization. At least some of these young people do contrapuntal thinking. We all know the teenager who simultaneously, or so it seems, does his homework while he is listening to the radio, carrying on a telephone conversation, eating his TV dinner, and patting the dog. Certainly such behavior means that he accomplishes much in a short time. And sometimes what he accomplishes may be noteworthy. His capacity for processing information may at times even approach the ability to handle seven separate concepts simultaneously.*

We also find that the young who accomplish things are well organized. They may have messy desks and work in a state of physical confusion; but most of them know where things are, and some of them know where they themselves are, as individuals. They keep lists and make plans; indeed, the most thoughtful make life plans. Life, as they schedule it, is very full on both the immediate and long-term basis. (Luther had frequent premonitions of death at an early age. He had so much to say and to do—as he had planned his life—that frequently he feared that he would not live to accomplish what he must. This became one of the factors which led to periods of deep sadness.) They live their lives rather than are lived by them. As a researcher I often found that they scarcely had time to be interviewed. But once they

*G. A. Miller, "The Magic Number 7, Plus or Minus Two: Some Limits on Our Capacity for Processing Information," *Psychological Review*, LXIII (1956), pp. 81-97.

began talking, they had much to say. Few of them are like Paddy Chayefsky's Marty, who was always lounging on the street corner with a group whose characteristic question was: "Well, watta ya wanna do now?"

The quantity of output might also be explained on the basis of energy. Many simply seem to have more energy than average young people. Lewis Terman called this ZQ—"zip quotient." They seem even to sleep with speed and efficiency. At least, parents who have bright young children say these youngsters go to bed late and wake up running. These same parents may find it difficult to face such nonflagging virtuosity day after day—especially in the cold glare of the morning and before they have had their first cup of coffee.

Gifted children in general show needs to deal with crucial issues and complex matters rather than with typical children's fare. Like Saint-Exupéry's Little Prince, they are concerned with matters of consequence and often have insights far beyond their years. The psychologists Lewis Terman and Leta Hollingworth found that extremely bright young people had a panoply of gifts. They were willing to battle with complexity and could relish the experience. They found abstractions such as good and evil, heaven and hell, to have elements of both delightful challenge and unrelieved horror.

A counselor once told me that, while he was bathing his five-year-old son, the little boy suddenly asked: "Germ warfare is pretty terrible, isn't it?" The father nodded affirmatively. The boy then queried: "The cobalt bomb could destroy almost everyone, couldn't it?" The father nodded again, at which point the little boy began to cry and sobbed: "Those people in Washington must be awfully stupid." As adults we are morally irresponsible if we shrug off these concerns or say regretfully, like the father in a recent *New Yorker* cartoon who sat close to where his diligent primary-age daughter was working: "Isn't she terribly young to be worrying about soil erosion?"

It has always been characteristic of the young Creative

Intellectuals that they were keenly aware of the sad state of the world and felt compelled to do something about it. Continually they asked why it had to be like that. In questioning the "why" of human relationships, many would answer themselves by saying that hostility and destruction were neither natural nor necessary. Man was by nature good. Contributors to a new mythology—the "Ethic of Caring"—they spoke the Gospel of Love (for Humanity), a gospel which is becoming The Word for large segments of the world's youth. In this, are they not following the example set by the founder of this Gospel? St. Luke has recounted (Luke II:42-43, 46-47):

> And when [Jesus] was twelve years old, they went up to Jerusalem after the custom of the feast.
> And when they had fulfilled the days, as they returned, the child Jesus tarried behind in Jerusalem; and Joseph and his mother knew not of it.
>
> And it came to pass, that after three days they found him in the temple, sitting in the midst of the doctors, both hearing them, and asking them questions.
> And all that heard him were astonished at his understanding and answers.

Because of their universal sensitivity, these young Creative Intellectuals are often deeply concerned about plants and animals as well as people. Large numbers of these children cannot tolerate the abuse of animals, as was true of Abraham Lincoln and Louis Pasteur, neither of whom, when young, could ever bring himself to kill one.

An outstanding contemporary who feels a close kinship with animals is the gifted young Englishwoman, Jane Goodall. Looking back on her childhood in Bournemouth, on the south coast of England, she reflects:

> My idea of Utopia was to go to the country and look at animals, or birds, or insects. I always kept notes on the way animals behaved. When I was nine, my mother took me to a lecture given by

> a man with a golden eagle. He asked if anyone would like to handle it—and I was out front before my mother knew where I was.*

Her determination to live with and study the animals in Africa was made clear again and again in her childhood and youth. Her day-to-day activities, self-directed and intense as is characteristic of gifted children, underscored these intentions dramatically. She compiled and published a small magazine, *The Alligator*, which was filled with animal stories and quizzes. In addition she started a natural-history museum at her home which displayed shells and some skulls of small animals as well as tortoises and guinea pigs. Outside the house a notice on the gate read: "Natural History Museum. Open to the general public. All contributions for old horses."

The way that she has worked has revealed her empathy and profound respect for animals and nature. Beginning in 1960 she spent months as a silent observer of the chimpanzee settlement in Gombe. Finally,

> Her patience and endurance overcame their shyness, and one day she quietly approached a group of six adults and four youngsters in the shade of some fig trees . . . the chimps continued munching the figs, with hardly a glance in her direction. She had made the breakthrough.†

In this age of apocalypse, when it is easy to feel that much of the knowledge taught in the schools is of no avail, we have benefited from scientific observations such as those made by ethologists. Studies of animal psychology, based on observations in the field, have been especially helpful. A recent and not unexpected finding is that animals, as is the case with children, do better in free situations. It is now clear that when animals are caged or in zoos, very often the fathers and sometimes even the mothers will desert their young and not

*Timothy Green, "Remarkable Woman: Jane Goodall," *McCall's* (August, 1970), pp. 46-47, 84-85.
†*Ibid.*, p. 85.

give them the care needed if they are to develop a zestful curiosity. All of this is beginning to change, however, according to studies now going on, where the animals remain in their natural habitat and it is the human beings who hide behind or climb the trees to watch them. When the higher forms of animals are left to live their own lives, father and mother cooperate and the young animal emerges as a more confident, shiny-eyed, and bushy-tailed creature than one who was raised in a cage in a zoo.

Thus it goes, and for the human kind as well. The young, particularly the Creative Intellectuals among them, do not do well in cages. They need to be free.

VI • Self-Actualization

Heaven lies about us in our infancy!
WILLIAM WORDSWORTH

What is clear is that the young Creative Intellectuals readily accept Schweitzer's idea of "reverence for life." Among those who have a knowledge of the history of human altruism, most would subscribe to the judgment of Norman Cousins (editor, *Saturday Review*) that Schweitzer "helped 20th-century man to unblock his moral vision." For the creative intellectual child (and for many other young children) it well may be that moral vision was never blocked. Many would appear to start out "good" and at the top of the hierarchy. Wordsworth made this clear as he told how the child arrived "trailing clouds of glory," but that later "shades of the prison house begin to close upon the growing boy." In other words the blockage comes later on when the veils of custom close in and obscure certain kinds of truth and reality.

From the earliest years these highly gifted children show an extreme sensitivity. Donald Hebb, the comparative psychologist, says that "as intelligence increases, so does sensitivity." He held that this is true both phylogenetically and ontogenetically. Despite the recent questions raised about the phylogenetic theory, it is generally agreed that the dog is brighter and more sensitive than the rat, and the chimp more intelligent and more sensitive than the dog; while, if you want a highly intelligent creature who can become a red-hot neurotic, human beings are second to none. Ontogenetically the child evidently is more sensitive than the infant as the adult is more sensitive and, the tests tell us, more intelligent than the child. Terman, whose research on the gifted extended through nearly half a century, believed these children to be vastly more reactive to the experiences of living than young people in general. They cannot tolerate physical punishment and often need only a word spoken to them to change their behavior or to withdraw from the scene of action.

At the adult level this same sensitivity persists as a humanizing force, extending through the imagination to include the welfare of all men. J.B. Priestley speaks of it as liberalism, which, he says, "is modern man's nearest approach to real civilization." He goes on to remark that such humane concerns can be sneered away, that the power-mongers can take over, and the secret police can destroy. The liberal ideals, as he sees them, are "life-seeking, life-enhancing, a protest, perhaps too late, on behalf of the feminine principle." This is the ethic of all psychologically mature human beings, irrespective of age or sex. It is the threshold, beyond which there stretches the highest of all levels of human development— what some psychologists refer to as self-actualization.*

Self-actualization is a pattern of ultimate growth that embraces the Socratic triad: the good, the true, and the beautiful. To paraphrase Fromm, this means:

> in science the search is for truth, in art it is for beauty, and in human relationships for love and understanding.

*Although this concept has been used by other psychologists (for example, Kurt Goldstein), it is probably best known because of Maslow's studies of the self-actualizing person.

Such an optimal use of intellect and imagination results in those rare combinations which were traditionally called Superior or Beautiful or Good Persons. In no sense do these terms refer to one who is narrowly developed. A Superior Person is an individual who is not just coolly cognitive, but is also developed in aesthetic and moral ways. Similarly the term Beautiful Person does not describe physical beauty or outward adornments. It signifies instead the ideal type of individual who has been traditionally respected by the Chinese and the Jews. Finally the Good Person is the one who does good works *and* has good character.

Self-actualization, so conceived, differs from genius in at least one important respect. The latter is also an expression of a very high order of creative intellectuality. But unlike the self-actualizing, the genius is not necessarily mature; nor does he or she always feel a deep social concern. Indeed some geniuses go so far in asserting their individual preeminence that they can be abrasive, aggressive, and intolerant. Certain ones can only be described as egocentric grandstanders, social dolts, or unmitigated cads, while still others are lonely, tortured souls. Such examples as Michelangelo, Beethoven, George Bernard Shaw, and Frank Lloyd Wright come readily to mind. This is not to say that the genius does not change the world about him. He does—sometimes for good, sometimes not. His very genius manifests itself in the ability to break through the parochialism of his culture. As Ernest Becker says, "[he] creates new meanings . . . cuts through old forms."* But this cutting may sometimes have a sharply ruthless edge. And, creative intellectual youth, like many others, are now wondering if the great inventors, those who reshaped the world in the name of technological progress, have in truth contributed to man's happiness.

By contrast self-actualization always involves a high ethical concern for the good of others along with insight into, and acceptance of, the self. These are qualities of the generous heart—which is more basic than the cultivated mind and

*Ernest Becker, *Beyond Alienation, op. cit.* p. 282.

stands on a plane above it. The self-actualizing are not good just in the conventional sense. Nor are they those whose pious self-righteousness denies the joyful use of capacities and rejects openness and expansiveness of spirit. They reside in the light, they live to the hilt, they are buoyant and open-handed. They respond in generous ways to others. When someone talks to them, they truly listen. They think well of others, always they expect the best of their family and friends, they empathize and encourage. Their human and emotional sides grow.

It is this kind of individual that the young people—at least the Creative Intellectuals among them—are looking for, as they seek good vibrations. Youth have been speaking out and reaching out to find better human beings and to become like them. They value a oneness with the community far more than the egotistical genius who asserts his individuality above all else.

The gifted young seem to recognize that magnanimity, the possession of a great soul, has become a condition of survival. Indeed they use the very word "soul" openly and without embarrassment. The Blacks speak of "soul music" and "soul food," and the young Whites reach for salvation. One gifted San Diego high school senior, whom I interviewed, put it simply and directly: "I am trying to find my soul." They search within themselves for what many are quite willing to call the "Kingdom of Heaven." All of this will reinstate "nerve" and moral fiber. And, if eventually they do discover such inner strength, they may be less apt to be demolished by the juggernauts of the modern world. The most sensitive of them are conscious of the forces that may mash and mangle. Some of their loudest protests may be directed against those who would crush their psychological bones.

These juggernauts are not hard to identify. Throughout history, in one civilization after another, the most fundamental clash has been between the philosophers and the kings. In spirit, and often in action, the peace-makers and the power-mongers have been at odds. Rarely, if ever, did the military potentate and the saintly sage see eye to eye.

Since the philosopher-generalists develop from among the exceptionally gifted of the Creative Intellectuals, their relation to the power structure is central to the theme of this book. No matter what form authority may assume in a particular society, and regardless of the basis of its power (whether in wealth, military strength, religious dogma, etc.), the Creative Intellectual cannot avoid the role of challenging its claims and criticizing its pretensions. For he is too intelligent to be deceived and too independent to be silenced. Tyranny may destroy him bodily; but his ideas are indestructible. The power-mongers can usually win the hundred-yard sprint, put Socrates and Jesus to death, or compel Galileo to recant. But in civilization's marathons the sages and the saints outlast them.

One should bear this in mind when observing the stance of the rebels, dissenters, and protesters among the gifted of today's youth. The reasons and the occasions of their revolt may be novel, as may also be some of their tactics. But the fact of revolt is as old as history. Indeed one need only go back a little over a century in the life of the United States to find a man who in so many respects was a precursor to the contemporary youth revolution—Walt Whitman. For a short time he went through the motions of conforming. He wore the Brooks Brothers' uniform of the day, the "sartorially in" frock coat and high hat. But in his middle thirties he left the straight life—unequivocally and finally, giving up all pretenses to middle-class convention in dress, language, and habits. It was at this time that he found a new self or, at least, introduced a new personality to those about, perhaps feeling the incubating self was ready to emerge from the shell into the full light of day. Abraham Maslow has indicated that this was the stage of life when Walt Whitman became self-actualizing; and Richard Bucke,* who was tremendously interested in Whitman, called this change the step into a new level of consciousness, the cosmic.

Up to this point Whitman's public writings had been awkward efforts to say the kind of things that other people said and in a fashion that was current and acceptable. The result is that his early publications are judged third-rate—feeble, turgid, and melodramatic.

With the publication of *Leaves of Grass*, however, Walt Whitman formally introduced his "self" to the American people. The work was original and its reception was one of outrage. For some time he had experimented privately with a new verse form—a hybridization of poetry and prose freely conceived and combining the earthy and explicit with the mystic and abstruse.

At thirty-five Whitman began setting the type for the book which, in many ways, marked the beginning of a new American tradition. Along with his change of name—earlier he had been Walter Whitman, Jr.—he now altered his style of dress. The rough clothes of the workman—belted trousers, hip boots, generally coatless with shirt open at the throat, displaying a colored undershirt—replaced his dandy's attire. A beard, as free as his verse, completed the effect. With his *magnum opus*, a slim volume of twelve verses, plus his new appearance, the legend began. Whether by conversion or calculated decision, he had projected a new image for the public to see. The language and style Whitman had chosen, like his new dress and appearance, were abrasively nongenteel. The response to all this was immediate—rejection. The reaction against his search for a more honest way to speak, his eschewal of sexual prudery, his flagrant insistence on "doing his own thing" and "telling it like it was" was violent and long-lasting. The New York *Tribune* asked "whether anyone—even a poet—ought to take off his trousers in the

*A late nineteenth-century North American psychiatrist whose studies of levels of consciousness have strongly influenced present day psychologists of human potential. (See bibliography at end of book.)

marketplace." It even referred to this declaration for self and humanity as "the slop-bucket of Walt Whitman."

In no way did the barrage of criticism deflect Whitman's efforts to find and be himself. He loafed intermittently, while, more or less continually, he invited his soul. He was, in fact, the prototype of what the British call layabout youth—and this at a time when the Protestant Ethic was in full flower, especially that part of it which prescribed long hours and diligent work as necessary for personal salvation. What is more, he was openly dissatisfied with a self-satisfied society which concealed its squalid underlife beneath a Victorian gloss of gentility. As a sometime journalist—he was in and out of work, on and off jobs—he managed pointedly to criticize aspects of the society that were not generally acknowledged to exist. He paraded where others concealed and protested where others condoned, denouncing prostitution and other social abuses as well as legalized chicanery in general. Disillusioned politically and socially, he thought the party conventions (local, state, and national) were moral disasters. Those who were political, if not crassly expedient and opportunistic, were apt to be pigheaded and fanatical Abolitionists or wrong-headed and morally corrupt exponents of slavery.

When the Civil War came, as it had been threatening to do, he did not join the troops. Like today's war resisters, he had many reasons which the general public judged to range from feeble to fabricated. He was, of course, forty-two years old and had been raised a Quaker. But the compelling fact was that he found discipline anathema and the face of war disfigured with obsequies and corruption. Like Florence Nightingale a few years earlier, he was already committed to nursing and had been volunteering his services in the hospitals in the New York area when he received word that his brother George had been wounded in the war and was hospitalized in Washington. To help his brother Whitman went to the capital city where he stayed on for twelve years as an unpaid volunteer nurse. During this time he lived in a marginal way, doing hack writing and often spending what little money he did have on presents for the patients. Unsurprisingly he found more acceptance for his nursing efforts than for his writing. In 1865, ten years after *Leaves of Grass* appeared, he published *Drum-Taps* and was attacked anew. *The New York Times* dismissed it as a "poverty of thought paraded forth with a hubbub of stray words."

Throughout his life, akin to other self-actualizing men of genius, Whitman remained remarkably and flagrantly inconsistent. One of his pronounced patterns was a projected image which today would be labeled unisex. He wanted to be thought of as boisterously and robustly male and would brag at length of his masculine appetite. Yet at the same time he affirmed that "to be a woman is greater than to be a man." This bearded republican who glorified male comradeship became noted for his tenderness and motherly qualities. As Louis Untermeyer notes:

> His divided nature sometimes made him misread the meaning of democracy, but equipped him with extra sensitivities and awareness of the infinite varieties of suffering, an elemental pity and participation.*

It was almost a century before the Whitman style of independently equalitarian dress and philosophy had more than occasional self-selected adherents, although there were many who dressed this way as a matter of course. Homemade clothes, threadbare and sometimes tattered; soup-bowl haircuts (or none at all); and bare feet: These were common patterns in nineteenth- and early twentieth century America, well within the memories of almost all of today's senior citizens and still vividly in the mind's eye of those in the Establishment whose origins are rural. Only with the beats of the 1950's and the hippies and diggers of the 60's, did Whitman's doctrine of brotherly love and his new life style (footloose and property-less), find hospitable soil. Whitman

*Louis Untermeyer, *Lives of the Poets* (New York: Simon and Schuster, 1959), p. 572.

should not be considered, however, a prototype for only one kind of creative intellectual youth, for he seems to represent them all. As he himself said: "I am large. I contain multitudes." He was a romantic rebel in the artistic tradition, an intuitive mystic with an Eastern vision, a humanitarian-altruist in the Good Samaritan mold, and a social critic with radical inclinations.

Who are our contemporary Whitmans? What is it they are thinking and feeling? What are they saying? And why are they protesting?

In 1960, before creative intellectual youth declared war on the Establishment, I polled a group of intellectually superior high school students to discover their opinions on academics and philosophy, and also their tastes and prejudices. At that time it was apparent that the attitudes, interests, and values of those who classified themselves as Creative Intellectuals were not those of the general public. Already they seemed to be saying that the larger society had its priorities reversed. A decade later these young people now of voting age, were in the wave front of the revolution, manning the barricades, ministering to the poor, living in communes. What are now being called the "new values," expressing the new independence and defiance of youth, were emerging already in the early 60's—writ large for all to read who chose to see. In fact the opinions of these young revolutionaries seem to have changed little, if at all, in this decade. However the young have become more vocal and their criticisms more pointed, while their knowledge and insights have enlarged. Thus we see that the Youth Revolution was being rehearsed in the minds of the young almost a decade ago, even though it was late in the 60's before the revolutionaries took to the city streets and before the numbers of those who stood up to be counted became a swelling tide.

To understand them as they subsequently developed into their many varieties, let us first look at a composite picture which draws together their general features. What follows is taken from the actual phrases which these boys and girls used to describe their attitudes and feelings in their essays, comments, test forms, and in the interviews conducted at the beginning of the decade of protest.

Poetry is a passion with me. But then I'm a reading addict. I'd even read the telephone book although I don't like the plot. Like Everest, "it is there." As far back as I can remember, I've read science fiction and philosophy, history, and religion. And I must admit that I've been in love with *Winnie the Pooh* for a long time. I always have liked things "over my head" better than the grade-level stuff the teacher said we should read. Dick and Jane just didn't speak to me, but I found that the great novelists did—even in junior high—and since I took French, I've tried out some French novels in the original. I must admit I prefer the nonrequired to the required; and, although I enjoy geometry, I also like to delve into ESP and magic, hypnotism and witchcraft. In grade school the teacher didn't dare send me to the dictionary. I'd literally "fall in" and "come to" many words and pages later, usually having forgotten the word I was sent to look up. I literally read at all times "while waiting for things to start and waiting for things to stop." And when I read I looked for deeper meanings and for complexities. Characterization, style, and form in literature appealed more than the 1-2-3 of action or the 3-2-1 of Space Age action. I want three dimensions or more. For me the two-dimensional, two-tone mock-up falsely represents a complex and largely uncharted world.

I like to stay open to possibilities and "consider many alternatives." So much of what we are taught in school seems to be the brainwashing approach of the Great Simplification. Some of the adults we know seem to say, "There are only two sides to every issue: wrong and right (or yours and mine)." This is the best thing about social studies—if you have a good teacher with an open mind he will tell you what to consider, but not what to think. Of course I like to "fool around with new ideas even if they're useless," "to learn new things," and to solve all kinds of problems—tic-tac-toe and chess in three dimensions, puzzles ad infinitum. And, as I look ahead, I want an occupation that allows, even requires, original thinking and also one in which I can work for the betterment of man.

I am interested in ideas and in how they are used. Obviously I am unwilling "to accept authority for authority's sake." Not only do I dislike arbitrary rules and regulations, but, what is more impor-

tant, is where these acts take us. We may not know how to resolve ethical issues, but we must consider them. I often "disagree
with classmates and teachers" and find that I do agree "with people who are unpopular or who hold ideas that are unpopular," if
these make sense. It is the inner person—his soul—that counts, not
his color, his dress—not even whether he is clean or not. So long
as he is a human being, he has a right to food and shelter and,
beyond that, to believe as he chooses. The people I'm interested
in must think and care.

The new and the exciting has an appeal all its own. More often
than not, I "prefer the unknown to the known ways of solving
problems or thinking." I want to "interpret the Bible" for myself
and I like to study other religions too. From what I know of it, I
would say that Zen has a good deal to offer. In fact if I could
break away and had the money, I'd like to spend some time in an
ashram or a Buddhist monastery. I've often thought of leaving
home, "running away" if necessary. Even "losing contact with
my parents" doesn't panic me.

But I don't always have to be doing or discussing things. I like to
philosophize, criticize, and plan a better world. But you can't do
this very well if you don't have time to think. And I also want
time to read and write—poetry, particularly, or articles in the
magazine we publish. Or to listen to music—folk, rock, primitive—
or to play my guitar. Sometimes I think I must be perverse—I like
things that are different, new experiences. I don't have to have
everything lined up and settled—predictable. In fact I don't really
like people who always do what you expect. I prize my own
uniqueness and so I want my friends to be themselves—unconventional and nonconformist, if they feel that way. Some of the fellows I like are frankly feminine, I guess you would call them
soft. They can be sensitive and tender, but ruthless too sometimes, and when they are hurt too much, they get bitter and cynical. Intensely aware, they are like finely tuned instruments. They
listen hard and look hard. I think I do too. The idea is to be passive and open and receptive at the same time. You can revel in
"being," you know, inundate yourself in experience, free yourself
from the system, break out of your capsule, tear down the walls
and the barriers. When you do this the outward and inward join
and then you can resolve the paradoxical and the contradictory.
Most Americans prize speed and efficiency, but forget that life
can't be judged this way. It's what you are and what you stand
for that matters, not how well you do things or whether they're
done on time. Ends are more important than means, but moral

judgments apply to both. "Killing people for peace" just doesn't
make sense.

From this composite self-portrait it should be clear that
the creative intellectual style can take many forms, and the
species may change with the year and the season. The revolt
of the youth to which many Creative Intellectuals have lent
their talents has expanded both outward and downward—in
some cases becoming diluted or even perverted. It has not
been constant, but always in flux. As the 60's waned the
children of Aquarius rose side by side with the Weathermen
and the Panthers. Each sub-group had a stamp and character
all its own, although the mass-media—and through them the
general public—tended to lump them together and made little
allowance for their genuine differences.

The morning headlines swing the opinions and fan the
controversy. They give us each day our daily "whipping boy"
or girl, and make no effort to deliver us or the young from
evil. The press wades interminably in the "slough of de-
spond" and somehow, today's media, these "undertakers of
the mind," miss completely Browning's point about the year
at the spring and the day at the morn.* The healthiest and
most irrepressible young people America has ever produced
(could it be all those vitamins and baby food?) still seem to
want the hillside to be dew-pearled and the lark to be on the
wing. If smog has obscured the dew and DDT done in the
lark, then something is awry. What is rotten may not be in
Denmark, but next door or in our own backyard.

---

*Robert Browning, "Pippa Passes"
The year's at the spring,
And day's at the morn;
Morning's at seven;
The hill-side's dew-pearled;
The lark's on the wing;
The snail's on the thorn:
God's in his heaven—
All's right with the world!

VII • The Diversities of Dissent

Those whom I am calling Creative Intellectuals have this in common: They object to the present social system and to the kind of human relationships, indeed to the very world view, which it supports or imposes. At a deep level they feel that the present culture is profoundly wrong and essentially dehumanizing. They ask that we again should become concerned about man's inhumanity to man. Seeking to make people aware of how far they have strayed from what is basic to their humanity, many of these youth who are the leaders of dissent are asking for changes which are radical in the sense that they reach the roots of the established system, but not in the sense of being altogether novel. Some students of the youth culture have observed in what are called the "new values" a central core which is derived from the democratic dream and the Judeo-Christian ethic. In this perspective the counter-culture is part of a reform movement, utilizing and reviving older traditions.

What is wrong is vividly clear, what is less clear is the way out. Moreover although the system in general is anathema to creative intellectual youth and their older counterparts, they level against it a wide range of specific objections. Similarly, their positive goals—which their critics claim to be generally lacking—are not all of a piece. Some seem bent on destroying faulty structures, while others work toward a Peace on Earth, Goodwill to All.

The methods of protest in the 60's varied, and so did the response. Beginning at Berkeley with the Free Speech Movement (FSM) in 1964, there was for some time an acceleration of abrasiveness, stridency, and raucousness. But as the decibel level of objections rose, so did the forces of repression, complete with bullhorn and siren. By 1970 muted tones were rarely heard on any side. In his Inaugural Address (January, 1969) President Nixon appealed to Americans to lower their voices. Within less than a year he was unleashing the discordant divisiveness of Vice President Agnew. However there still remained gentle souls who quietly raised questions—for those who would pause to listen—as to the wisdom, ethics, and practicality of using violence to accomplish change.

Protest has taken many different forms. Some wanted to smash the system, thinking they could change the basic structure through political confrontation and revolutionary action, and then replace it with something new. Others wanted to correct the system by continuous criticism and exposure of its flaws. Others again preferred to improve the system by doing good works within it. Still others have chosen to withdraw and design a culture of their own. In all the groups to which these diversities have given rise there are Creative Intellectuals who are leaders and many others, not necessarily Creative Intellectuals, who are followers or supporters.

From the kinds of action taken the major divisions would appear to lie between those who would follow the outward route and those who would take the inward. In some ways the militant activists (the extremists of the outward route) who try to change the basic structure seem the most radical of the creative intellectual dissenters. However they are still concerned with *running* things. Their actions show them to be task-oriented and preoccupied with power. This means that in certain respects they still accept the mainstream of the older culture. Many of them, in fact, live by stern moral codes, practising the very Protestant Ethic which they ostensibly repudiate.

In contrast the "hippie" movement, which attains its extreme form in mysticism, is essentially an inward one, a renunciation of society by those who move away and cultivate inner experience. Instead of the heavily cognitive and intellectual emphasis which the militants so often use (and which is much like the emphasis in the prevailing culture), they tend to stress aesthetic experiences and to believe in the power of love. Couched in the current psychological vernacular, theirs is a belief in the psychology of *being*, whereas the focus of the militants seems to be more on *becoming*.

Between these two extremes of militant and mystic, various shades of activity and quietism are expressed. Among the young scientists, for example, there is a growing and discernible number who assert—contrary to typical "scientific" stances—that the knowledge which their research discloses is in fact value-laden. But it supports the wrong values. They ask whether discoveries can be of "value" if they do not increase human welfare and further the cause of all Nature. The most outspoken of the scientists have become reformers and are unabashedly humanitarian. Finally there are those alienated, non-involved whom I shall call romantic rebels. Don Saxon is a case in point. Jean Jacques Rousseau is their archetype and the fictional Holden Caulfield their recent model. Many writers, musicians, and artists come within this category.

I propose to take a close look at these subgroups, beginning with the militants and continuing (in this chapter and the next) with the other groups which pursue an outward route. Following this will be a discussion (Chapter IX) of those who are inward-directed. This division is used, of course, with the preliminary caution that groupings of human beings into types are conventions—and, in this sense, they are abstractions and sometimes exaggerations. A classification of types tends to focus on differences. There is wisdom there-fore in Henri Bergson's reminder that "none of our intellec-tual categories apply precisely to the things of life. In vain we try to fit living realities into our conceptual frameworks; all the frameworks crack; they are too narrow, too rigid to contain what we wish to put in them."*

THE MILITANTS

The militants are readily defined and easily recognized. Their opposition to the established system is apparently total; their methods of registering protests and seeking change are dramatic and often violent. They revolt because they are revolted. They destroy from disgust or despair. Although many of the youth who participate in militant activities and who provide the leadership are the children of middle-class homes, often of upper-income parents, they are alienated by their very affluence. (Witness the opening scenes of the movie *The Graduate*.) Marx, Engels, Lenin, and Trot-sky, it should be remembered, came from similar social backgrounds, so the phenomenon is not so new.

These antecedents suggest something else which invites serious reflection. Many of the most militant—and especially those most active in the leadership—are highly gifted intellec-tually. Many do extremely well on intelligence tests; their college-board scores are frequently in the 700's and their IQ's well above 140. Further, despite the fact that they have been curious and questioning since childhood, they were often reading addicts† and were so well informed that many teach-ers gave them high grades despite their penchant for dissent.

In the conventional grading patterns of our colleges and

*Quoted by Charles de Gaulle in Le Fil de l'épée, Paris: Éditions Berger-Levrault, p. 17.
†Marx spent many years doing research in the British Museum.

universities these have been students with numerous A's to their credit. Their attitudes and actions, whatever they may be, are not associated with inferior reasoning, nor do most appear to have the "sick minds" their critics impute to them. Mental health has for some time now been defined as finding a commitment, which many of them seem to have found. Although alienated from the major society, they frequently have immediate goals, and at least a few have long range plans.

The paramount question then is: What turns them into militants? What is it that persuades them to resort to violence? The answer would seem to be that what Alice did in fantasy, they have done in fact. For them, the images of the ad-men, the artifice of the public-relations specialist are meretricious and dishonest. Such arts do not reveal the reality, but veil it. And the gifted adolescents, reared in an environment of material comfort, judge its essence to be shallow or hollow. They watch a father entrapped in the worship of what William James called "the bitch-goddess Success," his activities predetermined by the assumption that what another wins, he loses—who understands the *zero-sum* game* but not the principle of synergy. They see a mother who allows her horizon to be bounded by the routine of the diaper-wash, country club, and P.T.A., but who may also read and reflect on the inadequacies and inequities of the "great society" and impart to her children a mood of questioning and search.

The militant has it all "handed to him on a silver platter," but spurns the proffered gift. He or she is first of all an idealist, in the sense of exploring ideas and espousing ideals. Militants are fundamentalists, for they think that as the causes of corruption lie deep, so do the conditions of change. Militants are activists, for they have rejected the notion that

*An analogy used in game theory to show that whatever is lost by one player (or side) is won by the other. No definitive theory exists for the *non-zero-sum* game where the gain of one player is not the loss of the other. Some have committed the error of applying the *zero-sum* analogy to international relations. But what is precise mathematically is not true humanly.

they will tolerate society as it is, and they see no reason why a better world should not be created here and now. Militants are moralists, burning with indignation and a sense of outrage against injustices which society sugar-coats or treats with indifference. From all this they then proceed to translate principle into action, "putting their bodies on the line."

At this stage they discover that the established system either yields very slowly or it yields not at all. They work for civil rights in Mississippi—and some are murdered. They espouse candidates for public office—and they find nominating conventions rigged against them (San Francisco, 1964; Chicago, 1968). They petition, at first to no avail, against the authoritarianism of academia; then when they disrupt its administration by "sit-ins" *en masse*, the instant response is tear gas and arrests.

The evolution of activists into militants was a phenomenon of the 60's. At the opening of that decade various of the youth, White as well as Black, started working for integration. The southern sit-ins began in Greensboro, North Carolina, in 1960, when a group of well-dressed and polite Black college students sat in at a lunch counter. Within a few months this very effective technique was used in various sections of the nation. Southern racism was being openly and effectively defied. Many young people and not a few old gave it their idealistic support. Both SNCC (the Student Non-Violent Coordinating Committee) and SDS (Students for a Democratic Society) were established at that time, and for a while the Blacks (still called Negroes) and the White students joined hands. Liberal professors, too, helped in many cases. This first phase came to its climax in the period 1963-64 which witnessed the assassination of President Kennedy, followed by the murder of two civil rights workers in Mississippi and the first of the campus confrontations conducted in Berkeley by the FSM. Not long afterward President Johnson launched his massive military intervention into Vietnam's civil war.

In the late 60's frustration verging on emotional desperation increased in the young who had begun with a doctrine of trust and a belief in participatory democracy. They became acutely conscious of their powerlessness in affecting the course of the war in Vietnam and influencing the party regulars in a national election, in getting a President to take note of a peace moratorium of 500,000 marchers rather than watch a football game. This mood, spiraling in bitterness and anguish, may have been what propelled these questioners toward extreme political demands and violent means. Some of the leaders could see no alternative but to fall back on Marxist dogma. Originally, the goal of the New Left was a society of participation. But, none of this offered an analysis of the social order and how to change it, whereas Marxism did provide these as well as a justification of violence.

To many of the youth the recourse to accepted political means appeared barren. Seeing Eugene McCarthy defeated, they rejected Hubert Humphrey as unthinkable—and all this in a year (1968) which had earlier witnessed the assassination of two more of their heroes, Martin Luther King and Robert F. Kennedy, both of whom had been outspoken against the war. Confrontation in the universities also became more violent in the spring of 1968. There were strikes, take-overs, sit-ins; but these achieved little or no fundamental change. Indeed many of the university authorities, after some initial concessions, became part of the national backlash and hardened their stance. But soon the erosion and crumbling of the larger system became apparent. In academia it seemed on the verge of collapse in the spring of 1970 when President Nixon ordered American forces to intervene in Cambodia. As if to justify Charles Reich's* warning that the system would self-destruct, the economy spiraled downward into a depression, while the Army had its Calley case.

Out of this decade of experience came the militant of the early 70's. This militant is a mixture of impatient idealist and disillusioned reformer. His own short experience has led him

*See *The Greening of America* (New York: Random House, 1970).

to the conviction that the existing system reposes ultimately not on higher values but on primitive force—and he has his scars, jail sentences, and martyred dead to add passion to this belief. Thence he draws the crucial inference which makes him the militant he is: Force will yield only to counter-force. The system must be smashed by the same violence as it employs. Since a few dissenters, however, cannot cope with the entrenched power-structure by themselves, they must "radicalize" the thousands who are more passive, enlisting their sympathies through confrontations. Some of these are deliberately designed to evoke repression and reaction.

In favor of this line of reasoning is the admitted fact—whether we like it or not—that violence does shock people into action and often produces a response where gentler methods were brushed aside. The burnings in the Watts district of Los Angeles were immediately followed by a massive inpouring of hundreds of programs to compensate, in some measure, for decades of indifference and discrimination. To the same effect after the first wave of major disruptions at the London School of Economics, a British newspaper commented sadly that university authorities were leaning over backwards to make hasty concessions to radicals of unconventional garb and hair-style when they had previously refused to respond to polite petitions from the well-dressed, short-haired and cleanly scrubbed.

But even if that is granted, the militants suffer from a fatal flaw. Having decided to oppose the prevailing culture by adopting some of its own methods, they run the danger of becoming assimilated by the evil they attack. If you mobilize power for a confrontation with power, can you escape from power's corrupting influence? If the history of mankind has always exhibited the same recurrence of power succeeding power, this vicious cycle can be broken only by the use of different methods. There is nothing to suggest that the resort to violence will ever bring about a world which is either brave or new.

THE HUMANISTIC SCIENTISTS

Quite another style of dissent against the system is recognizable in a newly emerging breed of scientists who interpret science in terms of the "new values." Science for them cannot be separated from humanistic and subjective thinking. It is an enterprise that must *always* have moral and ethical overtones. They agree with Brooks Atkinson that the "roar of progress deafens the ear of conscience" and infer from this that we should diminish the noise and sharpen our hearing.

Most of the scientific workers and the committed professionals are probably still following the patterns of the nineteenth-century model and are attempting—in the grand manner of the old euphemisms—to do their research in empirical and value-free ways. The conventional scientist-scholars continue to accept science as it has been defined for the last three or four centuries. In the eyes of critical students this means to pursue "data" and "objective facts" by the approved techniques. This has been the quickest path to the degree, as well as the surest route to promotion and prestige for the neophyte researcher and junior professor. The name of the game was, of course, "publish or perish"—but the rules were more finely drawn than that phrase implies. One had to write in the fashionable jargon with statistical tables for garnish, so that the "learned" journals would publish the moribund prose.

This value-free science, as the young humanistic scientists maintain, has typically neglected to question the social and political implications of its own discoveries. There has been a passionate concern for theory and method, along with a dispassionate neutrality about the fate of humankind, of nature and our animal kin. Most of these old-school scientists still do not seriously question the technocratic imperative. As someone has said they all seem to have been mesmerized by the sounds of their own words and are caught unwittingly in a "doctrinaire lockstep toward moral oblivion."

In the late 50's and early 60's many students, responding to the pressures of the Sputnik era, enrolled in science and engineering programs. By the mid-60's, however, science, particularly science for science's sake, was being criticized as aseptic téchnology. It may even be that the new high school science programs (designed to teach our most gifted young "to think like scientists" so that the United States could outmaneuver the Soviets in the "space race") taught them actually to think like great scientists. That is to say, they learned to think critically and in terms of larger issues, and not in the typical cant of the rank and file professional.

This helped prepare a group of young scholars to question the basic premises which they had been taught. Since many of the students who were guided into science were also the most gifted, they were apt to be Creative Intellectuals. As such they were sensitive individuals who could not wall themselves off from the world. This, they felt, was what many academicians do who remain in the narrow confines of the departmentalized jungle—that "darkling plain . . . where ignorant armies clash by night"*—and who refuse to look over the horizon at emerging problems.

The most able among the young scientists have begun to look at science quite differently than the majority of their professors. They have turned to Catherine Roberts and *The Scientific Conscience*, as well as back to Rachel Carson. Furthermore they are listening to the new Jeremiahs of the environment—Paul Ehrlich and Barry Commoner—as well as revisiting the older poets and philosophers—Loren Eiseley and René Dubos. Science, as a way of thinking, is coming back to its humanistic beginnings. And some are remembering that even the great Newton had his humble moments.

Ecology has been called "the subversive science." Those who saw, as did Aldous Huxley, that "ultimately everything is related to everything else" had already begun to believe that many things should not be done even if they could be. They recognized that it was the basic research of scientists

*Matthew Arnold, "Dover Beach,' ll. 35-7.

which had set the stage for nuclear weapons, herbicides and pesticides, for highways that ribbon the earth and skyscrapers that browbeat the man on the city street, for industries and automobiles which poison the air he breathes. By the early 70's the humanist scientists had become aware that Big Science (Frankenstein's Little Brother?) had spawned a biological revolution that threatened to produce monsters-at-will. Did not James Watson, who helped make the double-helix accessible, himself warn against its evil potential? The possibility of test-tube babies and "cloning" breathes down our necks and clouds our picture windows. And Huxley's magnificent sop—the love scene on the bearskin rug—seems to have been lost at the laundromat. It is 1984 all the way. Brainwashing? Operant conditioning? Or those ultimates—sensory deprivation and dream interruption?

But, as we have seen, there is a rising chorus of philosopher-scientists and their young disciples, who are greatly concerned about the quality of human life and all of nature. At the beginning of the 70's, studies of environment were being developed on many campuses. Typically these cut across disciplines, sometimes as many as twenty. For instance, Michigan State University's new Center for Environmental Quality is headed by a physiologist, John Nellor. Even some of the engineers, in a profession which has been accused of simply "following orders" and disregarding the more aesthetic and human parts of life, have at last become concerned. The engineering department at Louisiana State University, for example, developed a survey course to deal with conservation and pollution. As Dennis Sustare, the leader of the Wisconsin Ecological Students' Association, remarked:

> The new awareness is a combination of things. Some see it as a question of the survival of mankind. Some see it as a way of attacking our economic and social system, and others just don't see songbirds in their yards any more, and they are wondering why.*

*"New Bag on Campus," *Newsweek* (December 22, 1969), p. 72.

Along with these other concerns, young scientists show an increasing inwardness. More and more they are influenced by the great archetypes of the new science—Einstein and Bohr, Heisenberg and Polanyi—as well as by poets and humanists. They are moving toward an acceptance in all things of the unconscious and the ineffable. For these Creative Intellectuals, science cannot be value-free. Each man, as they well know, discovers himself and reveals himself in his work, and is responsible both to all men and to himself.

Among many of these humanistic scientists—whether mature or immature—the search for empirical certainty and clearly-drawn limits, for the rational argument and the operational definition, is branded a lost cause. Their new insight reaffirms a very old one, simply that in fundamental ways the world is, and must ever remain, mysterious and undetermined. The old science, which omitted the human concern, may itself be on the way out. Slowly, the human species senses it must be reunited with the universe. There is a striving to rejoin the nerves that have been severed and to reknit the broken bones. When mankind is healed and whole, we may yet attain a transcendence which unites the good, the true, and the beautiful.

VIII • The Humane Protest

The ethical stance which is so marked a feature of the philosophical leaders among the militants and the humanistic scientists is even more prominent among two further subgroups of Creative Intellectuals. Though closely related to each other, these are yet distinctive enough to deserve individual treatment. Their common trait is a profound humanitarianism—a desire to work directly for people. The most dedicated feel an equal concern for all mankind and willingly take up the gauntlet against discrimination in any of a variety of forms. Where they differ is in the kind of action through which they express this concern.

THE HUMANITARIAN ACTIVISTS

Like his more mature prototypes, the young humanitarian activist is determined to "take arms against a sea of troubles and, by opposing, end them." He investigates, exposes, and denounces—stumping the country, testifying before Congressional committees, thundering in the market place, and fulminating in the mass-media. This is critical analysis in the best tradition of Lincoln Steffens and Ida Tarbell, a blend of the muckraker and the knight in shining armor. Fairness, justice, and honest dealing are the standards to which he appeals. He is fully prepared to prescribe standards and police them so that such ethics will be maintained. But he does not present an image of a society fundamentally restructured.

Ralph Nader is the prototype of contemporary humanitarian activists who are working at the cutting edge (or crumbling ledge?) of the problems. He has launched a series of investigations into big business and big government on behalf of the American consumer and, at least in the minds of the less radical, he provides a model of dedication. For some he is the battling zealot beyond comparison. They point particularly to his lone stand against the Detroit auto industry—and to the fact that he won. Many have worked with him as volunteers or for a nominal income. In the late 60's Nader's Raiders fanned out among the agencies of government, pored over the reports of congressional committees, conducted interviews, compiled statistics, and assembled data. And these activities accelerated as the 70's began.

Nader is not the hero for all youth. The more radical, for example, have felt that he was ineffectual and that patching would in no way correct the fundamental flaws in the system. And of course, at the opposite extreme, the exponents of "Free Enterprise" have objected to his "nosiness." But many of those in between have lauded the careful research and the rigorous documentation that have characterized the work of Nader and his young cohorts. Undeniably, their research has placed on the defensive both industrialists and government bureaucrats (the ministering priests of the corporate state) who work against the public interest.

THE HUMANITARIAN ALTRUISTS

The humanitarian altruists among the creative intellectual youth agree with the activists in their diagnosis of what is wrong with present-day society. But their prescription is more positive and less polemical. They believe in good works. This preference became strongly evident after John F. Kennedy was elected President. In the mid-60's, Mervin Freedman—reporting on an extensive study of college youth—indicated that many not only were Creative Intellectuals in the cognitive and affective modes, but had a strong social conscience as well.* They saw the need and the possibility of establishing the ethic of social service as a powerful motive in modern life.

There were other early warnings of this new wave, of the welling up of ethical concern. In an essay prepared in 1960 for the Golden Anniversary White House Conference on Children and Youth, Liston Pope commented: "It seems obvious that the coming generation will be far more sophisticated about social possibilities than their parents were."† Five years later teenagers seemed to be fulfilling this prophecy. In the fall of 1965 *Time* magazine reported that in that year "folk rock—big-beat music with big-message lyrics—had taken over." These lyrics were concerned with everything from the PTA to Vietnam, from racial integration to domestic morality. As *Time* put it:

> Where once teenagers were too busy frugging to pay much heed
> to lyrics, most of which were unintelligible banshee wails anyway,
> they now listen with ears cocked and brows furrowed. The rally-
> ing cry is no longer "I wanna hold your hand," but "I wanna
> change the world." ‡

This expression of social conscience, which became more and more apparent among adolescents in the 60's has been manifest for some time among the young Creative Intellectuals. Certainly we cannot deny that the initial response to

*Mervin B. Freedman, "Roots of Student Discontent," *The Nation*, Vol. 200 (June 14, 1965), pp. 639-643.
†Liston Pope, "Traditional Values in Transition," *Values and Ideals of American Youth*, Eli Ginzberg, ed. (New York: Columbia University Press, 1961), pp. 229-235. (Reverend Pope is Dean of Yale University Divinity School.)
‡*Time*, Vol. 86 (September 17, 1965), p. 102.

the Peace Corps and the Civil Rights Movement demonstrated the importance of the ethic of social service. Many observers in the mid-60's saw these trends as good signs; only a few diagnosed them as a direction antithetical to the major thrust in our society. Freedman commented perceptively: "I am convinced . . . that if we can refrain from blowing ourselves up in the next decade or so, college youth will make this a much better world."*

Nevitt Sanford, similarly, perceived the aims of what he called the "best students of the present generation" as quite different from the goals of the generation that was manning the Establishment. He remarked that many of the most able young people of that time (1965) wanted "to be educators and reformers." They wished to nourish their own "humanity and that of others."† Also in the mid-60's two more social scientists, Fishman and Solomon, further documented this desire of able youth to serve—and not just for a summer or as a pastime. "Youth," they noted, "are talking increasingly about fusing 'movement' work with a developing career line."‡

It is characteristic of youth to be concerned about what goes on around them. But the humanitarian altruists go further. They want to change the world—a world they never made. They want ideals to be acted upon and decisions to have a moral base. They feel that their parents, their schools, and their government have failed. They recognize the violence, the enslavement to technology and the impersonality of the age, but—for a time at least—they resist bitterness and spiritual blight. The healthy organism does not readily settle for the cynical view. These gifted and spirited youth expect

---

*Freedman, *op. cit.*, p. 643.
†Nevitt Sanford, "The Human Problems Institute and General Education," *Daedalus*, Vol. 94 (Summer, 1965), p. 661.
‡Jacob R. Fishman and Frederic Solomon, "Youth and Social Action: An Introduction," *The Journal of Social Issues,* Vol. 20 (October, 1964), p. 24.

something more from life than "business as usual." When the schools fail them, they search the byroads (sometimes as far as the uplands of Nepal and Tibet) for ways to discover their better selves.

There can be no question by now that these young people have an emotional hunger, not only for belonging, but for fidelity to humanity, to ideas, to truth, and to goodness. They seem to understand, as many scientists do, that the human race is orchestrating evolution at its own peril—and that, as a result, they themselves, along with the rest of mankind, have special responsibilities. They feel that those who see the light must act upon the ancient apostolic word: "Be ye not conformed to this world, but be ye transformed by the renewing of your mind." (Romans 12:2)

The young are more apt to respond to the mystics and the saints than to their own teachers and parents. Many understand and accept the possibilities of cosmic consciousness and the validity of such feelings as those expressed decades ago by Whitman:

> *The ocean fill'd with joy—the atmosphere all joy!*
> *Joy, joy, in freedom, worship, love! joy in the ecstasy of life!*
> *Enough to merely be! enough to breathe!*
> *Joy! joy! all over joy!*

("The Mystic Trumpeter")

Susan Druding, a young Ph.D. candidate in biology, wrote not only for many of her Berkeley counterparts, but also for an increasingly idealistic student population throughout the nation:

> I have great hopes for my generation, despite all the doom sayers. And even more for the next one. I think people are feeling more concerned for each other every day. I am convinced that we are all "destined for joy" as a French poet once said, even though there seems to be a permanent conspiracy against it.*

*Betty H. Hoffman, "How America Lives—Coeds in Rebellion," *Ladies' Home Journal*, Vol. 82 (October, 1965), p. 170.

Of course we do not know what the possibilities for realization of this kind of speculative thinking will be. However, there seems to be no doubt but that there are pressures from idealistic youth and from many adults for such altruistic change, as there are also the more basic pressures welling up from "the wretched of the earth." Certainly it is hard to deny that the explosion of world population and the increase of intercontinental travel produce an unprecedented need for human cooperation on the scale which the philosopher Oliver Reiser has called "world unification."

As a group, these activists of the word and deed are extremely well read, well informed, well educated. Unlike some of the more radical youth, they are willing to work through conventional channels, but this does not indicate faith in the system. Most have done well in school and many have begun on advanced degrees. As a result they can and do use their education as a weapon. What is more, they belie the usual observation that the young do not know how to put in a good day's work. In a general reaction against the excessive PR-consciousness of their parents, these young altruists tend to shun publicity and individual credit. But in certain ways they are their parents' children—reliable, hard working, thorough.

Contemporary creative intellectual youth, in short, generally agree with Harvey Cox,* with dissenting priests, and many of the ecumenical theologians, that service to the community rather than attending church service is the true worship of God. By 1970 law students, even at universities which had traditionally supplied the Establishment law firms, increasingly showed concern for justice in its original meaning, and were repulsed by those trends and images of law as a game in which a Mr. D. A. cleverly wins "by any means." Many young lawyers came to donate their time to those who needed their help instead of accepting as clients only those

*Harvey Cox, *The Secular City* (New York: Macmillan, 1966).

who could pay handsomely. Medical students* similarly began to give free medical service to the poor. Frequently they preferred to work in public health rather than fill their private coffers, to place healing above fees. Objecting to the prevalent image of the professional as a money grasper, the altruists among the young Creative Intellectuals included in their criticism those academics who "sold out" as consultants or researchers for corporations or for the Department of Defense. They said, sometimes in clarion tones, that the money changers had invaded all the temples, including the one of learning.

If it is true, as Gordon Allport has said, that "the fire that hardens the egg melts the butter," this is exactly the group that has been melted by the hardships which they see the world facing. To complete the picture one young humanitarian may illustrate the characteristics of many. A high school student whom I knew as a result of my research in the public schools was a girl named Diane. When I first met her in 1962 she was a slender, dark-haired ninth grader, described by one of our young psychologist-interviewers as "a girl with twinkling eyes and a sparkling personality, [who] probably would not conform to the teenage ideal of beauty, but is, nevertheless, a rather pretty girl." Diane's mother was then married for the third time and there were two young stepsisters. Always there had been an extended family. In fact many of Diane's most vivid memories were of her preteen years when she and her mother lived with the mother's parents. The grandfather, a man with many enthusiasms, with a strong appetite for living and indomitable good humor, remained a strong influence. Perhaps unconsciously she emulated him in many ways, for various of her values and intellectual interests reflected his.

Confident and self-sufficient since early childhood, Diane

*Michael G. Michaelson, "Medical Students: Healers Become Activists," *Saturday Review,* Vol. LII, No. 33 (August 16, 1969) pp. 41-43+.

spoke frankly of her abilities: "It was in the second grade that I started getting good grades in school. I just decided that I was going to be one of the best kids in the class. That's very easy if you make up your mind to it." She always liked to think about ideas, writing the important ones down in a little notebook. Religion did not escape her critical eye; she began early to question some of the basic tenets of her church:

> I don't think my catechism teacher liked me very well. She was going to prove to us that the Catholic Church was the only church, and I was speaking for all the different religions because I felt that I didn't care what religion you believe in, just so you believe it. My poor catechism teacher. I had her so confused she couldn't even remember if there was a God or not. I have trouble accepting all the dogma of the Catholic Church. They feel that when women get married it is to raise a family. I don't agree with our Church on a lot of things and *this* idea is ridiculous. I'm in favor of birth control, which the Church is against. I'd like to talk to people about this, but it is a taboo subject; most people just will not discuss it. I feel that planned parenthood is good.

> There are a lot of things against the Catholic Church with all its money and power. Religion is more or less a business, and like all businesses, you have to have the people pay the way.

Diane felt the whole world had touched her life rather than just particular people or a particular locality. In her view: "The more you talk with people the more you see their point of view. I like to get their points of view, especially if they are broad-minded." She reflected that young people of her age often seemed to lack such openness and that many didn't even have a point of view. By the time she was in the tenth grade Diane had declared herself a Democrat: "I don't have enough money to be a conservative Republican!"

Many things laid claim to Diane's time, including books and ideas, people and their problems. As a result she had to plan her days carefully. "However," she said, "I don't plan them so carefully that I exclude the unexpected. I want to enjoy the unexpected and the unplanned, too."

Above all else Diane wanted to make a positive difference in the world and believed that what everyone does affects everyone else: "It makes me feel funny just thinking about it and just realizing how much power the average person has which he is not aware of."

She was convinced that it is possible to find something good in everybody, and that cooperation and interaction will make the world a better place in which to live. These endeavors must be the responsibility of everyone: "Having done one thing for one person, no matter how small, and having cared for someone and having someone care for you—that alone makes life worth living."

But Diane did more than talk about caring. As a tenth grader she tutored unskilled workers every week in a training center set up to meet their educational needs. Her comment was, "These people are really quite intelligent and only need a chance." From such experiences she concluded that everyone should do as much as possible to help others.

Despite her soft heart and tender mind, Diane had toughness and resiliency. As she said, "I am the adult in my family. As a child—I was the only child then—all the adults would come to me to discuss their problems."

Diane considered herself to be forthright and independent and liked these qualities—in herself and others.

> I admire honesty in people. I like people who stand up for what they believe. Right, wrong, or indifferent, you should stand up for what you believe. My folks used to think that I had too much independence because, you know, I didn't want to be around them. And my mother was separated so I was alone all day, and I did whatever I wanted to and they felt that I had too much independence.

Although Diane noticed a certain lack of openness in the young, she felt there was actually more prejudice among older people:

> I can't get over how narrow-minded some people are, and how small their world is and how small they think. What the next door

neighbor is doing—that's their world. I can't see that. As long as
there are prejudices, there are going to be men like Hitler to make
use of them.

I think the next generation, possibly, is the generation that's going to iron out some of the racial problems in the U.S. 'cause I
think kids that are coming to school now are much more liberal
than their parents. I know I am.

In short Diane thought that there was a change taking place
in human beings, an evolutionary groundswell that might
change their destinies. As she said, "I think that people don't
know what they can really do until they're pushed into doing
it. Think how much genius people actually have when they
need it."

WOMEN'S LIBERATION GROUPS

When Diane entered college in 1966 the Peace Corps which
she had planned to join when she was older was already
suspect, and even Vista and the Job Corps seemed to be
corrupted by institutional interference. It was not until her
junior year that she discovered kindred souls, young creative
intellectual women, who spoke a language she understood—
that vocabulary of social reform which has become known as
the Female Liberation Movement (FLM). In this revolt of the
second sex she found others working for what she had always
wanted—freedom, equality, sisterhood. She came to see the
role of women as crucial to the new dimensions of revolution
and liberation which had concerned her since entering high
school. At first she belonged to a campus chapter of NOW,
but later switched to a more radical group, W.I.T.C.H. (Wom-
en's International Terrorist Conspiracy from Hell), whose
manifesto depicts witches as fighters against the oppression
of women. "Witches have always been women who dared to
be groovy, courageous, aggressive, intelligent, nonconformist,
sexually liberated, revolutionary."*

*Julie Ellis, *Revolt of the Second Sex* (New York: A Lancer Book, 1970),
p. 57.

Despite the seriousness of these women in revolt and the fact that they include some of the most intelligent and creative in the country (Ti-Grace Atkinson who also found NOW not radical enough, was a doctoral candidate in philosophy at Columbia), those who took this avenue of dissent found themselves shrugged off with sniggering condescension. By early 1970, however, the media were giving extensive coverage to the cause. Although the titters and snide remarks continued, some of the press treatment was objective and fair. In an issue of *Time* magazine (August 17, 1970) there were as many as six separate references to Women's Liberation.

Just how does all of this fit into the picture of radical social change? If the Creative Intellectual is most apt to be the major change agent in society, can girls and women qualify for either role? Have not men let it be known that they are the ones who run the world and have dreamed up all the major creative innovations? Why have women so rarely made their voices heard? Do they lack intelligence? New ideas? Self-confidence? Or is it simply that no one is willing to listen?

It is possible to look at the Woman Problem in two ways. We can follow the usual pattern and see what they have accomplished, how many are in *Who's Who*, and who runs the country; or we can look at those girls who are the counterparts of the most able boys, those destined to be leaders and agents of change, to see what particular talents they have and how they might use them. In looking at the record of public accomplishments, we must admit that women make a poor showing. But when we study the talents and predispositions of gifted girls, our conclusion has to be quite different. There is a vast discrepancy between the promise and the fulfillment.

If one accepts the American value system and equates money earned with "success" (have we not perverted the concept of "beautiful people" to mean those with great wealth rather than those with great souls?), women come off badly. Within the same occupation, women were paid only 50-60 percent of what men were receiving. White women make considerably less than Black men, while Black women, suffering from a double handicap, are at the bottom of the totem in terms of pay.* Even in the Civil Service, supposedly color blind and prejudice-free, women were reported in 1968 as holding only 1.5 percent of the top-grade nonappointive positions. Salaries, as reported in the census studies for 1967, showed only 5.2 percent of White women earning $7,000 or more, in comparison with 41.5 percent for White males and 9.5 percent for all non-Whites.†

But what about ability? Perhaps women really do catch on slowly and work in plodding, noncreative ways. After all, they have been assigned to do much of the repetitive, tedious work which society needs done. And they are expected to do the housework, although some have come wholeheartedly to resent this assignment. While observing the ninth-grade experimental class in which Diane participated, I recorded the following conversation between her and an undersized, prepubescent boy named Jim.

Jim commented, rather facetiously (Diane later described it as fatuously), "Women belong in the home, doing all the dirty work."

Diane responded harshly, "What do you mean?"

Jim quailed a little but kept on with assumed bravado, "A man's home is his castle, and that's where the woman belongs."

To this Diane replied, "That belongs in the Dark Ages and that's where *you* belong!"

At this early adolescent level, and in fact all through high school and over a period extending from 1954 to 1964, we found more girls who answered the descriptions of "gifted" and "creative" than boys. I realize that a woman who looks for Creative Intellectuals tends to find what she wants, as do

Ibid., p. 103.
†*Ibid.*, pp. 106-7.

all researchers. But I did have many male coworkers, and all of us agreed that there were numerous stars among the girls. Actually most research on the gifted reveals as many girls as boys. Paul Heist, at the University of California at Berkeley, reported as early as 1960 that the most able young women in the colleges that he was studying showed themselves to be more intellectually disposed and creatively inclined than a like sample of college men.

In my studies in Lansing, I had used many of the same instruments that MacKinnon (in his studies of creative adults) and Heist had used. During those years I tested, studied, and became friends with many gifted girls in the schools. Just as the literature had described them, they were "more of" people—exuberant and irrepressible. At least, almost irrepressible, for later I found that some of the most outspoken and forthright lost their self-confidence in the process of being schooled and socialized.

Violetta Chavez was a well-developed nine-year-old in the third grade at Maple Hill when I first knew her. I had gone to observe a most remarkable teacher, Mrs. Rousseau, who would soon retire. Unlike some teachers who seem to turn out flaccid white mice, trained incompetents, Mrs. Rousseau's entire room could only be described as creative, year after year. That day Violetta gave a report on the greater galaxies. Now I try to keep up with scientific theories and read the *Scientific American*, but Hoyle had always eluded me. Violetta, on the other hand, approached the topic with confidence and comprehension. We all sat up and listened.

After class was over she came up to greet me, carrying a bedraggled red coat and looking me straight in the eye as she asked, "What kind of a doctor are you?" I responded (assuming that the children must think I was at the school to administer polio shots), "Oh, I just study children, I'm not a medical doctor." Violetta didn't flinch as she came back with, "When I grow up I plan to get my Ph.D. too, but I haven't decided whether I'm going to be a physicist or astronomer." Her tragedy was that she left school in junior high, consigned from then on to the ranks of migrant labor. Her parents felt that a girl did not need an education and certainly the family needed all the money her work could contribute.

In the formal research I did in 1960-61 (and had begun informally in 1958), I asked students to describe themselves, particularly to specify their intellectual, aesthetic, philosophic, and altruistic interests. These studies continued through 1964, and year after year the girls tested higher on interests that had been found by Donald MacKinnon and his coworkers—such as Frank Barron and Ravenna Helson—to be those of creative writers, mathematicians, scientists, and artists. They were also much like the creative college students whom Heist was studying. They were more interested in aesthetics, more original, more mature socially, more philosophical, and they enjoyed complexity more than did boys of similar ability and age.

The girls* were far more apt to read or write poetry, to enjoy art and go to museums, and to listen to music (particularly classical). They also indicated, more often than the boys, that they wanted schools to offer more freedom for discussion and that they disliked rules and giving unquestioned obedience. Further, they did not expect to give up their rebellious ideas when they matured. They wanted to be "different." More footloose or foolhardy than their brothers, they were quite willing to venture far afield from house and hearth, to visit exotic and strange places. They did not believe that what their parents or government told them was

---

*On the other hand, all too many girls—particularly the Studious—are convinced early that they should not participate (let alone compete) in a man's world. Medicine, law, and engineering are generally considered "out of bounds" and girls who are brash enough to force their way into such programs often find they are discriminated against at almost every step. Generally the girl doubts her competencies long before college. Fifth-grade girls in a year-long study conducted by Paul Torrance were already convinced that girls can't solve scientific problems, even after they had solved such problems as well as boys. In *Discrimination Against Women,* Hearings before the Special Subcommittee on Education of the Committee on Education and Labor, House of Representatives, 91st Congress, Part I (Washington, D.C., June 17, 19, 26, 29, 30, 1970), p. 170.

always right. Nor did they have any intention of accepting the world as it was.

It is undoubtedly these girls whom Patricia Cross and Mildred Henry have noted in their studies of creative college students. Both have commented on the fact that creative students, more often than not, were dissenters. In fact Dr. Cross reported that young women were generally more widely represented in activist groups than men.*

Why then, with so many ways to dissent, have such a large number of creative intellectual young women moved into the FLM? One reason, many say, is that they have been treated as "stoop labor" and flunkies in most activist groups. They were expected only to take orders, not to give them, and were accorded scant recognition for long hours of hard work. A second cause may well have been their growing realization of the prejudice against them in the universities and in the labor market generally.

Unhappily most of the dreams of these girls who have already been graduated have come to naught. They encounter discrimination at the point of entry into college and increasingly when they face the outside world. In the competition for places in graduate school, fellowships and scholarships are given parsimoniously to even the most able of these young women, and only a few places in doctoral programs are assigned them.

Dr. Cross reports that women who graduate from liberal arts programs have often been dissatisfied with how they were educated. More women than men have been interested in liberal education, but they also would like to have a "living" wage. However, statistics showed that in the late 60's woman graduates of four-year colleges earned about the same as a man with an eighth-grade education (a little over $6,500). This is in contrast to the typical male graduate who

---

*K. Patricia Cross, "College Women: A Research Description," prepared for the Annual Meeting of the National Association of Women Deans & Counselors, Chicago, Illinois, April 5, 1968, p. 7.

earned $11,795.* Further, the higher education which might have prepared the young woman for a professional role is often denied her. My high school study in 1960 disclosed that 59 percent of the creative intellectual girls "hoped for" graduate school, but only 16 percent thought it possible. As education has worked out, many were able to get a "fifth" year, but even that did not make a great deal of difference in obtaining professional jobs.

It is often said that women are educated, but then "drop out" of the job market. In 1966, 80 percent of the women over forty-five with five years of college education were reported to be working, and in a later survey it was found that 85 percent of women with Ph.D.s work full-time.† There seems to be little basis to the claim that advanced training is wasted on women. If they do not work, it may be that jobs are not available. Women are more vulnerable to unemployment than men. In 1969 almost twice as many women as men were unemployed.‡ With the recession which deepened in 1971, it was estimated that perhaps as many as two million women who wanted to work are unemployed.

It is small wonder that resentment simmered in these women who had better grades, whose test scores were as high as those of the men, and in some cases higher, and who showed a more creative and independent bent than an equivalent male sample. On this point, the psychologist, Richard Farson, is quoted as saying that violent outbreaks by women can be expected because of a "great reservoir of rage . . . just under the surface."§

Discrimination Against Women, op. cit., pp. 22-30.
†*Ibid.,* p. 198.
‡*Ibid.,* p. 23.
§Richard Farson, "Rage of Women," *Look* (December 16, 1969), pp. 21-23.
pp. 21-23.

IX • Outside the System

The militants, humanistic scientists, humanitarian activists or altruists, and women's liberation all have this in common: They take the outward route to change, seeking salvation by acting in their various styles on the world around them. As Creative Intellectuals and change agents, they both contrast with and are complementary to those who have chosen the inward route. These heed the voice that said: "The kingdom of heaven is within you."

THE ROMANTIC REBELS

The artist can be said to be the seismograph or—as Flaubert put it—the disease of the future. For this reason those who are most representative of the youth revolution are the artists. In contrast to the scientists, at least those of the high *Teknik*, who separate and compartmentalize and search for the smallest unit of everything, the young-as-artists, fresh from the paint pans, like to blend colors and bleed edges. They take out walls, break down fences, and pronounce everything to be part of everything else. While the American businessmen stress competition, efficiency, and material consumption, the New Youth seek to cooperate. They are happily at sixes and sevens and extol loose ends and free form. Always they keep impedimenta at a minimum; what can be put in a knapsack is more than enough. Spit and polish are unnecessary; slickness is anathema. The Establishment (Military-Industrial-Government-University) lauds power and bigness, self-righteously it sees and accepts America as the appointed policeman of the world. Its members kill by the numbers and bomb by the computer-program, interpreting morality as obeisance to flag, to police, to authority.

The young dissenters speak of "One World" in which "All Men Are Brothers." They hold killing—including that of plants and animals—and unquestioning obedience to men and symbols to be immoral. Nothing, they think, should be done by the form or by the number or at a distance. What they seek is confrontation, which means they want to talk face to face with the university president rather than receive a mimeographed memo. As the young are saying, the behemoth of science and technology, of military super-powers, with its heel planted on the throat of nature, has its priorities reversed. It does not bear inspection. But if one holds one's nose and looks anyway, what is seen is pure madness. The good things—the beauty of nature, the joy of simple fellowship, easy leisure, uncomplicated love—are brutalized or bypassed. The implication of all this is self-evident: Nothing short of starting over again will do.

There is, of course, no guarantee that the reaction of the young to the "world as is" may not prove to be so violent that their "world in the making" will fail by new extremist commissions. In any case when one makes allowance for the usual ebb and flow of events, the probability is that not a few of the new plantings will take root and flourish. But what are these changes at every hand? How does the world look on its ear? What is the view of the up from the down? Are there insights we can derive from the current mood in the society as interpreted in the arts?

While most things are clouded over, some are crystal-clear. Boundaries—separating the arts and dividing them from life—are definitely down, perhaps forever. And the few that remain are being endlessly rearranged. Asked why she mixed art with politics, Joan Baez commented: "There's no way to separate things." Life, including all peoples and the world of nature, is all of a piece—a seamless web. And art is life, or the other way around. Contradictions do not exist once you have Niels Bohr's complementarity principle firmly in mind. Or they go hand in hand, existing in easy symbiosis. Answers are not "either-or," but "both-and." Most of reality never meets the eye—it stays behind the scenes (Northrop Frye's *Educated Imagination*, Michael Polanyi's *Tacit Dimension*) inexplicit and inexplicable.

Art nowadays is off its pedestal. There is no beginning, no end, no center, but rather the kaleidoscope, the collage, the everything-at-once of multi-media. Several dimensions are better than two. The line is superior to the squiggle; but curvilinear is more true than linear. Art is a vortex—it sucks you in. Any medium, therefore, will do. The artist Christo and unnumbered University of Sydney art students wrapped and tied a mile of Australian seacoast (in pale-beige polypropylene) as a climax to the 60's. Is he the ultimate Kidder, put-on and send-up—a mad Bulgarian sent from behind a rusting Iron Curtain to confuse and demoralize us all? For sure, the spectator is collaborator *and* artist.

Ceasing to listen to the established artists, in the late 50's youth began producing its own. And these, particularly the poets and musicians, radicalized the generation and produced a distinct genre—the New Youth. In poetry, form gave way to feeling and to message. Back came the troubadours.* Music and verse were sung and read in public, in coffeehouses, and in the rain. Direct communication with the audience was

*For the most part, the references to the new music came from two sources: Karen Murphy and Ronald Gross, "All You Need is Love. Love is All You Need," *New York Times Magazine* (April 13, 1969), pp. 36-38, Robert A. Rosenstone, "The Times They Are A-Changin': The Music of Protest," *The Annals of the American Academy of Political and Social Science* (April, 1969), pp. 131-144.

always sought. Messages could be scathingly unmistakable
("The Times They are A-Changin' ") or so ambiguous as to
demand of the listener a new frame in space and time. As
Sopwith Camel says, "Stamp out reality before reality stamps
out you." Records for the young became big business and
innumerable radio stations played nothing else. The music as
well as the lyrics blasted most would-be complacents out of
their comfortable apathy. The horrors and methods of war
were excoriated.

You know that peace can only be won
When we blow them all to kingdom come.

The young knew all too well the fatal error of making "a
desert and calling it peace"—the indictment leveled by the
British Queen Boudicca, against the Roman imperialists.
Along with many of the great philosophers of the ages, they
saw, with Santayana, that when we live at all, we live in the
imagination. Perhaps here was where one could begin a new
and better life. Each could start by finding his "own world to
live through," which would suffice even if, as the late Jimi
Hendrix suggested, "the sun did not rise and the mountains
fell into the sea." The personal reality inside one's head was
an inalienable right of each, and it could also be a delight.
Out of this might come the new Utopias where each would
try to "love one another right now" (written by H. P. Love-
craft and sung by The Youngbloods). No longer would Nature be "ravished and plundered" (Jim Morrison of The
Doors).

Although these messages seemed direct and clear, this is a
generation whose very character defies definition. Its visual
arts take many forms. Rarely do they allow the other senses
out of their reach and grasp. Trial marriages abound across all
media. What is more, these are realigned nightly and the
generic names are legion. This age has been termed that of
the "put-on," with reverse humor as its sign and password. It
is low-key (shaggy-shaggy dog), yet blatantly and raucously

sexual. But in the next breath the age becomes allied with the sublime. Religion (ecumenically speaking, of course) is reborn.

Around another corner, the temper of the times is said to be antirational and McLuhanish. Books tell less than the truth and take too long to read anyway. Certainly there is little time to read when one belongs to the first generation that "isn't sure it will have a future." Communication must be more immediate and more valid; nothing short of using all of the senses will do. Careers must be shunted aside for causes—Armageddon won't wait. Thus routine and authority must give way to the things that matter, such as heart and soul.

Moral and ethical ideals (those words that were scarcely used on Sunday a decade ago) are discussed openly. Authenticity is expressed in one's choices and life style, while simultaneously all is obscure and evanescent.

The folk-rock festivals of the late 60's, including those in Woodstock, New York, and on the Isle of Wight showed how much the scene had changed. Gone was the mindless screaming which earlier in the decade had greeted the music and singing of pop idols. These festivals were a reminder that youthful discontent was not limited to small groups. Youth was searching for a sense of community—something not readily available in the impersonal American society. They insisted that the music and the pot are relatively unimportant. The true worth of the festival, the returning pilgrims said,

> was the prevailing feeling of camaraderie, sympathy, even agape— with food, water, and shelter being shared with strangers. Americans demonstrated that they can, after all, experience solidarity and coextensiveness.*

There was the hope that many of the young could live by a code of mutual cooperation rarely observed before in large groups of people. At Woodstock as many as 400,000 were subjected to traffic jams, rain, and soggy fields. Yet they

Saturday Review (September 20, 1969), p. 69.

remained friendly and helpful, sharing their food, blankets, and conversation. Similarly, commenting on the festival on the Isle of Wight, the English correspondent Granville Wilson said,

> There was no hysteria, no desire to clash with authority, no outward displays of defiance. It was an orderly congregation of mainly articulate teenagers who say that they feel alienated by society and its reliance on the satisfactions derived from consumer goods.
>
> One girl at the concert said, "We are not religious, but we are looking for a leader." This quest for leadership frightens some British sociologists, who fear that all this youthful idealism could be exploited in the interests of Communism or Fascism.
>
> The fear seems to have been exaggerated. Certainly none of the teenagers interviewed expressed any interest in politics. They also said that they would not vote for any of Britain's political parties. Nor were they interested in political revolution.*

In later festivals, however, some new and tragically different features insinuated themselves. At Altamont, California, in 1969, the Rolling Stones invited members of the Hell's Angels motocycle groups to attend and to help in "keeping order."† The Angels did so, in their own fashion. More than one person was beaten or seriously injured in the mêlées that erupted, and a young Black was stabbed to death in full view of the onlookers, in fact within twenty feet of where Mick Jagger, of the Rolling Stones, was singing "Under My Thumb."

By 1970, both in the United States and in Europe, the possibilities of huge commercial profits were being exploited by greedy promoters and by some of the bands themselves. And their were also the drug pushers, with their open peddling of "acid" and heroin. Timothy Leary pointed out how Altamont differed from Woodstock—in the prevalence of hard liquor as well as the heavier drugs. In fact, Jagger

---

*Granville Wilson, "Forum," *Oregonian* (September 17, 1969), p. 27.
†The foregoing is based on Ralph J. Gleason, "Aquarius Wept," *Esquire* (August, 1970), pp. 85-92.

himself, while on stage, was taking swigs from a bottle of Jack Daniels. Local authorities and some of the residents in nearby areas came to show increasing hostility to the festivals, with attempts to limit the attendance and impose other restrictions—to the point where these became not so much occasions for togetherness as issues of confrontation.

What is clear about all this is that the young want to survive. They feel that they may not, unless the world wakes up to the tremendous problems which everyone must face. The most alienated among them are full of self-pity. They seem rootless, removed from the public and national life. Desperately they cling to sexual relationships. But a very great many—and there are a lot of young people around nowadays, if you haven't noticed—continue trying to inform their elders of what must be done before it's too late. And if the elders will not budge, the young know they will win— sooner or later—anyway. Population statistics suggest it may be sooner than we think. Some estimates suggest that by 1972 the largest part of the population will be under 25. All they have to do is "keep the faith."

THE HIPPIES

From the romantic rebel to the hippie is a short but significant step. The former sometimes finds himself encapsulated in his own rebellion, engaging in protest as a style of life and making "revolution for the hell of it." But the hippies and their descendants have gone beyond this. They found their peace in a love culture. Theirs has been a positive affirmation and expression of a set of values radically different from those of the "straights" and the "squares." It is a moot question whether the hippies presage a more human future, a counter-culture, or simply represent what some have called a reverse culture, harking back to an outdated past. The incontrovertible fact is that they stepped outside of the dominant American life style of the decade of the 60's and developed a recognizable sub-culture. This contained ele-

ments adapted from the ancients and the primitives and from
the child's world.

Generally the nascent hippie begins in his early teens to
turn aside from the habitat and artifacts of his parents. He
sees the crust of culture as a barrier to discovering himself
and to authentic relationships with his contemporaries, as a
wall between the individual self and his true sensations. Thus
he begins to resist mass or community or even family encul-
turation. He prefers to be socialized in a more tribal way, by
the hippie culture, since he sees this as more natural and
honest. Here the child's vision can be regained in Bob Dylan's
terms:

Ah, but I was so much older then. . . .

The hippies reject the social order and, although they
occasionally show missionary zeal, generally they try to
transform it by setting a different example (à la Buber).
Typically they withdraw into their own enclaves, literally
retreating from the clamor of commerce and going back to
the bamboo groves, as the Chinese have said about their
poets. They feel these acts are not an escape from reality, but
instead a coming to grips with it. The reality they sense is
that of nature—including the coldness, the dirtiness, even the
hunger—in its unprocessed forms, in all of its abrasiveness and
pain. This offers them something far more real than the tinsel
and glitter and the clashing gears of mechanical society. The
hippies view it as the difference between loving nature and
destroying it. Their desire is to return to simple ways, to
volunteer poverty, to tribal groups, and to the appealing
imperfections of the handcrafted. They glimpse a vision of a
free and joyous world which, by its very model, could liberate mankind from its tortured timebinds and heal the all-too-
prevalent carcinoma of the soul.

These values which are becoming increasingly important
are not new. Essentially romantic, the hippies seek unity in

all things and condemn dichotomies just because they divide.
As one of them explained:

> We are against the worship of things, especially those with built-in
> obsolescence made for conspicuous consumption. Instead, we
> value the old. In the past, things were built to last. There was
> handwork. There was individuality and a natural beauty. Home-
> made or home-grown food, as well as all else that is natural, is
> best. We try to make our own bread and grow our own vegetables
> if at all possible.
>
> We hold genuine relationships with others to be the supreme value.
> As with the Fox in *The Little Prince*, "it is the time that one
> wastes for his friends that makes them valuable." Hard work and
> getting ahead are not valued as much as knowing how to live.
> Thus most hippies choose to live in poverty. If you work, it
> should be at something you want to do and the work should fit
> your own schedule. You should not warp your life into a required
> work pattern: It is better to do work where you are needed by
> someone. It must be remembered, however, that many hippies
> work very hard. We build log cabins, raise our own food—when
> we can—and even grind our own grain. And we share all we can.
>
> Schools usually try to put you into an occupational niche. They
> are said to be practical, but I doubt it. What they are about adds
> up to a way to get money in order to lead what society calls "the
> good life." But by dropping out of school and shucking the occu-
> pational straitjacket, it becomes possible to value other things,
> *e.g.,* objects you make, such as beads or sandals, or something
> you develop, such as friendship.

During the two years 1966 and 1967 the visionary hippies
tried to institute in Haight-Ashbury their view of the Good
Society. Perhaps because the group was attracting new adherents and also because their life styles were so flagrantly
anti-Establishment, by the end of this period the hippies had
become the target of a systematized official persecution. As
Michael Brown has interpreted the situation,

> The rationale was, and is, that certain deviant behaviors endanger
> society. Therefore, officials are obligated to use whatever means

of control or persuasion they consider necessary to strike these forms from the list of human possibilities.*

The severity of the repression was due, in part, to "the attractiveness of the hippie forms" and "the lure of his way of life," including "the role of drugs as temptation."†

The police terror, as Brown described it, consisted in "street-sweeps" (in which the police cordoned off an area, waded in with clubs, then made arrests), raids on hippie "pads" (to look for runaways or drugs or enforce the health or housing code), and such a "para-military assault" as was conducted in Berkeley in May, 1969 (when police used rifles in the streets, killing a man; and a helicopter sprayed a broad area of campus and city, including the hospital, with tear gas).

The effect was to drive large numbers of hippies from the cities to the hills, to the deserts, and to other rural areas where they could set up their communes with less official interference.‡ As they receded "from the eye of the media" their culture appeared to grow in strength. In addition the hippies responded to persecution by diversifying their forms, including "religious-political, visible-secret, urban-hill, communal-individualistic." Some have even taken the extreme expedient of going "underground" (in the reverse way!) by

*Michael E. Brown, "The Condemnation and Persecution of Hippies," *Trans-action* (September, 1969), p. 38.

†*Ibid.*, pp. 38, 39, 46.

‡This is not to deny that there were many communes in the large cities. For example as *The Economist* reports, "Two places with comparatively large numbers of centres for communal living are San Francisco, in California, and Washington, D.C. . . . Washington is more typical. There are now close to one hundred communes in the city and its suburbs, with between 800 and 1,200 people living in them. Most of the members are local people, who either grew up or went to college in the area. The typical urban commune is in a terrace house in a decaying neighborhood." (*The Economist*, [December 13, 1969], p. 50.) A commune involving several thousand people in the city of Berkeley was described in great detail by Trudy Rubin in an article, "Counter Culture at Berkeley," (*Christian Science Monitor* [January 22, 1971], p. 9).

shaving their beards, trimming their hair, dressing conventionally, and *outwardly* conforming to the standard culture.*

Whether in a commune or as "odd" men in a straight world, the hippies have tried to live within the framework of their core values. John Howard lists these as "freedom from hangups about property, status, sex, race, and the other Furies which pursue the normal American."† Many would go further than Howard and say that their concern is with survival, their own and that of the species. That is why they speak so movingly of a need to love the land. Certainly they have been treated with as much angry prejudice and bigotry as most religious dissenters. In fact Brown goes so far as to say that their treatment can well be compared with the savage repression of the early Christians by brutal Roman power, and the barbaric onslaught of the Nazis on European Jews.‡

The hippie has much in common with other sub-groups. He has an ethic and a humanitarian concern. He is the altruist and the romantic rebel combined. But it is this other quality, the similarity between his culture and the manifestations of a religion, which leads some of the creative intellectual youth to yet a further stage. For in the true hippie, latent or dominant, resides a mystic.

THE MYSTICS

Many of the more contemplative observers of the youth revolution are able to see in it something more than youthful high spirits or bad manners or "infant depravity," uncontrolled and unchanneled. They see the young as talismen of a great and fundamental change in values. Some are suggesting,

*These statements are based on Michael Brown's report, *op. cit.*, p. 37.
†John Robert Howard, "The Flowering of the Hippie Movement," *The Annals of the American Academy of Political and Social Science* (April, 1969), p. 48.
‡Brown, *op. cit.*, pp. 37-38.

as has Willis Harman (director of the Educational Policy
Research Center in Menlo Park, Calif.), that this is a "Second
Copernican Revolution"; or, as Abraham Maslow observed,
"[We are] in the initial throes of a transition even greater
than that of the Renaissance." The latter goes on to predict
"the almost total loosening up and redesign of institutions."
And it may well be that this turmoil, to which we all are
witness, is not only a profound social movement, but, in the
terms of the sociologist John Seely: "[one] with essentially
redemptive or religious overtones."

It is the hippies whose external appearances have demonstrated the emergence of a different culture, although in
many cases the inward aspect (conversion) is not yet complete. They may not have found an earthly paradise, although
they are convinced that the old ways lead to "hell on earth."
But many are still unsure as to what they must be and do as
persons—how they must focus their lives and on what. In this
generation, unlike the past, an ever-increasing number have
broken through the fog banks of the materialistic culture and
the confines of rational thought. They have shaken off the
shrouds and blindfolds. Seeking to discover ways that society
and individuals might be transformed, they are searching for
a higher level of human development. Those that reach this
will stand out as beacons, transcending the autonomy of the
Creative Intellectual or the originality of the genius.

In the past such individuals have been considered saints.
Their essential quality has been that they moved beyond
egotism or selfishness. "He that loseth his life for my sake
shall find it." (Luke 9:24) Like the hippies they cultivate the
inner experience, believing in the power of love. But their
selflessness takes them beyond the conflict the hippie faces
between "doing your share" and "doing your own thing." In
contrast those who have become whole are selfless in every
circumstance of life. They are not "in conflict," either within
themselves or with others, because conflict is no longer an
alternative.

Typically the Christian saints have loved their enemies. The Buddhist carries this concept of oneness with all even further. His commitment to this ideal is so complete that he does not even recognize the existence of enemies. Through spiritual training or self-control such persons, as Huxley says:

> are able to be aware continuously of the divine ground of their own and all other beings; secondarily, as a means to this end, to meet all, even the most trivial circumstances of daily living without malice, greed, self-assertion, or voluntary ignorance, but consistently with love and understanding.*

Control and manipulation are to be avoided. Government is irrelevant. The world in which they live may have lost faith; but for them there is a unitive ground infused with godliness.

The mystic realizes that distinctions are illusory. Along with the romantic rebels he sees that boundaries are artificial and block the way to understanding. Logical thinking creates unnecessary dichotomies and separations. All severances create pain. Thus "life is pain" and only the mystical experience can make one whole again.

In the view of Steven Goldberg, Bob Dylan has found The Way in the Taoist sense.† Goldberg also believes many others among the young are searching for what could best be called religious redemption. As he says, "We have all always been out on the street, but it is only at a time like this that any great number of us are sufficiently troubled to realize it."‡

An artist can bring us back home again, his creations can give form and meaning to the chaos we experience, if—as in Dylan's case—he himself has seen and perhaps taken the road to salvation. The artist and the prophet can, as Goldberg suggests,

*Aldous Huxley, *The Perennial Philosophy* (New York: World Publishing Company, 1945), p. 43.
†Steven Goldberg, "Bob Dylan and the Poetry of Salvation," *Saturday Review* (May 30, 1970), pp. 43-46+.
‡*Ibid.*

ignite our faith. Dylan, perhaps more than any other contemporary poet, is capable of the words that can ignite this faith. . . . It
is only when one realizes [this] that the faith which precedes
salvation becomes necessary and possible.*

As mystics do, Dylan feels that the struggle for insight into
the cosmos and into oneself must come before efforts at
social reform. Such efforts, whether made by the Weathermen or those reformers who eschew hammer and tongs,
cannot "lead one to the Light which shines within him."
Goldberg continues: "[Dylan's] vision concerns the God
within and without. Society is left to shift for itself." In his
songs of the late 60's, through parables and poetry, Dylan
revealed his growing compassion and his acceptance of the
flow of life. Goldberg is not at all sure, however, that Dylan's
followers have yet learned or

> have even the vaguest conception of what he is singing about.
> [But] no doubt many of them are at least aware that Dylan is
> sending out clues.†

In contrast to Bob Dylan, but standing on an adjacent
promontory, Joan Baez has become a serious social critic—so
serious in fact that she refuses to pay that share of her
income tax designated for war expenditures and has built the
Institute for the Study of Non-Violence. Through her actions
and statements, it can truly be said that through the 60's she
gave the youth revolution its redemptive and religious overtones. In fact she appeared both to represent and transcend
the diversities of dissent. In an interview published in 1970
she emphasized, over and over, the sanctity of life.‡ She
holds such sanctity to be closely related to sanity, which she
defines as *"seeing* again, seeing each man as your brother,

---

*Ibid.
†*Ibid.*
‡ "Playboy Interview: Joan Baez," *Playboy* (July, 1970), pp. 53-64+.
Quotes in this section are extracted from this interview.)

getting back your vision, so that you wouldn't do harm to another." It is her view that not only violence, but even the rhetoric of violence, is wrong. "When you do violence to another," she observes, "you're also doing violence to yourself; you're diminishing your own humanity. . . . There's no violent way to get people together in brotherhood. It's like killing for peace. It makes no sense."

The imperative is that people find the vision; "if [they] can really *see* themselves and others, they'll find ways to take care of all the problems of living together." People who have not lost their vision, or those who are in the process of getting it back, "make it clear they want peace." They will talk, as she says, about brotherhood, about humanity, about people not being hungry any more.

Accused of being idealistic, naive, escapist, she replies: "I'll tell you who's impractical and escapist: Anybody who thinks we're going to survive this century if we continue as we are . . . what we're doing now isn't just imperfect. It's insane." She not only pleads for an end of violence but also asks that we take the positive step of becoming world citizens, that we all become brothers and forget our narrow allegiances to the nation-state. "Is it practical to be so tied up with the nation-state mentality that we couldn't get food through to Biafra?"

Whatever we try to do should make things better, not worse. Apathy does not help; neither do violent acts or language:

> you wonder which is worse- sitting around doing nothing or screaming dumb things at policemen. Somehow, nobody asks, "Does anybody on this campus want to go off and start a real school where we could actually *learn* things?"

Not only should there be more free schools and free universities, but we should make efforts to help all who are oppressed—including policemen. She sees continual evidence that people can and do change and that this is possible at any time in a person's life. In the past few years she herself has changed greatly so that she now lives more simply and more according to her principles. For her, as for Karen Place, a University of Oregon student writing in 1970, Revolution is a hopeful word.* As Joan Baez reflects:

> The thing that keeps me doing the things I do and makes me think they may work, in spite of everybody's argument about human nature [that we are from birth bad animals] and in spite of the wars and exploitation, is that I've never in my travels met a person who didn't want to love and be loved by other people. I think that need can be as powerful a force as any of the forces we've been talking about. That's the force I try to work with. *It's there.* The makings for the revolution I'm talking about are there. [The problem is that no one trusts the other person] but we do have a base: that need that everybody has to love and be loved. [I do, of course, get discouraged at times.] It's then I think: What if the revolution never happens? Well, I want to have lived my life in such a way that I won't regret any of the things I have done. So even if we never reach the goal, I'll at least have attempted to live a decent life all the way through. I'll at least have kept on trying to reach people, trying to keep myself open, so that I can be reached, trying to be kind, trying to learn about love.

Perhaps it is Joan Baez, the prototype for so many of our creative intellectual youth, who has recaptured the dream and again glimpsed the way which Lao-tse and Jesus had discovered before. This was, as Lao-tse saw it, "aligning one's own forces with the forces of nature, casting off customs, laws, values, symbols that blind one to the reality that underlies them." Then one is ready, with Jesus, "to renounce the effort to achieve power over other men or over the forces of nature, in order to seek the kingdom of heaven, where the law of love prevails, and the good of one's neighbor is one's own good."†

---

*Karen Place, "Revolution is a Hopeful Word," *Old Oregon* (July-August, 1970), pp. 15-17.
†The quotations which describe the thoughts of Lao-tse and Jesus are from Lewis Mumford, *The Transformations of Man* (New York: Harper and Bros., 1956), p. 86.

X • The Rearing-up of the Young

My research leads me to an inescapable conclusion that post-World War II child-rearing practices have fomented the youth revolution. The primary change agents are to be found among a group of able and imaginative mothers, particularly those of children who later became Creative Intellectuals.

Some say that motherhood is the last sacred thing to go. Apple pie has been suspect ever since they started spraying the young apples with DDT, milk is known to be a prime carrier of strontium 90, and the backbone of bread has been reduced to a pablum consistency. The flag has been defiled and God is either dead or exiled. Certainly He has fled the churches. It has become clear at last, as many have long suspected (particularly writers and playwrights in the tone set by Philip Wylie), that American motherhood is basically flawed. The more cynical might say that our society is finally desacralized and "science" can now reign supreme. Gerald Sykes called sex the last green thing. However, as everyone knows, that too has browned and withered under the klieg lights and in the dissection rooms—at the hands of Kinsey's interviewers, as the how-to-do-it pages of the sex manuals were prepared, and finally in the contemporary vogue for pornography as literature and for the sex supermarkets. Reason is triumphant and the last of the old mythologies is dead.

By instituting new patterns of child-rearing, and perhaps even of conception, future revolutions may be averted. Huxley in *Brave New World*, Orwell in *1984*, and Skinner in *Walden Two* had previously taken cognizance of the dangers of letting the unmonitored mother raise her young, but their warnings had gone largely unheeded. In fact during the past two decades free and easy ways of living and child-centered (translate: "self-determination by the child") practices have come to be ever more characteristic of certain American homes. And under all the freedom and the self-expression lies a corrosive honesty (some call it cynicism) that has led the mother of creative intellectual persuasion, either openly or covertly, to question all leadership and authority.

With all this she retained an idealism that caused her to search for better ways to live. It is important to remember that the mother and her attitudes are a dominant influence in the home because she is the one who is there. The child and the adolescent have their say because this fits the psychological theory which many middle and upper middle class mothers have generally embraced.

Whether this prior revolution in the home which nurtured the youth revolution was planned by such women is a moot question. Certainly both revolutions are worldwide and are spreading—from the upper classes to the under classes.

Undoubtedly there are other causes of this widespread revolt, some apparent, some unseen and unknown. Perhaps we might say that both groups of Creative Intellectuals—the mothers and their young—are simply extremely reactive and sensitive organisms directly responding to the overpowering currents from the sub-cellars of the society, like the Freudian image of the "Id Rampant." Leave the gates unguarded and the force will rise and overwhelm. However it is entirely possible that this particular group of sensitive women have felt a deep (perhaps unconscious) resentment toward the system. Although it no longer kept them barefoot and pregnant, it exiled them to suburbia and did little about solving or even recognizing the larger problems in our society. The life of koffee-klatching, envelope-stuffing, and chauffering-the-children that became the pattern in the 50's soon began to pall for the brighter and better-educated postwar mothers.

This mother is both WASP and MICE (Middle-Income, College-Educated). And in her incisive tutoring of her young she clarifies James Reston's point "that the mice of the world aren't taking orders from the cats any more."

The emancipation of women speeded by World War II was not about to be surrendered by this group. Almost all continued to read and think. At least half of them remained in the working force, primarily in social work and teaching, while many of the rest were serving society just as significantly as volunteers. These latter spearheaded many of the movements that improved the quality of life in the community—or at least were efforts to slow down the despoilers and the polluters (violence in the media, destruction of the physical environment, etc.). Such women doubted that preoccupation with trivia—*i.e.*, the kind of barbecue for the patio and the make of the two cars in the garage—could be the "good life." These were the ones who could not get the serious social problems out of their minds. For them dreams of a genuinely improved society became the order of the day. They read the women's magazines and the popular books on humanistic philosophy, theology, and psychology that suggested other and better ways.

Many of these young women were seriously questioning the distortion of values in the affluent society of which they were a part. Getting ahead in the world tended to reduce one's humanity. In all too many homes father was using all of his climbing and shoving muscles in the "rat race." He wanted to run in the higher circles and vie for the juicier rewards. Thus he was rarely home. This cut into the ecology of the family and made it a sometime thing. Mother reasoned that, if "togetherness" and a functional "participatory democracy" in and of the family were so important, then the father should be a part of it all and spend more of his time in the home. For many such women the affluent life had begun to pall. As a society we thought our major problems were the Blacks, the poor, and the young. Women were considered the least of our worries. Relegated to the material comforts of their homes, they played their endless stereotypes, complete with the "woofer and the tweeter." The fact was overlooked that these mindless activities left their educated imaginations free for significant thought.

But the signs of their discontent were there for those who had eyes to see. Ashley Montagu's *Natural Superiority of Women* brought him an instant success on the lecture circuits of the women's clubs, and purchases of Betty Friedan's *The Feminine Mystique** made it a best seller. The erosion of the old dogmas was slow but sure. Success and status did not appeal to those of a philosophical bent. Finally the men-folk themselves destroyed the notion of their superior wisdom by the insanity of the Vietnam war, for which they were willing to conscript the sons their wives had reared.

A certain sector of the Establishment finds this hypothesis —that women and the matriarchal home are the prime cause of the youth revolt—all too believable. As the claims go, women have been underhanded and devious since time began, since clocks first were manufactured and since history was made by males who selected what they thought were significant happenings. John Knox wrote that women were not only perfidious, but stupid as well. Even in this century a Frenchman published a book entitled *Are Women Human?* where he made the case that they are the "missing link." But, as one wit commented, "If women are underhanded and men are overbearing, we need a *third* sex!"

For those who accept this pattern of thinking, it is only a

*(New York: W.W. Norton & Co., 1963).

short step to suspect that women are our "enemy of bed and board," the not-so-secret agents who have been undermining the very scaffold of red-blooded Americanism. To this group of women-suspectors, the problem of counter-insurgency takes on the nature of warring with moles in Oregon and termites in California. How do you deal with such under-miners without exterminating them? Isn't this just another version of a *zero-sum* game?

Paraphrasing what Sam Levenson said a number of years ago: While men were making decisions about the important things in society—when and how much to escalate the war in Vietnam, settling the official family policy on the Berlin Wall, and running the bulldozers that leveled out the irregularities of nature—the wife and mother took care of such unimportant things as choosing the books that junior would read and selecting the college that he would attend. Father had yet to learn that the Keys to the Bunny Club were not the Keys to the Kingdom.

While husbands were husbanding the market place, the Critics of Women (COW) had begun to suspect that the weaker sex was subverting the country. Mother and child, say the more outspoken COWs, are the basic unit of subversion. Those Clairol ads which ask, "Does she or doesn't she?" and show vibrant femininity paired with innocent childhood should address themselves to the theme of sabotage, not hair color. The enemy in our midst is nothing so obvious as the town's identified Communist or Weatherman, complete with unkempt beard and hair, homemade bomb, and FBI file. Instead it is the radiant young mother walking from the village mall to her station wagon with *Harper's* and *Saturday Review* in her shopping cart and junior in tow. Just open those magazines or the new *McCall's* of the late 1960's and you will find Eugene McCarthy putting war in its place— and by 1971 a section devoted to developments in Women's Liberation, and a column by Betty Friedan.

The female anthropologists have been known to despair of our society and to suggest that we mend our ways—if there is

still time. Several have repeated the well known comment
that: "Ours is the only major culture that has moved from
barbarism into decadence without going through a stage of
civilization." Of course there are suggested nostrums. Not a
few male COWs among the anthropologists have proposed
that the only hope for American society is immediately to
adopt the patterns of the Manus and, by every means, (see
earlier reference to Huxley, Orwell, and Skinner for some
"civilized" ways) alienate all children from their mothers as
soon as possible. They have echoed the opinions of Sigmund
Freud, Martin Luther, and the Catholic Church that the first
five years are the telling ones. Benjamin Bloom's *Stability
and Change in Human Characteristics* simply documented
this in terms that the academic psychologist could accept—
that there was indeed an impressive array of facts as to how
the child fathers the man. Nor could there be any doubt that,
in the America of the 50's and 60's, it was the mother who
mothered that child.

But why, we may ask, is motherhood suddenly suspect?
What proof is there that the demonic subtleties of the child-
rearing practices of these well-educated, well-heeled women
have subverted the young and turned them—at least many of
the most gifted among them—against the Establishment?
What are the sources of these belief systems that have proved
so disrupting?

THE HOME AND MOTHER: SUBSOIL
FOR THE ROOTS OF DISSENT

The age-old responsibility of the mother has been to raise
her young to fit into a particular culture on the basic prem-
ise that the culture is somehow "good"—or at least acceptable. The gifted and politically liberal mothers of today's
student dissenters seemingly have been unable to conform to
this classic role. First the typical mother in this group feels
today (as she felt when her children were young) that there
are some basic flaws within the culture as it is packaged. She

has even gone so far as to suspect the infallibility of our leadership, to question our national goals (particularly the importance of the GNP), and to lack faith in the church as a source of solace.

With such attitudes the well-educated, "cultured," well-read mother raises her children to have both the aptitudes and the essential intellectual skills of social critics, of what Noam Chomsky has called "free-floating" intellectuals.* Perhaps inadvertently (or possibly not so inadvertently) the children were exposed to their mothers' personal dissatisfactions with the existing order. All this had its effect on the most precocious of the young who have latterly been in the vanguard of the protest movement. These were the ones who had the freedom to read the periodicals and books on their mothers' coffee tables and nightstands as well as the funds to buy more of their own choosing. Similarly, as is the wont of gifted children, they were absorbing the records and films that became more and more common in the post-industrial, cybernated society.

Magazines of social commentary found their largest market in these homes where parents ranked in the top quartile of Americans in terms of years of education and intellectual skills (at least as these are tested by those intellectual workers called psychologists). The mothers in this group belonged to that elite which reads without moving its lips and were more apt to peruse the articles than the ads in *Esquire* and *The New Yorker*. The cartoons particularly gave them the message. And the children became early devotees of the wry with the dash of bitters. One rosy-cheeked, well-fed, five-year-old, Karen by name, literally doted on Charles Addams. Her favorite reading was the *New Yorker Twenty-Fifth Anniversary Album*, a collection of cartoons.

While the innocent ones lapped up Saul Steinberg as well as Charles Addams, the mothers read *The Organization Man*

*Noam Chomsky, "The Responsibility of Intellectuals," *The Dissenting Academy*, Theodore Roszak, ed. (New York: Random House, 1968), pp. 254-298.

and *The Status Seekers*. But they also sought out stray fragments of hope and literally devoured the prophets of human
potentiality. A mother who is not an optimist has little
reason to do her level best at mothering. Thus Camus—at
least in his later essays—appealed more than Sartre. She
knew, of course, about *The Lonely Crowd*, but she also
remembered *Little Women* and *Magnificent Louisa*. She remained appalled by Hitler, but could still be exalted when
she read about Schweitzer. The sociology of Pitirim Sorokin
and C. Wright Mills was much more to her taste than the
sociologists of statistical samples. Norman Cousins and Marya
Mannes made eminent good sense. They did so in the 50's
and the 60's, and they still do.

There were many descriptions of a better world where
men, women, and children were self-directed, not alienated.
She could and did read the blueprints for Fromm's *Sane
Society* and thought she understood what differentiated the
milk from the honey mothers, as he described them in *The
Art of Loving*. She counted all those days as Red Letter when
she achieved that state of joy which placed her in the "honey" category. C. Wright Mills' *White Collar* told what was
wrong with the bureaucracy and how the individual lost his
way, and probably his soul, in the complexities of the social
fiction, but he also pointed out a better way, one that
bordered on the Taoist. His ideas dovetailed neatly with what
she remembered of Wordsworth and that trio of lyrical treats
—Byron, Shelley, and Keats—from the days when she took
Lit. 310, the Romantic Poets, from a long-haired professor.

In the late 50's another romantic was heard. Paul Goodman published his *Growing Up Absurd*. It was just like the
cartoons in *The New Yorker* said. But Goodman did not
leave us out on a cliff or strapped to the tracks as the freight
train roared in. He said in *Compulsory Mis-Education* that
the schools were doing it all wrong and suggested a *Community of Scholars*. All that was necessary was to take Wordsworth seriously—to experience the beauty of the world and
simple human affections.

As a teenager in a *New Yorker* cartoon in 1957 put it, "Okay, so Dr. Schweitzer didn't get swallowed up in the rat race. Name me three others." By 1970 those who saw the young radicals reading *Catch-22* and frequenting the movie *M*A*S*H* may well have felt that the battle against the inroads of cynicism was lost.

At Christmastime in 1960 I worked long and hard completing a chapter entitled "The Development of Talent" for an international yearbook of education that was centering on studies of the gifted.* When it was finished, complete with 86 footnotes, I sent it to my daughter at Reed College, hoping she would read it. But her schedule did not allow. Instead she gave it to her roommate who spent a full day tearing it apart, sentence by sentence. She said that she agreed with my ends but not with my means—her verdict was that I was a "muddled romantic."

Perhaps the new social commentators of the 50's tended to corrode and undermine the young more than those of us who still maintained a link with the more pastoral times of the early twentieth century—those long-ago times when children were not exposed directly to the calumnies of their fellowmen on the daily television. We, as parents, also might have been led into a temporary feeling of relief now that Hitler had been overcome. Perhaps we did not understand as clearly as did the young what Charlie Brown meant when he said, "We have met the enemy and he was us."

Although outspoken social protest may not have been common in the popular songs prior to the 60's, there were records to which the student dissenters and their mothers were exposed in the 50's that set the stage for the Beatles and for Simon and Garfunkel. Before Senator Joseph McCarthy died, the Canadian Broadcasting Company had released (in a plain cover) a record entitled "The Investigator," a scathing criticism of how the Torquemadas of the power structure treat people who think, especially those who dream of a

*"The Realization of Talent among Children and Young People," *The Year Book of Education* (London: Evans Brothers Ltd., 1962), pp. 366-87.

better world. Tom Lehrer's first songs were recorded in the
50's (copyrights 1952 and 1953) and, with "I Want to Go
Back to Dixie," he set the stage for civil rights unrest as he
sang nostalgically about missing the old-time lynchings and
putting his white sheet on again. He loved the very flaws of
that boll-weevil land with its medieval laws intoning: "Be it
ever so decadent, there's no place like home."

Fred Allen and Goodman Ace came forth with their acid
commentary of the time, and by the mid-50's Mort Sahl
added his voice. It was during the Eisenhower regime that I
heard him comment:

> Of course President Eisenhower should have gone to Little Rock
> and taken one of those little six-year-old colored girls by the hand
> and led her right in through the school door. His problem was
> that he could not figure out whether to use a straight or overlap-
> ping grip.

Those of us who worked for that kind of pluralism called
individualized and personalized instruction had some funds
to look into the problem of talent loss and Arkansas was not
bypassed. The story that was told to one researcher was that
a family (just at the time when the pressure to integrate was
welling up in Little Rock) had moved to St. Louis. There the
schools were already integrated in a piecemeal way. The
mother knew the penalties of undue haste. She deliberated
and did not buy a home until she finally found one in an area
which had a total of only six little colored children enrolled
in the neighborhood school. The next day the family's pride
and joy, a bedimpled six-year-old girl, Tommie Sue, began
her education. Upon the child's return home, her mother did
not bother to ask, "What did you learn?" but proceeded
directly with the social catechism, "Who did you eat lunch
with today?"

Taken aback, Tommie Sue stammered, "Well, Mommy, I

had lunch with six little colored children." To which her mother responded sharply, "How could you? There are only six colored children in the whole school!"

This was too much. The little girl burst into tears, "But Mommy, you wouldn't want me to eat lunch with those damnyankees, would you?"

Although the films of social criticism were considered off-beat in the 50's, they were there and the better educated people were seeing them, particularly the mothers and their children. Out of the horror of war and the anguish of rebuilding shattered lives, moviegoers in Europe and American became willing to let the cause of humankind, especially the poor and the downtrodden, seep into their consciences. Immediately after World War II the Italians set the theme with films like *Paisan, Bicycle Thief, Bitter Rice,* and *Shoe Shine.* Similarly the Scandinavians in Bergman's *The Seventh Seal* and the French in Cocteau's *Beauty and the Beast* contributed to a growing sense of abhorrence at man's stupidity, hypocrisy, and inhumanity. This was also the time when England's angry young men took to their tongues and John Osborne's *Room at the Top* was put into film. The contemporary movie *I'm All Right, Jack* also exposed the rising materialism in which each individual thought first and foremost of himself. Foreign films became popular in the United States because they were concerned with issues. The slick, superficial Doris Day movie had already run its gamut—"from A to B." The once-regal roar of the MGM lion was becoming threadbare and feeble, a mere whimper of its former self.

The first major American movie in which parents became villains was *Rebel Without A Cause* in 1955. In the same year *The Blackboard Jungle* portrayed the ineffectiveness of the school system and the helplessness of its victims; and *On the Waterfront* spoke to the problem of corruption in the urban society. Thus a trend began which gathered momentum in the 60's. Films spoke to a rising public interest (particularly of youth) in social criticism. Nothing was sacred. Authority figures, the social elite, the older generation, the religious hierarchy, and the business establishment—all were shown as black at heart or at least a dirty gray. These films, of course, did not depict feelings and attitudes that were not already in the air. They could not have been successful unless there was an audience waiting for them.

XI • The Background of the Mothers of the Dissenters

In the late 40's and early 50's the mothers of the dissenters were the young women who still lived with the memories of the Depression and of World War II. In her own teenage years in the late 1930's one such young woman reported rarely complaining about having to make her only coat from a woolen mill remnant or putting in eight-hour days (at everything from stoop labor to waitressing and tutoring) while she worked her way through college. She was deeply concerned, however, about solutions to the "larger issues" which she thought through in the meetings of the silent Quakers and expressed by signing the Oxford Peace Pledge. Having faced these large problems in her own youth, she was anxious to escape from the old unsatisfactory patterns of life and to help her children avoid them. The causes to which she had decided to devote her life were the elimination of injustice, bigotry, and war—in the nation and in the world at large.

In the conflict of her thought, dissatisfaction with the major society was countered by the conviction that better life styles were within reach. Never before in history had

humanity been able to invent a present and a future, and, if
we were botching the magnificent opportunity we should
shake ourselves—hard—count to ten, and start over. Perhaps
we were valuing the wrong things, investing our national and
personal birthrights foolishly. The cloud at Hiroshima had
not dispersed completely and new storms were gathering, but
there was optimism abroad too.

To understand the mother's reactions of skepticism and
idealism—the questioning arch of a brow as well as the
resonance of hope in her proud-mother tones which later
became the ambivalent attitudes of the young revolutionaries, her children—we should look at her own educational
experience. This is the group of women who went to college
and most of them graduated. Earlier they had lived through
the harsh realities of the 30's and, upon enrolling in the
humanities and liberal arts, sought to understand more about
this phenomenon as well as the war which had haunted their
youth.

The historians whom she read in college, the elder Schle-
singer, Beard and Commager, writers such as Theodore Drei-
ser (particularly in *Sister Carrie*), Sinclair Lewis (both in *Main
Street* and *Arrowsmith*), and the journalist Lincoln Steffens
in his autobiography did not spare the Robber Barons and
the Babbitts, but they also suggested ways—tortuous perhaps
—to enter a promised land. After college the young women,
especially those in social work and teaching,* found hope in
the writings of mental hygienists and such post-Thorndikian
educational psychologists as Edgar Dale and Arthur Jersild.
Dale was also a social scientist who wrote *How to Read a
Newspaper* in 1937. In this he suggested how to avoid being

---

*Some of the liberal arts graduates began to question the fairness of a
system that encouraged women to work as students in history, literature,
and languages, but rarely offered them an opportunity on the college
faculties as teachers in these fields. For example, at the State University of
New York at Buffalo, in the large faculty of arts and letters where most
women students concentrate, there is not a single woman full professor
(*Discrimination Against Women, op. cit.*, p. 153).

taken in by the "slanted" adjectives of *Time*'s pejorative
descriptions of political personages. However in other publications Dale showed his idealism by proposing that education must teach people "to think and to care."

In *Search for Self* (1952), Jersild described the wholesome,
healthy person as one who does not need to cheat, steal, be
cruel, or take advantage of others. He stressed that this did
not mean the lack of emotion. In fact one could not be
creative without emotion, and it was important to be creative. Maturity and control are not the same thing. For
maturity it is necessary to be spontaneous and to live fully—
to be really able to enjoy things, to love, to laugh, to feel
genuine sorrow. His implication was that this is not what goes
on in the market place or in most classrooms. In reading such
books the young mother could not help but ask if life didn't
have something better to offer than getting ahead in the
world and making money.

Looking to the past for authority and direction was no
solution. Surely, despite the sanctions of society against such
acts, thinking for oneself was in order, and this thinking
should include the making of plans for a better future—a
world without war and where quality of life was given precedence over quantity of things. Wendell Johnson (a popular
writer, speaker, and general semanticist of the 40's and 50's)
reported that people used to remark, "If it's good enough for
grandpa, it's good enough for me." But he went on to say that
it is not good enough for us today nor was it really good
enough for grandpa. After all, grandpa went through two
world wars. Johnson stressed that it was possible for all to be
clear-eyed and confident. It was not necessary for people to
be neurotic and unhappy. His message was, "Let's stop standing downstream and pulling out the bodies—let's go upstream
and see who's pushing them in."

Empathy now became an important concept. This was
stressed in the women's magazines, in the liberal arts courses,
in education, social service, and nursing. It meant "seeing the

world through another person's eyes." The relationship of physical disorders to emotional disorders was also emphasized. Psychological illness was seen, at least by the better educated, as no more related to innate depravity than was physical illness. The writings of the 50's pointed out again and again that everyone had flaws. A Canadian film of the period was entitled, *We're All Handicapped.* This blanket category undoubtedly included adults as well as children, rich as well as poor, men as well as women, the system as well as the individual. Imperfection was part of the human condition—an idea which the young, as well as their mothers, undoubtedly found highly acceptable. Since they were so often treated as second-class citizens, it was comforting to know that even the master class was flawed.

The new psychology, influencing and influenced by the new mother, also affected the child in many ways. And the latter, as a responsive organism in the post-industrial society, helped to write the psychology that explained his behavior and even the books that gave prescriptions for his rearing. Expressive education is said to be the wave of the future in the schools, but mother and child had already been trying it out—riding, perhaps somewhat precariously, on the crest of the wave. For the past twenty-five years the emerging values of what has been called the counter-culture had emphasized finding oneself, expressing oneself, and living fully in the now.

Beyond freeing the child and his emotions was the need to provide him with an evocative and challenging environment. This was attempted by increasing the number of artifacts available to him. For a number of years now preschool children have had dance-along, sing-along, talk-along records and by 1969 they had "Sesame Street." As they grew older, they had allowances that made it possible for them to buy things for themselves and as a result they amassed large record collections.

By the 60's the pop records did more than merely reflect the youth culture, they served as a radicalizing force. And, since they were and are played very, very loud, this music must have influenced the mothers as well. How could they have escaped?

The words and the music asked society to stop in its tracks and take a long hard look at itself. The message was that the game was up. The smoke screen with which the Establishment surrounded itself was seen for what it was—*smog*. By now the fact that the technocratic society, complete with "defense" mentality, was working against the best interests of human beings was screamed from the rooftops. The conglomerate was openly stigmatized as a "rat race" where the "white collars" were smudged and wilted from corruption and meaninglessness, and all too many of the WASP males were part of the nine-to-five brigade in the "lonely crowd."

By the 50's the young family had moved into the suburbs; and, after the austerity of the Depression and the voluntary belt tightening of World War II, there were signs of relief. Sleekness was extolled and plumpness arrived unannounced. Filet mignon and New York cuts began to take the place of hamburger, and T-birds were bought at premium prices when the Model T had once sufficed. Conspicuous consumption became a way of life for many. Obsolescence was the revolving door in which more and more consumer goods perished. The pied pipers of fashion design called for change at the drop of a hat. The costumes shifted with the same maddening frequency that afflicted the sets.

But the one-time liberal arts major felt uneasy about it all. As we have seen she was now reading the radical social philosophers. Poverty was rediscovered. Michael Harrington wrote *The Other America*. Madison Avenue, through advertising, had been capitalizing on the new markets—first the mother and then the teenagers. Initially it seemed that a retreat into the family and the building up of togetherness would ease the anxiety that had been left over from the Depression and the war years. However the fact that the father in these affluent homes was away more than ever and that material possessions did not satisfy the spiritual desires meant that a kind of unease and anxiety hung like an ill omen on the horizon. In the early 50's there was the Korean War to remind the mother that mankind in general and Americans in particular had not solved their problems. Even if she had wanted to follow Voltaire's advice and "tend her own garden," or lose herself in the intricacies of bridge, the ever-present radio and its big brother, television, would not allow these anodynes to be a complete reprieve.

In fact television, that happy hunting ground of the Madison Avenue adman, invaded and "occupied" the privacy of the living room, bringing with it the "fine" arts of public relations and the dishonesty of the boardroom. There on the screen, in full display, all stops open, was the "$64,000 Question," its participants wired and controlled and the answers rigged in advance. The credibility gap really began in the late 50's with the tragic exposure of Charles Van Doren, while the real villains—the men behind the scenes raking in the profits—remained unscathed, anonymous.

At the same time the popular literature on mental health was ever more abundant. There the young mother could find prescriptions for handling personal problems and raising her children. But she had already become suspicious of all formulas. Religion, which had been the supreme antidote for her own mother, no longer satisfied. Well before the radical clergy of the 60's took to the idea, she was feeling that the ministry should come down from the pulpit, out of the confession box, and into the streets. She was concerned about how to shake off ancient prejudices and other atavisms of the mind, which still clung to the main body of churchgoers like tarnished haloes.

Prior to the 50's there had been the facile prescriptions of J.B. Watson and the precise delineations of Gesell, side by side with the apparent profundities of Freud, that arch-priest of oversimplification. The facile formula, the pat answer, the Procrustean couch were increasingly probed for what they concealed or failed to tell. These gifted and sensitive women had realized that life was much more complex than anything like the how-to-do-it manual had so far suggested. They began to feel that they should live free-form lives and "hang loose." The important thing was to be one's self and to be honest. In this way the children would be harmed less. In the view of the new woman it was apparent that authority and prescriptions had not worked either in the larger society or in the home. Was it not time, therefore, for a new style and a new society?

Although there were a few years when a large family was fashionable and "togetherness" joined "expressiveness" as a dominant psychological theme, it was not long before many of the more thoughtful mothers were hearing a new message at the PTA meetings and were taking it seriously. The spokesmen of the social services and psychological agencies were spreading the same doctrine that the mothers heard from other sources. There was a convergence of messages. Let the child express himself and speak out. "It was better to have a child talk back than to sit and brood." "Talking problems through" was suggested as a way for the mother to deal with the child at home just as it had become a common way for the upper middle class mother to deal with her own problems—on the analyst's couch.

The reticence of speech—of strong, silent men—that had been valued by a pioneer society was replaced by loquacity. "Talking out," as well as "acting out," was felt to be therapeutic. Criticism of the social order became freewheeling and easier to make. Phrases to express such attitudes were coined already and through the music of protest these became part of the adolescent vocabulary. The therapists had made efforts to bring the unconscious to the fore for several decades but the new music seemed a quicker, surer way. Now the unconscious of the adolescent (and of his mother when she was within earshot) was assaulted regularly. If one could not improve the world or find a new one, at least one could escape to the inner self.

Part of the distrust that the mothers came to feel, as they explored the situation or mulled it over unconsciously, may

have been due to the fact that they were better educated
than women had ever been before. Each was potentially or
absolutely an intellectual and hence a critic of society.

Already we have noticed that gifted youth of the 50's were
aware of the studies on the authoritarian personality. Undoubtedly their mothers were too. Certainly there was a
continuing concern that men such as Hitler and Stalin and
Mussolini should not rise to power. There was a widespread
cognizance of the dangers of being a True Believer. The
war-crime trials at Nuremberg were followed all too quickly
by Senator Joseph McCarthy's intimidations of the American
public. The total demagogue package did not fail to horrify
these gifted women who were seeking a good way of life for
themselves and their families. They were fully aware of the
dangers that all of these things could hold for the mind and
spirit.

Skepticism was also mounting in another area. Science and
technology no longer seemed to have the answers. In fact
their basic worth was being called in question. Granted that
these forces were ever gaining strength in the industrial-
military complex as well as in the universities, nevertheless in
some sectors of the larger society and among able women in
particular, the suspicions spread that these very forces had
been responsible for the devastation of World War II and the
Korean War. Had not Einstein remarked at the time when the
bomb was dropped on Hiroshima that "Everything on earth
has changed except the thinking in men's minds?"

Women were ever reminded that they were continuing to
live in a Garrison State and that for the first time in American history, except for periods of general war, men were
being drafted into the Army. Also need it be said that women
were never really comfortable with machines? They did not
understand how the washing machine, the TV, and the motor
in their car worked—and, what is more, they did not care!
With the advent of the new statistics, and the fact that
well-read individuals knew that this was "the century of
probability," and that one "educated guess" was probably as

good as another one, even the venerable scientific method and logical thinking appeared increasingly fallible. Since women had never been expected to think logically and usually were told they didn't do well at it, they secretly applauded the New Critics of Science. Mutiny against the method was spreading. Perhaps there was still a place in this world for intuitive thought, feeling tone, and aesthetic sensibility.

Finally the young mother began to doubt the importance of the achievement motive. She became keenly aware of the ambiguities of progress—what technologizing our society was doing to the world and what working hard and getting ahead was doing to her husband. Her dreams of togetherness were more often than not shattered by the fact that her husband, if a rising professional or businessman, had to work long hours and was separated a great deal from her and the children. Surely he deserved a better kind of life than that and so did she and the children. These feelings, plus the fact that she felt a gnawing anxiety about the ascendancy of machines, made her long for another life style.

When the young began confronting the system in the mid-60's, were they not continuing a revolutionary ferment which had long been incubating in the doubts and disillusionment of the mothers?

XII • Teachers and Schools As They Are Now

It becomes ever more clear that the schools are the next step in the new generation's development of new goals and values. It is here that the youth culture is formed; here that students meet the great ideas of the past and can be, if fortunate, caught up in learning; here that the most outstanding teachers inspire the young to become their best possible selves. Yet we have found that many students, including many of the most gifted—and particularly the Creative Intellectuals—find school uninspiring and irrelevant. Although "cool" behavior has been lauded in the past, youth now consider commitment and involvement more important. Schools should be part of life and teachers should show unmistakable signs of being alive. Moral fervor is more impressive than the threat of a test or a trip to the principal's office. The authority of the textbook and the teacher—as is the case with papal and presidential power—is just not enough.

There is little doubt but that the American society stands, if not on its ear, then precariously near the brink of profound social reconstruction. The old mythologies are disintegrating, and great, hungry vacuums have emerged. The young are looking "for a leader" and for ideals to believe in. A reaffirmation and a shoring up of old values or a marshalling of new ones is clearly indicated.

Teachers can, and in some cases already do, step into this gap. Students find themselves nearer in their ways of thinking to these mentors than to most adults in their parents' age groups. Schools—which occupy large shares of the time that youth has at hand—are generally as good or as bad as teachers make them. Thus it becomes vital in any study of youth also to look closely at what teachers and schools are like now, and then at what they might be. What would be the ideal teacher and the ideal learning environment if education accepted as its primary goal the development of better human beings?

Since World War II, preparing for an uncertain future and for careers that come and go with alarming rapidity often seems pointless to the more perceptive young people. Teachers feel the demands of youth. They are also aware of the resistance to all of these desired innovations by the older taxpayers, members of the standard, traditional world. The latter want the young to sit quietly and learn their lessons— along with love for flag and country, respect for parents and elders, and willingness to comply with all the usual conventions—and work within the system. But for teachers the young audience is closer at hand, nearer of age (since many teachers are young, too), and more open in its desires. As with theater audiences, these students want to involve themselves in the play and improvise the drama. As with the new environmental art, they want to become part of the action. For many the themes on which education generally focuses— reason, technology, and methodology—seem divorced from reality.

The burgeoning human problems—anomie, alienation, valuelessness, violence—suggest that, in addition to the need for refinement of sensibilities and intellect, teachers themselves should be particularly mature and wise human beings. There is a growing opinion that they should be conversant with aesthetics as well as able to practice at least some of the less occult arts of the psychotherapist.

Although there seem to be rather clear needs for teachers with intellectual talent and social sensitivity, the issues of how to train and select them, how they should function in the classroom, and how children learn best are far from settled. Viewpoints about learning range across a broad spectrum. Strikingly at odds are the humanist-educators, who feel that learning primarily occurs as a result of facilitating relationships (Goethe: "We learn only through those we love"), and the technologist-educators, who claim that teachers cause anxiety and are less flexible than the hardware (Oettinger: "Students seem to prefer the undivided attention of the computer to the neglect by the individual teacher"). My view is that teachers are crucially important, both for their knowledge and wisdom and for their ability to relate to others. How they feel about learning and about their students can retard or facilitate the latter's capacity to learn, as well as help students grow toward self-understanding and mutual cooperation.

Teachers who are excited learners can communicate this to their students, but teachers who themselves found school a hard grind and continue in later years to read or study only under duress also communicate *these* feelings and attitudes.

Mrs. Jones, who worked with Don Saxon when he was in the fifth grade, also had a group of gifted third graders. Her own interests in observation and experiment and inquiring into all manner of natural phenomena were never far below the surface. She did everything—from the common experiment of demonstrating the expansion of air by heating a pop bottle capped by a balloon, to showing the youngsters how to make a mobile by precisely calculating the length each wire should be and just how close together the shapes could be suspended.

One day the third-grade group catapulted into the library, tipping over the wastebasket and knocking the Hans Christian Andersen diorama askew. They had suddenly realized that there was a monstrous hole on the playground, and speculations were rife as to its origins. The sixth-grade teacher, having overheard the beginnings of the discussion, had moved in on the group and informed them flatly that the hole was simply land behind a terminal moraine which had been left by a glacier that had pushed down from Canada in the Pleistocene epoch. In fact the same glacier or one of its companions had probably carved out the Great Lakes. At the time of the last big glacier movement southern Michigan was a terminus.

The little group of gifted doubters and dissenters, who were learning to ask questions even about "final" answers, did not accept this pronouncement gracefully and were sure there must be some better answer.

Mrs. Jones saw this as a teachable moment, a time for formulating questions (hypotheses) and for testing them. Bill said he was sure the hole was the remains of the foundation of an old building that had been torn down. In fact his brother had seen the wreckers come. Becky speculated that it "just might be" a crater left from a volcano. Only the budding young scientist, Inge Sorenson, was willing to test the sixth-grade teacher's theories.

The next step was to decide how the truth could be determined. What were ways of knowing? Ways of finding out? The more studious suggested consulting encyclopedias, the budding social scientists thought interviewing "old timers" would be the right way, and Inge decided she would find a means to test the validity of the terminal moraine theory.

Encyclopedias supplied information about volcanoes, and it was quite clear that the North Central states were a very ancient area—the land had not altered fundamentally for millions and millions of years—and there were no volcanoes within a thousand miles. The young social scientists found that no one in the area had a memory of a large building except Bill's brother. Led by Inge, the systematic observer, they examined the flora, fauna, and geology of the area. Finally Inge had a flash of insight as she looked at a young maple tree almost six inches in diameter that grew in the center·of the "hole." "Bill," she asked, "just how old is your brother?" It turned out that he was ten, and Inge informed Bill that the tree could not be less than thirty years old. That same day she picked up some reddish rocks and compared them with the small rock fragments on her cardboards on which her collection of rock samples were attached. There was no question but that the rocks from the hole in the playground had a strong iron content and had probably been pushed down from Michigan's Upper Peninsula. No one could remember seeing rocks of this kind before in the area. Somehow Mrs. Jones was always able not only to allow but also to stimulate students to be eager learners, continually searching for truth in its manifold varieties.

Similarly the teachers who profess to love young people, but obviously do not, cannot help but reveal their true feelings. Such implicit attitudes come through as an unspoken contradiction to those the teacher avows. Even the less perceptive students interpret the situation: "What she is speaks so loud that I cannot hear her words." Sometimes the ways and power of love are a little strange. Mrs. Snell was my daughter Karen's fourth-grade teacher and had told me repeatedly when she saw me at after-school meetings or at in-service workshops how much she loved children. Her face was open, ruddy, and quite without guile, and so I never doubted her sincerity. Thus I was a little surprised that Karen said the children were careful not to stand too close to her. I probed further: "But Mrs. Snell says she just loves children."

"But that's the trouble," Karen expostulated. "Whenever we're near she grabs us and then she hugs us, and you know she's a very big woman. And she wears a steel corset, and when she hugs us it hurts." Perhaps she was, as Karen implied, not only good-natured and hearty, but also just a little insensitive.

The attitudes of teachers—shown by gestures, voice tone, and other ways still unfathomed—are probably more important than the words they say. Albert Mehrabian did some interesting research in the 60's which confirmed this. As he put it:

> The verbal part of a spoken message has considerably less effect on whether a listener feels liked or disliked than a speaker's facial expression or tone of voice. . . . In fact we've worked out a formula that includes how much each of these components contributes to the effect of the message as a whole. It goes like this: Total impact = .07 (verbal) + .38 (vocal) + .55 (facial).*

Miss Patricia Brod, a sensitive and intelligent elementary teacher, reports that when she was teaching a group of third graders she was dismayed to find that *Streets and Roads* was the reading text from which she was supposed to teach. This book was almost identical, despite revisions, to the *Streets and Roads* that she had been forced to read at least five times when she herself was in school. It was her decision not to talk about this, but simply to pass out the books and have the children read "as usual." After only a few days seven-year-old Shelley, referring to the books that were being distributed, said, "Miss Brod, you don't like that book, do you?"

The reply was, "No, Shelley, I really don't. But how did you know?"

"I don't know. It's just something about the way you pass them out."

A year later Miss Brod reflected again on the sensitivity of children:

> I hadn't realized how much my students learned from the expression in my eyes until I broke my glasses and found it would take a week to have them replaced. Since I'm very nearsighted, it was necessary for me to wear my prescription sunglasses in the classroom. As the week went by, more and more of my second-grade students complained about the sunglasses. "We can't tell what you're thinking when you're wearing those dark glasses, I wish you'd take them off."

*Albert Mehrabian, "Communication Without Words," *Psychology Today* (September, 1968), pp. 53-5.

It may be that the eyes are the windows to the teacher's thoughts as well as being "the windows of the soul."

My assumption is that a school, a classroom, or even an informal gathering, needs self-actualizing leadership if significant learnings are to take place and students are to feel that something has happened which was worthwhile. The atmosphere should be one in which the teacher suggests and guides, but where the initiative to learn and the energy required for continued learning come from the student. First and foremost learning is the *learner's* responsibility. As the teacher comes to know students as individuals with distinctive hopes, desires, and interests, she can guide, encourage, and educate in the ancient sense of "leading out." Martin Buber has explained how this might be done:

> It is only when someone takes him by the hand not as a "creator," but as a fellow-creature lost in the world, and greets him not as an artist but as comrade, friend, or lover, that he experiences an inner reciprocity.*

In contrast to the rare setting that fosters such self-directed learning, the atmosphere in the majority of classrooms is authoritarian or prescriptive. Authoritarian leadership is based on the role status of the teachers, who count on receiving respect simply because they are in a position of authority. This is in contrast to the real authority that comes from a recognized superiority of experience, knowledge, and insight. Only such humane authority is capable of wisely directing and utilizing growth and change. Too much of today's education is heavy-handed. This is in direct contrast to the fact that all children—and particularly the most sensitive and individualistic—respond best to the whisper of suggestion, not the shout of command. For wisdom is to know

---

*Translation by Herbert Read of a lecture given by Buber in 1925 in Heidelberg and published in Read's. *Education Through Art* (London: Faber and Faber, 1963), p. 286.

how little one knows, and teaching at its best communicates both charity and humility.

Since the early writings of John Dewey most liberal educators have held the democratic classroom to be ideal. Almost a century later, however, the truly democratic situation is rare. In classrooms, as in student government, democracy too frequently exists in name only. It should be understood that an acceptance of democratic procedures does not mean underwriting *laissez-faire* approaches or undirected permissiveness. In other words what is purported to be democracy cannot come about without some planning and some direction. Even in the free school, Fernwood (which will be discussed in Chapter XXII) where the students designed their own curriculum, there was a solid core. No group can be softly amorphous all the way through and survive. Somewhere there must be a spine and, more important, a brain stem. From this comes the life philosophy, the guiding direction. The primary relationships—the sense of communion—that are established must embrace not only a mutual forbearance but a positive kindness. The feelings and the rights of the other must always be uppermost in one's mind if oppositeness is to be overcome.

In every classroom, even those at the graduate level, there are disturbed people—sometimes just out of the mental hospital, sometimes on the brink. The teacher can foster group cohesiveness and help generate a warm atmosphere that can make a difference. She can encourage acts of simple kindness such as listening carefully, accepting and trying to understand what may be only superficially stupid or bizarre remarks. And she can refuse to allow the sharp-tongued to lash out at those who are shy and gauche and clumsy. If the class has become a group, its members will not sit alone at the refreshment break or recess unless they want to. Certain students, sensitive and humane, will become teacher surrogates and will look beyond the clusters to search out the lonely and the unnoticed. Even though their own interests may not appear to be directly served, they will move into the void and break

bread with the outsider. They will come to sense the difference between those who are sensitively enjoying silent communion with the moving branches on the tall evergreens and
the others who sit alone because they are afraid.

The democratic classroom must be a carefully designed
and synergic organism where there is an ongoing balance
between individual and group needs. In such a situation
students can learn not only to realize their own individual
potentialities but also to be mutually helpful and truly democratic. As Dewey pointed out, if we really want to help
people live together democratically, then we must recognize
that "democratic ends demand democratic methods for their
realization."*

As do most writers on education, I accept the democratic
dream and the themes of altruistic expression central to all
major religions and philosophies as desirable directions of
growth and as suitable goals for education. Edgar Dale, as we
saw, translates this more specifically to mean: Teachers
should help children learn to think and to care. John Gardner's view is in essential agreement: We must seek excellence
in a context of concern for all.

The fact is that, while most people accept the democratic
ideals at a slogan level, many would openly contest such
interpretations as those of Dale and Gardner. Probably only a
few teachers have thoughtfully designed programs where critical thinking and ethical concern are central. As Don Saxon
said when he was in Mr. Hewitt's room, "These school people
say thinking is good for children, but they don't teach us
how, and they don't give us anything very important to think
about."

And the records written in blood in the city streets, and by
the hunger and poverty of the "forgotten fifth," point to a
lack of effectiveness in teaching compassion. Paralleling the
realization that we too seldom teach thinking and caring, is a
growing recognition that teaching facts is no longer a mean-

*John Dewey, *Freedom and Culture* (New York: G.P. Putnam, 1939),
p. 175.

ingful activity. The major burden of the argument is that there are too many facts, that they change with an alarming frequency, and most of them are forgotten with alacrity.

Teaching children how to learn by themselves and encouraging them to continue learning and thinking and reading with unabated zest and curiosity seem far more desirable than the usual presentations of facts and conclusions. Even more important, however, is the need to build situations where the essential dimensions of understanding oneself and caring about one another will emerge. But the existing state of affairs is such that few teachers do these things and probably few know how. Further, they are not apt to learn these new behaviors unless their own attitudes, interests, and values change, and they probably will not function with the needed aplomb and *élan* unless their self-concepts improve.

To explore some common dimensions of the attitudes and abilities of teachers I interviewed a number of them as well as university students, and reviewed the literature on the teaching profession. From this descriptive source material I developed a typology which I hope will be helpful in thinking about teachers as they now appear to themselves and their young charges. If we can accept that there are at least three dominant American Ways which have produced three quite recognizable student types,* then it will not be difficult to see that teachers, too, generally fall into the same categories, as do all human beings. This is all said with full knowledge of the Whitehead dictum: "Seek simplicity and then distrust it."

---

*In presenting these types [both of students and teachers], I fully recognize that they are not hard and fast, that actual individuals straddle some of the divisions, that all individuals differ, and that their major emphases may shift in the course of time.

XIII • The Three Types of Teachers

THE SOCIAL TEACHER: SUCCESS ORIENTATION

What salvation was to medieval man, competitive success is to modern man. At the turn of the century Edward Spranger postulated in *Types of Men* that the drives to acquire material things and to want power were two universally held values. For those seeking success by the standards of the affluent society, this still holds. The teacher who hopes to become the school administrator—and thus wield power and control purse strings—knows that the route to the top is through organizational channels. His preference is for "running things," not for questioning ultimate goals. He defines progress more in terms of movement than of destination. His focus is on means—technological innovation and an ever-accelerating GNP—rather than ends. These entrepreneurs of the classroom, who accept the organizational goals of growth and power, and who adopt obedience, manipulative personal relations, and opportunistic behavior as their norm, are apt to succeed if they have moderate ability as well as a modicum of energy and a large amount of self-confidence. Although they give lip service to individualism, their route ahead is clearly marked as one that demands acquiescence to authority and obeisance to convention. Individualism, thus, means looking out for oneself.

Accepting things as they are, the success-oriented teacher works out a scheme of action within this framework. Since he delegates as much work as possible, his talent need only be minimal. Influence, through sociability and conviviality, is important. He respects the powerful and successful and tends to display a typically authoritarian hostility to minority groups.

The description of the success-oriented teacher which follows is constructed from interviews which I conducted with a broad sample of teachers of all types.

> This is a practical teacher, rather than an idealist or a man of ideas. His values are materialistic, and truth for him is what he sees, not what he seeks out. He values promotion and pay, and status in the eyes of the larger society. He is anti-intellectual and lacks strong loyalty to friends or fellow professionals. He's not above cutting someone down to build himself up. He is out to win, no holds barred. All cultural history is sometimes depicted as a battle between the Philistines and literati, the fatheads and egg-heads. He himself is a Philistine. In his personal relations he is superficially friendly—hail fellow, well-met. For him success is an amalgam of luck and expedient behavior built upon crafty clever-ness with a scaffolding of charisma and cajolery. His characteristic style is simple and objective—a "slogan mentality."

> He wants to run things rather than do the work; to be best liked or chairman of committees (but not the workhorse or idea man). He does not actively (openly) rock the boat unless this approach will lead to material success. Does not "fight" reports. Instead he complies with the bare minimum. Does not work for educational change as a result of conviction or philosophical view or research evidence, but is apt to get on the current "bandwagon" since he wants to go places. Dislikes philosophical discussion, particularly avoids "examining" values, ethics, morality, "knowing himself."

Has open contempt for peaceniks, hippies, and assorted "bleeding hearts" and "do-gooders."

In college he was not BMOC but wanted to be. Lacked connections, brains, looks, or something else for entering the business world directly. Was not above conniving, apple-polishing, and cheating. Accepts the affluent society's definition of success. Wants a job that pays well and has status. Teaching was and is a second choice. He wants to be more than a teacher.

The success-oriented social leader girl may teach immediately after college, but since marrying into the affluent society is important, she may realize her best route is through lower-level white-collar channels in the business world or via stewardessing. Often the social leader girl, wife of a not-too-successful businessman, will come into teaching as her children approach college age because she needs funds. Generally she is a suburban koffee-klatcher—often active in clubs, bridge, and decorating her house according to the dictums of the women's magazines—but not in humanitarian or civic causes, reading, theater, music, art. She tends not to like lower-class children. These children don't have "good backgrounds"—often they smell, say bad words, and mumble, slur, and commit syntax errors when they say them. They do not know place names or geography, nor do they care much. Further they have not been read to and don't know how to sit still. They lack minimum frames of reference. But there are also other young people who don't appeal. The success-oriented teacher rarely likes creative intellectual students who have read and seen and thought too much. She can accept social leader and studious types, but even with them her teaching is perfunctory. Like her male counterpart, she is not a great teacher and does not aspire to be.

These social leader teachers are bored with that part of their work which calls for intellectual effort. When they receive student exercises and test papers, more often than not these go into the wastebasket—unread. In fact, they find it difficult to keep ahead of the students in the textbook. As a result many class periods are spent having students one-by-one read the assignment a-paragraph-at-a-time, round-robin fashion. This usually can be relied on to consume the class period, and when the bill rings, all the students who are still awake sigh and pass on.

During their free periods these teachers clump in the lounge (after all, they don't have to make preparations) where they smoke and gossip. Here their social leaderism can come to the fore as they discuss the most intimate and lurid details of students' lives and comment caustically on other teachers. Their conversation bristles with belittling remarks about the poor old workhorses who take the "curriculum" seriously and the "pointy-headed" intellectuals whom they identify as "liberal Communists."

THE STANDARD TEACHER: PROFESSIONAL ORIENTATION

In the eyes of the larger world, the Standard Teachers often seem timid and mousy. They give the appearance of being less mature than the aggressive and extraverted social types, those who aspire to be administrators. Belonging to the Standard Traditional World, they look to convention and conscience for guidelines in thought and action. This Mr. or Mrs. Milquetoast is seen as an over-conformer, toeing the line and obeying the rules. At the irrational-conscientious level of character development these adult versions of the studious child are less apt to use others for their own ends than the Social Leader, who is a teacher-cum-administrator. In the world of traditional values others are not exploited knowingly, and there is little expectation of immediate personal reward. Things are done because they are the right things to do. The Standard Teacher is always ready to take responsibility, often with a touch of unction and a garnish of "I know what is best"—for the classroom, often for the school, and sometimes for the community. Concern is rarely voiced for changing the world—except back to the "good old days." However in the best of the Standard Teachers the Protestant Ethic continues to flourish, and their lives are ornamented by duty and obligation. Material success is important, but it should be won honestly—by hard work and without undue deviousness.

Unlike the social leader teacher who is adaptive and opportunistic, the Standard Teacher is studious and professional, conventionally idealistic and quite moral. He has incorporated the voiced standards of his own teachers and parents and honestly believes that keeping the child busy is necessary for his mental and moral health. Children are cautioned not to have "idle hands" and are upbraided if they "stargaze" or "window-watch," "sit around" or "kill time." Instead they are exhorted to "make the most of their time" and not "let the grass grow under their feet." This teacher has more the "proverb" than the "slogan" mentality.

In Freudian terms the Standard Teacher harkens to his superego which emits the voice of conscience and assorted guilt feelings which are translated into rules for the unruly. The ebullient child who is an excited learner needs to be brought into line. He must learn to do only so much and very little more. Thus he is not allowed to do tomorrow's work today, and it is a capital crime to read next year's book. Similarly the low-gear learner must be urged to move ahead and hopefully to catch up. Going slowly in the hard book is often more approved than reading a more appropriate book that is different from the rest of the class.

Standard Teachers tend to standardize everything. Procedures and lesson plans follow a pattern which is often worked out laboriously over the years and has no fuzzy areas or soft spots where a child's imagination can wander freely. Boundaries of time, space, amount, and kind are continually set. An art lesson can be as precise as a parade-ground drill:

> 20 minutes to do a picture. Draw it on a 9 X 12 piece of manila paper. Put it in the center. Fill up the page and put your name in the top right-hand corner. Use only one sheet and draw on one side. Make an animal. No people. No hanky-panky.

In its most extreme form, SOP (Standard Operating Procedure) becomes one way—the teacher's way is the right way. Thus "all the eggs are in one basket" and much time and energy are expended in their production. It's "The Eggs and I" against the world. (Once a teacher, all of fifty years of age but bedecked with genuine tears, approached a young university lecturer asking, "Do you mean to tell me I've been teaching spelling wrong all these years?" No amount of explanation that there were *many* ways to teach spelling—the lecturer's way, the teacher's way, and others—seemed to heal her wounds.)

These are some of the phrases typically used by the persons I interviewed to characterize this kind of teacher:

> Does the expected well. Fits the role, the stereotype. Goes the Horatio Alger way. As a teacher is well accepted by older teachers, the hierarchy, and the administration. Gets reports in on time. Follows rules. Runs a taut room. Not too friendly with children. Keeps an appropriate distance from youth; thus may grow old before his time. Often seems self-righteous and may foster dependence. Needs authority. Demands and gets respect. Supports teachers against children. Knows right way to teach—usually involves texts, tests—can explain this and convince parents that "good teaching" is being done. After all, it's the way they were taught. Thinks his task is to give answers rather than to raise questions. Covers work in syllabus. Reads texts, students' papers, and exams. Not much beyond. Lectures or has recitations. Dominates all verbal interaction. Prepares students for next year's work, next year's teacher. Education is the same as it was for him when he was a child.

> Tended to be studious in high school and college. School was a hard grind. If one were not highly gifted or somewhat devious, this was the only way to get the grades that made it possible to get the certificate and the degree. Was conditioned to accept what parents, elders, teachers, and books say as gospel. Conducts self with care in all public places. And monitors leisure with care, too. Guilt feelings are rarely in abeyance. Thus monitored, has had no time to read widely, participate in "culture." Understandably lacked the developed tastes, interests, habits to participate in the world of the arts when he began to teach. With his nose to the grindstone, tends to stay at "kitsch" level. Tastes are banal and undeveloped. Concerned more with career and profession than authenticity as a person. Being professional stands in the way of being real. In upper grades and high school tends to be subject- and discipline-oriented in the most conventional terms. The near horizons, not the far reaches of the discipline. In the primary grades is reading and busy-work oriented, not child-oriented. There is something intrinsically good about keeping children busy

and not letting them look out the window. It is also desirable for them to be clean and neat—after all, "Cleanliness is next to Godliness." Times are set and rules are made for cleaning desks, washing hands, and marching through the halls. These are as much a part of the curriculum as reading.

Such restricted behavior patterns wall off the Standard Teachers and their young studious alter egos from free choice and free thought. In their classrooms traditional conceptions of the world and the *status quo* of behavior are never challenged by design and rarely by chance. There is little time or tolerance for student self-examination, contemplation of alternative actions, or raising serious questions. Thus there is a modest husbanding of the human condition in terms of protective socialization. But little is done to help the young learn to live in the present or the future, nor is there a concern for the kind of social action that might safeguard the human estate. Tradition—doing things the right way and teaching by the book—is all but irresistible.

With the years the authoritarian tendency may firm up to a degree which can blot out openness to the new, tolerance of ambiguity, acknowledgment of complexity, and the more passionate commitments. Life as the Professionals live it can be grim, and secretly they may mourn never sensing intellectual or spiritual triumph or giving in to outright joy. But they do not admit to this in public.

THE SELF-ACTUALIZING TEACHER: CREATIVE INTELLECTUAL AND EMPATHIC-ALTRUIST ORIENTATIONS

The Self-Actualizing Teacher is a rare and, as the day-to-day reality of teaching goes, sometimes an unhappy breed, although his characteristic stance is often optimistic. In general he is idealistic and responsible—traits which are expressed in terms of concern for both the larger and the local community. Unlike the Standard Teacher he breaks with tradition and precedent. He believes all (his version of humanity-at-large includes teachers and students) should think for themselves and in terms of what the world is now and what it might be.* He is concerned about the human condition and the human estate, the private world and the public domain. He hopes to improve the present society by putting ideals into practice and working toward such goals as liberty, equality, and fraternity. His is the creative intellectual world inhabited by some scientists, many humanists, the Upper Bohemians, the ecumenists, the old liberals, and the New Left.

No institutions, schools included, were made for those who aspire to self-actualization. Just as Rousseau saw society as the enemy, so do the Creative Intellectuals still resist the inevitable prison of constraint erected by law and dogma, rules and regulations. Yet school is a place where ideas and children can be found. Both can be delightful.

On the better days—when the intercom systems are quiet and textbooks are on the shelves—duty and pleasure merge in such a way that both teacher and students are conspicuously, self-consciously, and joyously engaged in learning. At such times work is play and learning is for learning's sake. Whether this is in or out of school does not matter. (With Ishmael, they might hold that "a whale ship is my Yale College and my Harvard.") Learning in these terms is not confined to the time-frame of the school or the space-frame of the classroom, but pervades the breadth and length of life. Nonverbal learning takes on great importance and, for those of generalist persuasion, nothing is irrelevant to anything else.

The Self-Actualizing Teacher does not plan to succeed through professional thrust and sortie or by economic pillage and plunder. Instead he hopes to leave his mark by having "the courage to be an individual." Some concentrate on

---

*By contrast, the Success-Oriented and the Standard Teachers tend to live in the past and in the present and thus do not see a need for helping students to plan a future. For them management will suffice. Often coping becomes the order of the day. Creative extensions of thought are rare. Utopian conceptions border on blasphemy.

social reform, others find and present themselves through the arts, and still others prefer the discipline of the sciences.

The dedication to truth, the stance of flexibility and forthrightness, is one that the organizational society and the institutionalized schools find abrasive. In the Establishment the questioning voice is more often heard as an anathema than as the accent of reason. Aware of these problems this teacher finds he cannot, in honesty and good faith, behave differently. He must continue to be concerned with ideas, creative change, and the ethics that underlie thoughts and actions.

As we have studied teachers who are seen as self-actualizing, more specific descriptions have emerged:

> There appear to be two major groups of these Self-Actualizing Teachers: the Creative Intellectuals and the Empathic Altruists. And among the Creative Intellectuals there are the Artist-Poet-Mystics and the Humanistic Scientists. (The former, a tropic plant in too temperate a climate, rarely survives long enough to become naturalized and tenured.) Sometimes these qualities merge in an individual, but more characteristically the urge to work creatively finds its emphasis in either ideas or people. Always the search for truth and authenticity is there. Theories and values (the democratic dream and the Judeo-Christian ethic) are taken seriously. It is the right of all to think for themselves, speak for themselves, become themselves. It is a duty as well. Success is viewed as being true to oneself. Styles of teaching become highly personal. Innovation is continuous, but never without concern for what premises lie beneath the change. Typically they work beyond textbook and curriculum: "I would be bored to death if I ever taught a class the same way twice." But topics have a familiar ring about them. The focus is apt to be on the Grand Abstractions and crucial, current, and controversial issues.
>
> The creative intellectual teachers most apt to survive are the Scientist Scholars. Being a change agent in science is safer than in the social realm. The Romantic Rebels have built-in problems. Their quest, for themselves and their students, is for a community of scholars and artists—in books and materials and in the flesh. In this search they take risks—try the untried, explore the unverifiable, ask the unanswerable.

Nearly always their interests are strong and their commitments passionate. They love to teach, but are often at odds with the other teachers and administrators. They use up their points early. With a beard. A lack of spit and polish. Scruffy but often flamboyant. Conspicuously irregular. A beflowered mini-bus with the bumper sticker of the week. Questionable friends. Morality is so important as to be taken seriously, but is redefined. They are often more concerned with honesty and integrity than correct behavior. They resist faculty parties, teacher gatherings, committee meetings. May also disregard or actively reject routine teacher tasks—keeping records, filling out forms. Being an administrator, for most, would be unthinkable. May not cover required work or may handle it very quickly. "Do your textbook this weekend and we will spend a month on the mystics." Apt to come late and stay late. Room may not be in chaos, but is rarely neat. Desk is piled high. Many things, including a wide variety of animals, artifacts, and books, casually inhabit the classroom. Students in their courses choose their own topics and emphases and the budding Creative Intellectuals—when unleashed—typically explore the tangential, divergent, and exotic. But since focus is self-chosen, both teachers and students work diligently and long.

Many of the creative intellectual teachers characteristically gravitate toward secondary teaching and specialty areas: art, music, science. However this is also the style of the best of English and social studies teachers. Many do not consider education as an undergraduate major because of the stereotypes of teachers and teaching. ("Those who can't do, teach." "Teaching isn't where the action is.")

The warm-empathic, humanitarian-altruistic teachers are also free spirits, but since they more often teach the young and less frequently question "conventional wisdom," the community considers them safer. Other teachers, however, may find their free and loving ways a threat, for the warm-hearted teachers respect the child and love him and hold him close—not at arm's length. The child responds and other teachers may be jealous or simply fear that fences between teachers and students will come down. Since most of these warm-empathic teachers reach out to everyone, the parents of children will often become their friends—a fact which can and sometimes does result in further reprisals from the other teachers who feel the culture of the school and of the home are quite separate. The most courageous and farsighted of this group move beyond the schools and work for the causes in the community, seeking to right wrongs in the larger society. The most unusual of teachers combine head and heart—are warm and altruistic as well as creative, excited learners, worldly and wise.

The Self-Actualizing Teacher is aware of the kaleidoscopic complexities of today's world, but is also cognizant of the need for unities. By suggesting frames of reference and unifying themes, these teachers try to prevent diffusion and fragmentation. Their students are encouraged not only to form immediate goals, but also to think in terms of distant goals and of such abstractions as the Good Society and the Good Person. At all times their respect for the young is clear in their actions and words.

The self-actualizing teacher tends to be contemplative and self-aware, open to growth and the possibility that he or his discipline or even his government might be wrong. Thus he continually sees himself as a learner, seeking truth just as the student does and critically reevaluating his own beliefs. Inquiry, discovery, and scientific investigation are his scholarly tools. In the realm of aesthetics and ethics, he relies on intuition, empathy, and insight.

Learning is seen by most of these teachers to embrace much more than the purely intellectual. This larger view is most strongly held by the artists and all those of a humane and altruistic bent. They are concerned not only with the inner-life philosophies and commitments to live by—but also with the larger world in all its manifold diversity.

XIV • How Teachers Get
That Way

If teachers do indeed make the school and are a vital factor in the lives of our children, are they not of crucial importance in determining what our society will become? Must we not think very carefully about how to select and educate them? Should we not devise patterns of education for teachers so that more will become self-actualizing personalities, wise and psychologically mature?

The good society will never evolve without the good person. That being so, how can our young become psychologically mature unless their teachers are? Can there be any doubt that the kind of people teachers are—the way they think and act and feel—significantly affects their students? Can youth know how to live in a democratic society of their peers unless they experience democracy, not only in the haven of the home but also in the testing theater of the school?

Whether the teachers are primarily concerned with reinforcing their power and position, following the prescriptions of the curriculum, or enlivening minds and stirring hearts will be mirrored in their students' responses—in stereotyped reactions or in intellectual ferment. Similarly a student's ability to accept himself and to love others can often be traced to the classroom climate and the teacher's personal warmth and empathy. Some have gone so far as to say that, as the schools operate at present, it is difficult for students to become—at least overtly—superior to those who teach them. Without models few students can excel at divergent, critical, and integrative thinking or be independent, expressive, empathic and altruistic. However, those gifted teachers who are self-actualizing have particularly great effects upon their students.

Although researchers have rarely come to anything like complete agreement as to what a good teacher is or how to find this out, there is a great deal of agreement among students as to the qualities *they* like in teachers. Further, these are very much the qualities which are stressed in the literature that portrays great teachers and are also found in the descriptions of psychological health. Good teachers *are* good people—in the sense that they are not sick or hostile. They enjoy their teaching, their students, and living in general. Their appetites are good, their eyes bright, and they are happy to go to school in the morning. More often than not, they feel revitalized rather than drained after teaching a class. (Of course if they must teach six classes in a row they get too exhausted.)

Slow students as well as bright, boys as well as girls, and both the young and the old want their teachers to be more fully human, psychologically mature, and self-actualizing. The Harris poll in 1969 reported that high school students prized the teachers who not only listened and understood but were free and open, who encouraged discussion and participation, who treated students as real people ("grownups"), who gave them responsibility, who were interested in them, and who encouraged them to probe, to challenge, and to speak their minds.* Research in counseling supplies additional information that further confirms what is effective in the inter-personal situation and what is not.

But, as we have seen, these are qualities which are hard for teachers to maintain. Their joy is ground down and the peaks of excitement are leveled off in the training mills which they pass through as they are educated, and which they are asked to staff when they receive their diplomas. In order to hold their jobs too many believe they must be neat and quiet and follow orders. They report that the janitor is often more important. (In at least one situation, a janitor managed to get a teacher fired because she let her first graders use finger paint every day and encouraged them to bring in specimens of weeds from the field.)

In extreme cases order can become an obsession and dominate the life of the school. The majority of teachers have been cowed by their college experiences, after which they move under the surveillance of their senior colleagues, the rule of the administrative edict, and the ever-watchful eye of the vigilantes of suburbia. Thus all too many become Standard Teachers. For them to remain or become Creative Intellectuals or Self-Actualizing Teachers takes the strongest of self-concepts. They are apt to be criticized at every hand—for the way they arrange their classrooms, their lack of adherence to the curriculum and textbook, and their free ways with children. If a few among them by sheer genius or strength of character become truly outstanding, if their pupils fall in love with school—and with their teacher—they may get so much adulation from the children that other teachers become jealous. By one means or another the message will be conveyed that the proper stance for teachers to take with children is at a distance. Student teachers report that they are told by their supervisors not to smile at the students until

*The *Life* poll by Louis Harris "What People Think About Their High Schools," *Life* magazine (May 16, 1969), pp. 23-39.

November. As a result of such views teachers all too commonly are inducted into a Cold War. All students respond to vitality and enthusiasm and resilient self-confidence, but no group needs this model more than the young Creative Intellectuals who discover anew each day that schools were made for the conscientious conformer, not for the eager questioner. Thus the Self-Actualizing Teachers, and the freedom and acceptance they offer, are a much needed antidote for the creative intellectual student who feels (and probably is) hemmed in and continually put down.

As children, some of these so overflow with knowledge and enthusiasm that they literally cannot restrain themselves —despite the sanctions which society places against them when they are most truly themselves. Already at age seven Andy had a penchant for using big words. He had an ongoing love affair with the dictionary and rarely could refrain from using whatever new words he discovered daily. Once when I was visiting his mother he had just come in from play and she asked him solicitously how it had gone that day. She had previously told him that he should use adult vocabulary when he spoke to adults and not with children. Visibly disturbed, Andy replied, "Oh, Mother, I didn't do so well today. I used the word claustrophobia because I couldn't think of a synonym."

The Creative Intellectuals search for the responsive environment. They want to find someone to share their esoteric enthusiasms, their love for the far away and long ago, their utopian dreams. Most find that it is only the teacher with creative intellectual inclinations who accepts and shares these ideas and tolerates such major deviations from curriculum and text. Beyond this creative intellectual teachers tend to read widely, as do creative intellectual students, and to be extremely well informed. As a result they never merely listen, accept, and respond. They also challenge, add to, shake up, rouse, resist—and the best do this without rancor or spite. Learning is a game that any number plays, including the teacher, who stands to be corrected at any time in the day.

The more humanely sensitive creative intellectual teachers show their emotions and their deep concerns, bare their souls, and disclose their fears. They do not try to conceal hypocrisies—their own, their community's, or their nation's. They resist being dominated and fettered by the school administration, the community elders, and the state course of study. When a child brings up a question about race prejudice, they never respond with "Ask your parents" nor do they turn a deaf ear. They do not put off the eager questioner with "That comes next year" or "You're too young to understand" or "We must get on with the lesson." Most importantly they are sensitive to what students know and want to know. They are never those teachers who are guilty of the crime (which bright young people find insufferable) of "telling us always and endlessly what someone else *doesn't* know." Instead they are, as Bertrand Russell has said, like artists, philosophers, and the men of letters who can only perform their work adequately when they feel themselves to be individuals "directed by an inner creative impulse, not dominated and fettered by an outside authority." Russell continues:

> It is very difficult in this modern world to find a place for the individual. . . . If the world is not to lose the benefit to be derived from its best minds, it will have to find some method of allowing them scope and liberty in spite of organization.*

As we have seen, most success-oriented and professional teachers do not accept, understand, or know how to facilitate these processes. As a result students generally are not exposed to self-actualizing behavior, to creative or intellectual commitment, or to a humane compassion. The pressures of the assignments that are made in the name of texts and guides (there often is a very thin line between enrichment and busy work) allow little time for the students to make

*Bertrand Russell, "The Functions of a Teacher," in *The Basic Writings of Bertrand Russell,* Robert E. Egner and Lester E. Denonn (eds.) (New York: Simon and Schuster, 1961), p. 442.

these discoveries on their own. Even if they are fortunate
enough to have found road maps and guidelines that they
would like to follow, there are no hours in the day in which
this self-directed exploration can take place.

Like the poor counselor, the poor teacher "tunes students
out" and the students usually reciprocate. Research during
the 60's on the amount of talk in the classroom has shown
that the typical teacher utters about 85 percent of the words
spoken. These are the teachers who talk at students, not with
them. Beyond that they do not let students express opinions,
they think they know it all or that it's all in the textbook,
and are apt to say piously, "I taught the subject, but the
students didn't learn."

For centuries this has been the classic model of the Grad-
grinds, but the students seem less and less willing to put up
with it. They have little patience with the dull, monotonous
drone of the lecture or the dead world it embalms. But the
question arises again and again—how can this situation be
changed? Practically all students dislike or, at best, barely
tolerate it, and the younger teachers are equally eager to
bring life into the classroom. They, too, still have blood in
their veins.

It is unfortunate, but true, that the education of teachers
has not prepared them to be autonomous, original, emotionally free, socially concerned, or characteristically able to use
the higher rationality. Their schooling has not made them
generally well informed, nor has it encouraged them to enjoy
reading and to read widely, to participate in the arts and the
general culture, or to proceed with self-development to that
point where they might become more fully functioning and
integrated. In short their education and perhaps their predispositions have rarely made them self-actualizing. This is not
to say that teachers could not come to have the appropriate
attitudes and behaviors; or that they could not develop the
requisite intelligence for living in and expressing the creative
intellectual style and the empathic attitude. However it
seems logical that they will *not* be apt to grow in these

directions—and facilitate such growth in children—if they have not themselves experienced an education which allows or prompts such growth. Most of the teacher education currently offered does not do this.

Many teachers come from homes where there is little expressed interest in what is sometimes called High Culture— the world of the ballet, the opera, legitimate theater, art exhibits, etc. American society has been called anti-intellectual and in part this refers to a lack of interest in the arts and in ideas. With intellectually able young people, however, I have not seen this to be so much a turning away as a lack of experience and not knowing how to participate. True, a few are influenced by Middle America's stereotype of the artist as effeminate, the very opposite of the proper male image—crew cut, jut jaw, and bulging biceps. But even though this ideal of proper maleness may have persisted through the 60's, I have found that education majors are shifting their loyalties. More than a few like artists and reject rigid sex roles. Most women and many young men (some even from working-class homes) who are in my classes are searching for different (perhaps better, at least more exciting) images, insights, and life styles.

Poster art and pop music, as well as thousands of unrecognized influences, have washed away barriers that previously existed. More and more, especially among the young people, there is a questioning of the ways of the Western World and particularly Middle America. Not a few are eagerly asking what the Eastern philosophies can offer. Perhaps the Creative Intellectuals who so often disdain school were influenced by their education in unexpected ways. George Wald, the biologist, and others have said the intellectual emphasis in some of the high school programs of the 60's has produced the brightest group of students the colleges have ever seen. But "teaching the students to think like scientists" may have cut both ways. The Sputnik-inspired programs which were to help us surpass the Russians may have brought the brightest students into mind frames not unlike the *avant garde* physicists and the ecologists—nearer to the mystic than the engineer. Science was being learned at the very moment the student was reading *The Catcher in the Rye,* the Tolkien books, and *Siddhartha,* and listening to Baez, Dylan, and the Beatles.

Learning to think like scientists the students came to see the old science as not so formidable and the scientists as not infallible. Summer programs as well as advanced placement (bringing college courses directly into the high schools) also made a difference. As college preparatory students in the 60's numerous education majors whom I later taught were influenced in these ways. Many had suffered from cognitive overload, too much homework, and a lack of art and music appreciation—called "Mickey Mouse" by some who were in charge of the Search for Talent programs—and they were ready for the affective part of life.

Many are suggesting we need to redefine education, that the new pattern will mean that boundaries between learning and living be erased. It is my view that life *itself* should be redefined. In a culture where there will be more leisure, it is important that teachers discover aesthetic as well as intellectual and altruistic interests that will make their own lives richer. And from this new vantage point they can lead their students into a rich and varied culture.

For these reasons, I have been making some efforts, probably not enough, to encourage my students to have many aesthetic experiences. Many joined their classmates in a group who went to a series of three ballet performances, which they not only enjoyed but were eager to go to again. Similarly, students responded eagerly when groups have gone to the Japanese gardens.*

Trips to art museums and galleries proved equally popular. For many, these were literally a foreign land inhabited by a socially elite audience and enigmatic artists. They needed to enter the *terra incognita* with friends and to be introduced

---

*There are several beautiful varieties—landscape, moss, and sand—clustered together on a Washington Park hillside facing Mt. Hood. These were designed and built under the guidance of one of Japan's finest artists in landscape gardening.

gradually to its language. Then, as one student said, "I couldn't stop wondering how many other fascinating places were available—if only I knew where to find them."

If we want students to be more independent, more humane, and more motivated to learn, then the character of teacher education must change. There must be a critical assessment of how we should educate teachers and who should educate them. Are the teachers of teachers well informed? Excited learners? Aesthetically appreciative and expressive? Empathic and altruistic?

As we look into the situation in the colleges and universities, it becomes abundantly clear that much of the college preparation of teachers is antithetical to and destructive of self-actualizing development (especially the creative intellectual style). It tends instead to lower self-concepts. Students are too frequently enrolled in large classes and taught impersonally out of textbooks. Wide reading in new sources and involvement in current controversy is often impossible. Work taken in the academic disciplines is more apt to be geared to those who will be specialists—majors preparing for research careers or graduate school—and not for those who simply want to participate in the wider culture.

Many academic professors belittle education as a discipline and do not want to teach its majors. Quite apart from this some actually may have little to offer the teacher in training. As a group professors are seldom exciting, optimistic, self-actualizing creatures. Nevitt Sanford reported in the fall of 1970 that he and his colleagues at the Wright Institute* who are doing research on college teachers find that their devotion is mainly to their profession rather than to their students. In other words they tend to teach the subject rather than the students! They do not see teaching as a profession, have no rationale for the way they teach, and lack a philosophy of education. As Sanford says, most of the faculty talk about

---

*The Wright Institute in Berkeley, California, conducts post-graduate multi-disciplinary research which is focused on social action.

teaching the way the man in the street talks about child training—they have all been children and have been raised as children. Their academic culture is not concerned with students. Thus college faculty members do not ask their colleagues about their teaching nor do they observe one another. Further it is considered bad form to be popular with students or to spend too much time with them or in class preparation.

Out of such an academic culture it is not surprising that many professors who really like young people and would respond with enthusiasm to broad intellectual topics become narrowed down by their profession. More than a few become complainers and nay-sayers, nihilists and weary cynics. They tend to be conservative about their disciplines and/or professions, although many stand ready to reform everything else in the world. As one intellectual put it, "All too many are self-appointed know-it-alls with tenure and the worst truly are effete, intellectual snobs." Moreover many are autocrats of the podium, teaching the word from on high. Students who would survive dare not speak out or talk back.

In arts and letters what is taught is more apt to be critical than appreciative, atomistic than holistic, fragmented than integrated. The background given in music is too often theoretical and thus may destroy the zest for trying. Students who are exposed to critical presentations of great music too often feel completely inadequate to express themselves in the face of such splendor and such erudition. Thus those students who are to become teachers reject and avoid what has been called the higher culture from fear, ignorance, misinformation—just plain bad teaching.

Little opportunity is offered for the expression of talent, as yet undeveloped, in any of the arts. Nor are students generally allowed to pursue creative projects as naive learners, where they may make mistakes and appreciate freshly and joyfully as children do. Yet it is only through such approaches that these teachers-to-be can move on to the higher levels of appreciation, where they will go to concerts and museums willingly. Realistically however, we must face another problem here: There is little encouragement or time for the teacher-in-training to go to concerts and museums. After all, assignments—from the chosen books, on specified topics, and done in the proper style—must be completed and turned in on schedule.

Teachers who come from lower- or lower-middle-class backgrounds and are using teaching for upward mobility should be introduced gently and tenderly into the broader culture. These are the teachers who need the support of a morale-building group which meets at frequent intervals. The great, eager rush for "encounter" sessions is proof that they—and many others in the population at large—need someone to talk to, someone to listen, time to find themselves, and an opportunity to make friends. And none of this is anti-intellectual; the problems of self must come first. But soon almost all are eager to discover and discuss the world and thus to move beyond the depths of self-discovery and the soft areas of human relationships. College, however, offers few of these experiences. In fact, it may do the opposite. It can wall the budding teachers out of the higher culture, as well as make them feel alien to themselves, and reduce their ability to relate to others.

Yet when all the negatives have been stated, much that is positive remains. Changes are in the wind and under way. Teachers are younger—five million new ones entered teaching between 1960 and 1970*—and they are better educated. Although students are unhappy with the American high school, it is apparently the administration or general structure that receives the brunt of their criticism. Most students in the 1969 Harris poll liked their teachers and felt that they would be more apt to find like-minded cohorts among them than among their parents—or particularly their parents' friends. Three-fourths of both teachers and students wanted the school to extend its boundaries and the administration to allow much more field work outside. Two-thirds of both

*Peter Drucker, "The Surprising Seventies," *Harper's* (July, 1971), pp. 35-39.

groups spoke of a desire to work directly with the community. It is undeniable that, when compared with most other occupational groups, teachers as a whole are less grasping and materialistic, more responsible and reliable, and more concerned about their fellow human beings. These are higher-order traits. They must be encouraged, and not discounted.

Aside from the Peace Corps and Vista (in their early years) and some of the training programs in psychotherapy and counseling, no large-scale efforts were made to screen and train for such skills and arts as establishing rapport, developing feelings of trust and unconditional acceptance, and helping the student work toward self-actualization. Certainly one would welcome more evidence that these qualities are displayed with frequency and are sufficiently valued by university faculties including those in education.

The changing demands of the society and the felt needs of public school teachers (and their most discerning observers) indicate that reconstruction of teacher education is long overdue. Through their education teachers should flourish as human beings and expand in mind and spirit. Range and level of intellectual talent should increase, awareness of the natural and aesthetic world should be sensitized and refined, and they should become more fully human in terms of concern for their fellow men and in mastering better ways to relate and to interact with them. For this to happen, teacher education must be not only individualized, but also made vastly more human and exciting.

XV • Leading Out and Letting Be

What I have to say about teaching teachers comes from both my practical experience and a good deal of observation and reflection. In part I am reflecting upon my own efforts to reach both teachers-to-be and those who are teachers.

My earliest attempts to understand what goes on in the classroom occurred the year I turned eleven and had the great good fortune to be taught by a most unusual teacher, Miss Rebecca McKay. I came to her as a new student, a country girl—younger and smaller than the others. The forty or so students in her classroom were mainly children from the small town of Amity, Oregon. Instead of an interloper I was a valued friend and contributor, almost from the beginning. On Fridays I was often chosen to read a poem or give a reading—both the class and Miss McKay apparently welcomed every slender, fledgling talent that I had. Never before did I have a teacher who, I felt, really cared about me, one who cared about all of her students. The result, as I think back on it, was that we all valued and stood by one another. I never missed a word in spelling that year and I later came to suspect that Archie Higgins, when he corrected my paper, simply changed the words that were wrong. Since he was always kind and thoughtful, how could I hurt him by suggesting he should not do this? The class also took it upon themselves to write to the state superintendent on my behalf, reasoning that I should not have to take the state final exams just because I had had too few years of formal schooling.

Perhaps none of this conveys the idea that Miss McKay was a teacher so remarkable that I can still close my eyes and see her gentle face with the graying hair drawn back austerely. It is my memory that she customarily wore only two dresses—a gray linen and a blue with crisply pressed clean cuffs and a collar attached anew each morning. Her voice was as unobtrusive as her appearance. Yet we all loved her and we loved each other. And, what I now see as of secondary importance, we all learned a great deal in the terms of what grade-school youngsters were supposed to learn prior to World War II. Never before had I watched someone teach, adapting lessons for the slow, quietly suggesting something special that the more able might enjoy doing, encouraging groups to work in dramatics or art. Reprimands were never necessary. Learning was a joy. I was so overwhelmed by it all that I decided to keep a separate notebook on how Miss McKay taught, what she said, and how students responded. But the notebook was burned, with all our family possessions, in a fire that brought our house to the ground one Christmas Eve when I was in my late teens.

Fortunately I was able to talk to Miss McKay in the late 1960's. She was, I believe, ninety-four years old then and even smaller than I had remembered, but very alert. She did not use a hearing aid or a cane, wear glasses or false teeth. As she put it, she was still using all of her original equipment. She continued to tutor neighbor children—helping out the slow readers—and children still loved her. But, as she said, she was slowing down. The year before she had let her driver's license expire and she was going to give up her position on the election board. On the other hand she had piled three cords of wood that summer and still did all her own work.

In awe, as always, of her human talents and wondering about her own reflections on teaching, I said that my memory was that she simply never had discipline problems. Could she recall any in the decades she had taught? Miss McKay searched her memory. One day long ago, when she was teaching in a country school and had perhaps fifty pupils, a little girl came on Monday morning in a state of mental breakdown and incipient wildness. Only by putting her arm around the child and holding her gently and close could Miss McKay keep her from screaming and tearing her hair. Not wanting to upset the hard-working parents who were putting in the fall crops, she kept the girl close by her side day after day for the entire week. On Friday afternoon the father came to get his little daughter and, with tears in his eyes, said, "Have you noticed anything?" Miss McKay replied that she had, but had not wanted to alarm the parents. In sobs, the father thanked her for her kindness. Together, teacher and parents arranged for institutional care—of the limited variety available in the 1920's.

Miss McKay was not only the beloved teacher of all the children, but also the friend of all the parents. And, I must admit, her influence has been such that after decades of teaching at all grade levels and through high school and college, I still find that I cannot discuss discipline problems meaningfully. Students at all ages respond to what Carl Rogers has aptly termed "unconditional caring."

Education is from the Latin *educere* which means "leading out." This is the function of the teacher of teachers as well as of those who teach the young. It involves, as Buber has said, taking the student by the hand and moving with him as counselor and, ultimately, as friend. The student is not left alone to choose without guidance or without possibilities from which to select, left, as Herbert Read so aptly said, "beating his wings in the void." Instead the teacher opens a cornucopia from which the student may choose and suggests guidelines for choices. Thus the student gradually comes to sense what is worth knowing, what ways or things are relatively better, and which are relatively worse. With these criteria he can make the most fundamental decisions—choices of life style and world view—as well as the minute-to-minute existential choices of which most people remain unaware.

The positive freedom which comes from a "letting be" is also needed by the college student. With a young child spontaneity may not have been repressed, and he may engage immediately and joyfully in experimental activity. His creative vents may still be open; his "instinct to originate," unimpaired. However most adults are already encased in walls of conformity built up by their school experience and their encounters with the larger society, even though these walls may not be as relentlessly confining as those sand barriers that imprisoned the "Woman in the Dunes." Some fairly young people draw back from the daylight of freedom as did the prisoners in Plato's cave; upon others, as Wordsworth expressed it, "shades of the prison house" have already begun to close. Many will only gradually comprehend the meaning of freedom and can only be "led out" by a gentle and persuasive teacher. Such students may actually prefer marching in file and lockstep in the monotone corridors to strolling in the meadows or running in the wind.

The reader may ask why, in a book which examines the development of the creative intellectual style, I choose to devote so much of my time to teachers. I can only reply, "because I think they are so very important." Most of them, in some ultimate way, are potentially self-actualizing; and I would judge that a sizable group, if given opportunities, would be drawn to some aspect of creative intellectual development. (In my experimental study of able high school students which began in the fall of 1962, a group only slightly more gifted than the average teacher, I found that, although only 20 to 25 percent chose to describe themselves at the outset of a special program as Creative Intellectuals, the number who were so inclined the year after the program was completed had risen by 40 percent.*) And, to be truly honest, I must add something that reveals an unpopular—even perverted—taste: I like them. I have been a teacher since I was eighteen (and did my student teaching when I was sixteen, but that's another story). At this juncture I am loath to admit that I have wasted my life.

I see teaching as the most satisfying and rewarding of vocations. That is what it is all about—it is a vocation, not simply a job or a profession. The teaching of a child by a mother; the teaching of the public by the artist and the writer, by the saint and the sage; the teaching of the young by the professional teacher—all can properly be done only by devotion. All teachers have the obligation to protect and to become friends with their students.

If we are concerned with self-actualization, and with the warm-empathic and creative intellectual development which are its precursors, we must focus first on the kind of human beings we should be. We should encourage self-actualization because growth of this kind is authentically human. In fact many of the humanistic psychologists use these very words and speak of a person becoming "more fully human"—by which they mean the growth of such qualities of the spirit as warmth, wit, imagination, courage, honesty, loyalty, and resilience.

In what must become a world society if the human species is to continue on this planet, more people must take what John Platt† calls "the step to man." For it is the healthy people, those moving toward self-actualization, who are best able to transcend the confines of a particular role (*e.g.,* teacher) or culture. If students are to be introduced to human aspirations, hopes, godlike qualities—teachers must be aware of these possibilities and must move in this direction.

---

*This program is described in Chapter XXI. The official report of this experiment is in Elizabeth Monroe Drews, *The Creative Intellectual Style in Gifted Adolescents,* Vol. II, *op. cit.*

†John R. Platt, *The Step to Man* (New York: John Wiley & Sons, 1966).

"Leading out" such captives may involve considerable pain for them unless their teachers are supremely sensitive. The teachers who guide those who have been kept fettered and hobbled in semi-darkness will have to anticipate their fears of free play. Such teachers must be continually open and permeable to what the students are trying to say, even if their only language is an imploring glance or a sudden shudder of revulsion. But they must also resist imposing new controls: Their task is to inspire and to release. In these ways the true teachers will profoundly change their students by the emotional impact of example.

The teacher must learn to balance the "leading out" and the "letting be." The student must learn that the world can be both free and meaningful, that there are no easy answers to hard questions, and that truth is more a direction than a point of arrival. Such understandings will probably be greatest in those times of open exploration of life in all its chaotic unpredictability. At such moments the student may sense the joy of coming to original conclusions, and as Einstein did, he may pause to revel in the mystery of the unknown. But these creative experiences are not enough. As Read says, "Freedom in education is nothing else but possessing the ability to be united." Students must learn that a vital part of education takes place at the intimate human level—finding friends, learning to work with them, sharing generously, appreciating, and being appreciated. And it is the teacher who helps the student to establish these vital ties with his fellow beings.

"Leading out" and "letting be" must always be complementary and symbiotic. At certain times and for certain students, one process will take precedence over the other. And the processes will vary considerably. "Letting be" can involve allowing a student to struggle with a problem when you as a teacher could "set him right" with practically no effort. Or it may simply mean providing a quiet and attractive setting whose beauty can seep into his soul and where he can make the first tentative gestures in establishing a new friendship.

"Leading out" can be done gently and solicitously, as we have seen, for those who have been psychologically blinded and crippled. Or it may simply mean helping the eager questioner find answers. But if the teacher has the skill and a taste for it, for some students it might involve a literal bombardment of Socratic questioning.

Those with strong egos respond well to these volleys. I remember two students in a particular class—Jim, a young man who had been a star football player as well as a counselor in the Job Corps, and a young woman, Lynn, who taught physics in a local high school. Both were sturdy mesomorphs with unusually quick minds and rather careless work habits. The rest of the class enjoyed the questioning, too, and perhaps came to understand the ethics (or lack of it) in "operant conditioning" by listening to Jim respond to my questions. And they may have gained insight into what the physicist, Michael Polanyi, meant by "superior knowledge" when Lynn did not receive an answer to her question of how to do a critical review. Instead, by questions, she came to realize she already knew that some books were better source material than others, and, in fact, was in command of the answers to all of her questions. The point is, that when Socratic questioning goes well, students are helped to discover what they already know.

Of those majoring in education relatively more women come from the upper middle class and many have an excellent liberal arts background. Some are truly gifted Creative Intellectuals with surprisingly supple minds. For them teaching by poetry and parable—as Dewey suggested—is often the most effective approach. A few will say very little all term in the large group discussions, but will produce superb anthologies and do outstanding critical reviews. In general women students talk less than the men and will need more encouragement. In a class of thirty I often have no more than five men but they do as much or more talking than the twenty-five women.

I have also observed that although some men like my

efforts to humanize and personalize education, some do not. On the other hand I have never had a woman make more than minor complaints and none has taken a grievance directly to the administration. Women, as some would and do say, may conform to almost anything. Or on the other hand they may feel that the personal approach in learning and teaching —discovering themselves and making friends, instead of competing with fellow students—is much to their liking. Many men, including not a few of my fellow professors, have told me they think "love" should be outlawed from the vocabulary of education and psychology. Respecting one's students and colleagues is acceptable, but never loving them! Academic professors seem to set their teeth against love even more resolutely than those who are studying or teaching education. At a recent national conference of university and college teachers I spoke about the youth revolution and about reforms in education that the young wanted. Much emphasis was placed on love, and I referred not only to Fromm and Buber but to the teachings of Jesus. Some New Wave professors liked it; but many of the Academics-as-Usual did not. A friend told me afterward that a man sitting next to her said, "I feel like throwing up."

All this is to say that if we are to change our ways of teaching teachers and perhaps of behaving toward our fellow men (and I, for one, think we will not survive if we don't), we may have to introduce the radical and uncomfortable idea that love must come in through many doors simultaneously. Someone has said that the Californians long for the Good Old Days when the air was clean and sex was dirty. It has been my impression that sex is generally a less dangerous topic than love. And people will talk about what is wrong much more easily and with more zest than they discuss what is right. Witness how many teachers' rooms become veritable cells for the assassination of student character and how few teachers cluster to extol the virtues of their young charges!

Some mental health researchers have claimed that psychologically healthy people have good memories of their childhood, and that the degree of one's psychopathology is reflected by the fact that bad memories block out the good. If this is true many people seem to have only a very modest degree of psychological health. On the scale of psychic maturity they are barely adolescent. If we accept the hierarchical theory of growth advanced by Abraham Maslow—and this agrees essentially with my own experience—then it is necessary that we give university students, particularly those who are studying education and will teach our children and youth, the kind of education that will help them meet their own emotional and social needs. Most people, admittedly, are not psychologically free to pursue such higher-order needs as learning for learning's sake or the search for beauty. In that case it is in no way a condemnation of teachers, the general run of whom are above average (but not markedly so), to hold that many of them need to be given the time and circumstances to work on self-discovery, to be original and creative, and to be united with others.

I have experimented with many ways in which students can gain insights into themselves and develop feelings of belonging. One of the simplest—almost at the parlor-game level—is to have them share their early experiences in that most formidable of institutions, the public school. Students can speak far more readily and movingly, I find, about "the worst thing that happened to me in school" than the "best thing." In fact many are hard put to remember anything good. Thus as a technique for students to get acquainted with self and others and, of course, as a means for me to know and remember each one of them, I will often ask everyone to tell the "worst thing." Eventually they will learn the positive by contrast with the negative. They may also need to experience a little exorcism of evil in the familiar Freudian sense. One's negative memories may be the psychic equivalent of bars on cages. For the firmly caged there may be a need to discuss how their prison or cave looks and feels before they will venture out into the open meadows and the green parks of freedom. The ways and powers of love, to use Sorokin's expression, may appear quite unlike the ways and powers of "real life."

The range of slights or gaucheness suffered, whether real or "remembered," is always eye-opening. Teachers' cruelties to students range from downright meanness—physical and psychological—to all manner of obtuseness and petty unconcern. One of my students, Lowell, reported that he was still a nonreader at age twelve and at that time was referred for special reading help. He remembers that for the two years just prior to this referral he had sat as assigned, in the back of the room, and was never called on once. His sad-voiced comment was, "I guess the teacher thought I was part of the furniture."

Mary moved to the mountains of northern California from Switzerland when she was ten. She spoke only German, was small for her age, and retiring in manner. Over the one-room school in which she and her brothers were enrolled there reigned a poker-straight, tinder-tempered old Scotsman. The small girl was much too frightened to engage in any of the subterranean teacher-hazing that was always in evidence: mocking smiles, gum wads shot heavenward from only God knows where, noises of uncertain parentage. But one day she was afflicted, as she said,

> by a crick in the neck which was sheer agony. Mr. McDougall was lecturing us and we were supposed to look straight at him, but my head stayed at an obstinate tilt. I tried to get it on straight by gyrating my neck, but to no avail. Before I knew what happened he was upon me and, grabbing my long braid from behind, dragged me—with no concern for my vertebrae—from my desk to the front of the room. He tried to wrest a confession from me, but my mind was devoid of all English. I could reply only in what he called "German gibberish." My memory is that I wrote a sentence which spelled out my sins a thousand times. Years later at a school reunion I saw Mr. McDougall again and he recognized me immediately and with ill-concealed venom told me how glad he was when I and my troublemaker brothers had moved away.

Some of my most gifted students tell the all-too-common story of suffering from untested accusations that they were plagiarists. Miles was an indifferent high school student, but somehow became greatly interested in the topic of alcoholism when he was a senior. He spent weeks researching and writing what turned out to be a monograph of almost publishable quality on the subject. His senior English teacher failed him on the basis of this very evidence, insisting that the work could not have been his. Nor was any appeal allowed. Up to that time Miles had not planned to go to college, but changed his mind at that moment, "to show her, the school, the world that I had the ability to do anything I wanted with my mind. I am now working on my doctorate in psychology all because my English teacher wouldn't believe that I had really written my long-term project myself."

"The worst thing that ever happened to me in school" does not, by any means, seek to implicate the teacher as culprit. My hope is that teachers, through sharing feelings with classmates, can begin to see what a tenderly sensitive organism the child and human beings, in general, are. Some may even become aware of the super-sensitivity of the Creative Intellectual. There are, of course, other benefits of looking back and looking inside. Self-understanding is not the least of these.

Character education may be a part of it all, but I have never been sure that this will always happen when the teacher follows the curriculum guide set up for this purpose. It is my view that such education happens in much more subtle ways. Generally in the events of life many things occur which may shape the conscience although the shaping may never be acknowledged or even known by the conscious mind.

Shirley remembered that the worst event of the days and years of her schooling centered about the milk money she brought daily from home. As a second grader she was given seven cents each day and handled it proudly and well. But one day she was overcome with an extra responsibility. Her mother had no pennies, so Shirley was entrusted with a dime. This was almost too much. What was she to do with it? How was she to keep it safe and secure, to prevent it from being lost or perhaps stolen? She finally settled on holding it in her mouth. But the inevitable happened. When she was called out of her reverie by a question from her teacher she was so startled that the dime slipped down her esophagus without a ripple. Clearing her throat, coughing, hanging her head down —nothing helped. And she did not dare tell anyone. She feared heaven-knows-what manner of punishment. Saying she was ill, Shirley passed up her morning milk and upon arriving home after school she told her mother—when asked about the three cents in change—that this had been stolen. But Shirley's problems were not over. Not only was she conscience-stricken about lying, but for years she was worried about her health, concerned that the dime might cause her death. It was not until the night she graduated from high school that she was able to confess to her mother and clear her conscience.

I, too, have often reflected upon these crises of conscience that children have. In the third grade I was somehow prompted to look at a spelling word on the paper of the boy who sat behind me. As a result I changed the spelling of the word on my paper and for the first time received a less than perfect mark. The incident was seared into my memory. In telling this a few years ago to Mike Grost while he was spending an afternoon in my home, I said that this cured me of cheating. As I phrased it, "I decided then and there to use my own mind instead of depending on someone else." Mike, at age ten, appalled that I would still think about this as I did when I was seven, looked at me steadily and said, "Wasn't it your conscience?"

Bruce Stern, like many contemplative and creative young people, thought his way clear of an activist, rule-burdened religion and imagined himself into a contemplative mysticism. He also contradicted all of my preconceptions about sex differences. He was slender in build and graceful in his movements. If he had lived at a time when profiles mattered in movie stars, he would have been easily mistaken for Leslie Howard. But his outstanding characteristic was a joyous acceptance of life and of the free style in education. He was an outspoken advocate of love of all kinds and of the joy that came through experiencing—particularly the tender things in the world: small wild flowers and young children. His university adviser, a former coach-social studies teacher in the city schools, had demanded that Bruce be assigned to someone else when the young man announced that he planned to be a kindergarten teacher and raved about a recent ballet performance that he had seen at the new civic auditorium.

In Bruce the new blurring of sex roles appeared in many guises. He was happy with his curls, his long lashes, and his variously hued turtlenecks. And, later in the term, he looked admiringly at the flowered trousers of the twelve-year-old musicians who provided a nontranquil interlude in the class retreat. In fact when the mother of one of the boy musicians said, "I didn't put my foot down when Josh brought home those pants, but I blew the whistle loud the other day when I found him in my closet trying on my blouses—to choose one to wear to school," Bruce turned to her, incredulous, and asked, "But, why?"

In telling about "the worst thing" Bruce recalled a problem that occurred because, coming from an Orthodox Jewish home, he was expected to eat no leavened bread or cake during Passover. "At ten," Bruce remembered,

> I was still a social and religious conformist. I played baseball because that was what boys played and I got hungry just like everyone else. Finally, one Saturday, we were all overwhelmed by a smell of freshly baked doughnuts that was drifting toward us. As if shot out of a gun, we raced in perfect T-formation and at top speed to the shop which sold them. And just as quickly they were purchased and devoured. Only after the deed was done and the doughnut downed did I realize my crime. I had broken the basic law of Passover. Surely God would smite me dead. Alternating

between convulsive fear and silent but fervent prayers for forgive-
ness, I waited for the blow to fall. But nothing happened. Divine
vengeance did not strike. What could have been the reason? I
started to have doubts. The doubts deepened. Was there really
such a divine law and a God who cared and watched? After two
days of terror I returned to normal, but my religion didn't. By
the time I was fourteen my only religious observance was going
through the outward motions to please my parents. Now that I'm
deep into Zen, I try to avoid all religious discussion at home. For
me, the distance between the rules and rituals of the Mosaic Law
and free-floating *satori* has been an easy trip.

The sharing of "worst things" is not only a means of
rediscovering the child within oneself, but also of coming to
understand all children better. Instead of an assortment of
faceless strangers, we all begin to be individuals. Through the
reflecting pool of our minds, we not only see each other as
we are now, but also catch glimpses of ourselves as children.

It is a truism that you keep more firmly in mind that
which you think about intently. Reflecting upon your students, for example, you will find you can more readily call
each student by name. This is a vital step that you must take
immediately since it tells them much about what they mean
to you. Yet calling everyone by name by the second class
session is not always easy. Often I make this task simpler for
myself by having everyone tell the class something about
himself that will make him unforgettable. He can invent it if
he wants to. Following this I find that it helps to read
through the roll soon after the first class meeting, before new
experiences have had a chance to intervene. As I look at each
name I pause to form a mental image of the particular
student in still and animated versions. This is the beginning
step for carrying them about in one's mind.

My students gain a great deal from getting to know each
other. Introduced as they are by vivid personal statements as
well as these vignettes out of the past, most of them seek, as
do I, to participate in a humanizing process that will allow
the roles and masks that we wear (as adults, and especially as

teachers) to begin to fall away. There are other roads to take that also helps us on this long journey in search of communion.

Americans seek endlessly for ways to find themselves. Many of the roads turn out to be detours and dead ends. The Expressways to Instant Nirvana may take us instead to a Road Show or a Junk Yard—as tragic as the Roadside Zoos billed as the authentic haunts of wild animals. None of these offer what mature adults, including my students, want. But this does not mean that there are no easy or pleasant routes to take, or that games and exercises do not work. I am speaking not of encounter sessions but of ways that a group of people may come to like one another. Making friends bears some similarity to, but is not the same as, the therapeutic process.

In a class where most still do not know one another I often begin by asking all students to find a partner, a classmate they do not know, but one they would like to be friends with. The assumption is that the choice will be mutual and each is to tell what quality of the other appealed, why he wanted to get acquainted. After these exchanges each tests his empathic abilities by telling his partner what he thinks he was like when he was young. Again these initial impressions are corrected in free interchange. (There is no requirement to tell all to classmates or to anyone else, but a chance to make friends if one feels so inclined.) Finally if it seems best to limit these conversations, each duet is asked to join another. At this point each member of each pair tells the other couple about his new friend. Such an activity may sound contrived, but it can work out amazingly well—involving everyone and getting far below the usual superficialities of talk at teas or cocktail parties. People almost always find out something new about themselves. A girl who has held an image of herself as a gangly tomboy may suddenly find she is seen by others as a Queen of the May.

My feeling is that such insights are relatively nonthreatening. Not at all like the shock experienced by one of my friends who attended a much-advertised encounter session. At the first meeting the group leader destroyed her with "one fell verbal blow," as she put it, and she caught the first bus going home. Her partner had described her to the group as a fluffy canary, gentle and ineffectual. To which the group leader acidly replied, "Don't let her fool you. She's a bitch. I can tell by the way she smiles." Fortunately, beneath the soft exterior there was a little iron and my friend came to see the incident as high farce. But sharp-tongued accusations based on little or no knowledge (or even on much information) can cause emotional breakdown. It takes very little imagination to see how the high casualty rates which Richard Farson says often occur in encounter groups can happen. I am not suggesting that we abandon self-disclosure or sharing with friends but rather that we be kind and gentle with each other. Particularly in those early stages of growth when the extension of self to another is tender and green, and the roots of friendship are only lightly anchored.

XVI "Show Me a [Woman or] Man Who Reads"

The kind of change that I have been suggesting for teacher education involves a new and, for some, a terrifying adventure. However most of the women and many of the men, including those who are already teachers and especially those designated as good teachers, welcome a chance to discover new ways of working with people. Equally new for some—surprising though this may seem—is learning to *enjoy* reading.

After studying the characteristics of fifty outstanding elementary-school teachers, the psychologist Philip Jackson*, reported that the best teachers are spontaneous and informal. They not only prize their own autonomy, but are concerned for the development of the individual student. Many speak in the terms of the missionary, telling about miracles that take place, transformations in children, and the "thrill of witnessing dramatic change." They talk of working from intuition and feeling rather than by reflection and thought. These are, as Jackson sees them, tender-minded romantics and mystical

*Philip W. Jackson, *Life in Classrooms* (New York: Holt, Rinehart & Winston, Inc., 1968), pp. 115 ff.

optimists, whose "view of children [is] definitely idealized and tinged with a quasi-mystical faith in human perfectibility." For such people (if they are kept out of the academic swamps) a psychology of human potentiality, rising out of transcendentalism and theories of cosmic consciousness, can provide the rationale for what they are already doing.

Such teachers, it seems to me, are good people who do and should trust their intuitions. What they see as right and appropriate is generally what is good for the child. With psychological health comes the ability to choose well, immediately, and without effort. Jackson speaks of the teacher being called upon to change focus 1,000 or more times a day, to make this many "inter-personal interchanges." Most of these involve some kind of decision on the teacher's part. She sees a child in anguish over a just-completed picture drenched in milk as a result of his attempt to get the plastic straw into the vent and knows compassion is the only humane reaction. Certain responses are all wrong—for instance, a sardonic smile that conveys, "You're clumsy just like your brother was," or a strained frown which tells the child, "This is the last straw. Why did you pick this very minute, just when the music teacher is about to arrive?" She must see the world through the child's eyes and somehow help him share the overwhelming tragedy of the ruined painting.

But this sharing of the child's world should not be allowed to blot out your vision of what he has done and what he can do, of his great capabilities that lie just below the surface or are perhaps sealed away from his consciousness in some subterranean place. The poor reader is usually handicapped by the fact that he focuses on what is wrong and can scarcely acknowledge that anything *he would do* could be right. He does not see that his flawless reading of "The quick brown fox jumps over the lazy old dog" is good and sufficient cause for jubilation. Instead, given over to self-flagellation as he is, he only remembers that he made verbal garbage out of the next sentence. He cannot laugh at his errors, nor can he put them in perspective. You, as his wise teacher, must show him how. You will somehow have to be large enough and sufficiently refulgent to give the timid and fearful the warmth, energy, and zest they need. You will protect, you will permit, you will encourage, but you will also inspire.

It should be apparent by now that not all teachers are prisoners of the *status quo* or laced into the straitjackets of professionalism. And—I have observed—many who are, do not want to be. As with people in general teachers would prefer to be known as individuals, not as representatives of the genus teacher. But how to reverse the trend? The river of tradition runs wide and deep.

My efforts have been more to divert the water than to swim upstream, although it may seem as if I am doing the latter. I have tried to redefine education by improvising a new pattern in the day-to-day, ongoing process of teaching. Mainly I have made small changes. The first thing to go was the textbook. Then student-selected readings* took the place of a list prescribed by the professor, although I continued to give out bibliographies so that students could see what I have enjoyed and thought important. Always discussion in the form of polylogue replaced the monologue of lecturing. But none of this was much beyond what many colleagues of mine (I would call them the better college teachers) were doing more than a dozen years ago when I became a professor in a large university. It was not until the early 1960's that I began to experiment by encouraging the students to *make* anthologies rather than *buy* them, by changing the dimensions of place, time, and materials, by creating situations where students would come to see themselves in new ways.

---

*Although teachers have little time to read, and some read only under duress, a few already have books in mind which they plan to add to what I call a "select-your-own-bibliography" and to read at will during the term or any time thereafter. These teacher-students often tell me that while they read many articles during the term they do little book reading at that time. After all, a term usually lasts only ten weeks; and teaching full time, plus taking university work, imposes a heavy burden. Many only begin to indulge their new appetite for books after the term is over.

To do all this I had to see myself as something less (or more) than a professor, and I had to explain to my students why I did what I did. Students have to understand that studying such subjects as the psychology of reading, learning, or human potentialities must mean that they comprehend these in relationship to themselves. They need to see that the heart of understanding all or any of these areas well is, first of all, to know themselves. But merely to discover and become one's self was never enough; one must try to become one's best possible self. This goal, I feel, is much more important than what most of my students have been led to believe are the aims of teacher training—stepping-stones for a certificate and, for a few, learning to learn and accumulating knowledge. Further, such an aim involves bypassing or rejecting many of the usual education routines—work sheets and formal lectures. To become better human beings people (teachers included) must shape themselves and take responsibility for choosing what to read and what to learn.

But they cannot choose in a vacuum. Without a range of tantalizing, even compelling offerings and unless the implications of choice can be understood, there is no "freedom to select." True, professors, as well as their students, need to be psychologically mature. But this does not and cannot mean that all will like the same things or will agree on all issues. Viewpoints of other professors and of the society at large will mean that each of us has our influence moderated, even if our views are not moderate.

Students have a right to disagree with these values and objectives. They may feel, for example, that participatory democracy is a kissing cousin, if not a little brother, of anarchy. If they disagree very strongly and reject being exposed to what they feel is a perversion of education, they are urged to take the same courses from other professors in other terms. The message is essentially this: "If the uncertainties and ambiguities trouble you and if you fear exposing yourself to the possibility of conversion—grab your souls and run."

Each of us has our own inimitable learning style, so that, when we are forced into a pattern that is not our own, we can become vastly inefficient or even psychologically ill. The most gifted and creative people are the most truly individual and, in the normal course of events, least suited for school work as it is assigned. "Easy books" are often made available for the slow, but books at adult level are rarely provided for gifted third graders who can easily read and comprehend them.

Similarly gifted college students complain that too many education courses are all pablum and contain no inviting textures or unknown ingredients. Nothing turns us against learning so quickly as the teachers who do not challenge us—perhaps because their knowledge does not extend beyond the perimeter of the textbook or perhaps because they doubt our capacity and deny that we are ready to bound ahead. Yet it is well known that the more gifted the student, the more willing he is to take the large risks. Even the Army does not expect all men to wear size nine shoes, but schools all too often force all people to read the same textbook at the same time.

Strange as it may seem many teachers—both the certified and those in training—do not know what they like or even what is good for them. Making anthologies, a project contributed to by the class as a whole and then prepared by each student individually, encourages, for most, this kind of development. The suggestion is that all ask themselves what they like to read, what ideas they agree with, and which they reject.

For every class a core of readings is selected by a committee of students who volunteer to serve as editors. These make their selections from two major sources—the new choices submitted by each class member and the core readings which previous classes developed. These latter now amount to several thousand pages. Eventually the editors compile a new core of readings for their own class consisting of five to six hundred pages. In these they generally try to emphasize special themes (the usual choices tend to underwrite creative and expressive modes of being) as well as to provide a balance of varying kinds—the solidly scientific, the frankly inspirational, the radical, the conservative, the satiric, the sentimental. Included are stories such as Tennessee Williams' "Grand," a touching account of his beloved grandmother, and Aldous Huxley's tale of "Young Archimedes," the small boy who was also a mathematical genius; poems of many kinds—those written by children and teachers as well as selections from Blake and Auden; book reviews and comparisons of such contrasting pictures of human nature as those of Carl Rogers and B. F. Skinner, or such conflicting ideas about animal nature as those of Peter Kropotkin and Robert Ardrey. There is no end to the varieties of format and viewpoints, but nearly always certain issues of fundamental importance appear again and again: Who am I? What is the nature of man? What is the world all about? This core of readings is duplicated and distributed to all the students in the class.

> Use it as a basis for your own anthology. The choice is yours. You may use all or part, a great deal or very little.
>
> The task is to take these materials—read them critically and creatively. Comment on the ideas presented, or make creative extensions of your own.
>
> In other words take each article in hand and live with it! Think about it. Look at its many faces. As you read these selections you will change your mind a thousand times. Through this process you will more surely come to know what it is you like and value.

The core readings are only the beginning. Most anthologies take on a decidedly individual flavor and many contain a rich store of materials which the student supplies—papers or poetry he has written in other terms and other years, old articles he has saved, new ones from sources he has just discovered. Some anthologies are prepared with such care—in format and design, as well as in content—that they are truly works of art. Certainly they are more interesting and have immeasurably more appeal, both for the student who makes them and the professor who responds to them, than the conventional textbooks. After all the instructor has presumably read the text before, and the usual routine of reexperiencing it through the facelessness of the IBM-scored tests does nothing to augment one's personal growth. In contrast it is impossible not to be moved and affected by the delightful, sometimes sharply trenchant, often pleasantly naive—but always highly personal—world of your students.

Each reacts to the same core material, but the comments, like the students, are all different. Although some articles become favorite fare for almost everyone and are chosen term after term, the "best-liked" articles of one student are rarely the "best-liked" of another. The variety of taste and the ways of expressing this are legion. Some will go into paeans of praise over John Holt's article "Schools Are Bad for Children," while others find his air supercilious and his condemnation of teachers far too sweeping. After all *they* too are good teachers—and who does he think he is anyhow? Some think "Student As Nigger" is saying it "like it is" and like it should be said, four-letter words and all. Others are so affronted by the language that the message completely escapes them.

All of this will help them think less about what they are to do (and how to do it) and more about what they ought to be. The result: Teachers will discover what they like and value.

One of the statements that the class receives goes to the heart of the matter. This is Carl Rogers' trenchant observation that he cannot teach, he can only learn. Like leading out and letting be, this view is part of the wisdom of both Eastern and Western sages, of Lao-tse as well as Socrates. As a teacher you are a fellow student, a co-searcher for truth. In the fashion of Socrates you are always open to new knowledge and fresh interpretations. As a good Taoist you learn how to stay out of the students' way. You learn not to make their choices for them. Remaining forever an amateur, you avoid the pitfalls of hubris, power, and authority and instead develop relationships of mutual respect and reciprocity.

In this new pattern of education the definition of learning is enlarged in many ways. A separation between learning and living is not acknowledged. Instead we explore Aristotle's concept that "thought by itself moves nothing" and go beyond this to Polanyi's view that all intellectual activities are influenced by one's feelings and values. All knowledge is indeed personal. Each sees the world differently than it has ever been seen before. And the more gifted and creative the mind, the more original the world view.

This special and private view that each of us has, as my readers (but perhaps not my students) will know, is what Northrop Frye has called the "educated imagination." In his book by that title, he argues eloquently that the real world lies in one's mind. We arrive there by reading and by becoming friends of artists and philosophers, knowing through them "what humanity has done and can do." This is a path that may be taken by anyone who is eager to release the creative intellectual self within.

XVII • Nothing Is What You Take It To Be

Students will normally learn best when their contributions of ideas and experiences are genuinely welcomed. My practice is to ask them to bring two things for the second class meeting—an autobiographical account of their learning or their reading (including how they learn and how they read) and a copy of an article, story, or poem they particularly enjoy. The first will serve as the beginning step in self-study and the article should be one they would like for their anthology. Each will also be on a committee. This serves not only to make the class student-centered and directed, but is also a way for students to make friends.

At the first class meeting some students form committees immediately while others continue to consider the range of possibilities I had proposed or to suggest other alternatives. Committees or small informal groups handle most class activities although I usually am the discussion leader. Committees are responsible for many things:

For planning and organizing the retreat (this should probably take
place on a Saturday or Sunday—or both—in the third or fourth
week of class) and for other special happenings;

For making surveys of and perhaps participating in cultural events
and helping groups and agencies in the community;

For reviewing films and arranging a film night;

For planning food for class meetings and special activities; and

For editing the materials which will be reproduced and become the
class anthology. (This committee should have their first meeting
as soon as possible since it takes time to read the selections, make
the choices, and reproduce copies of the basic set of readings that
all students will receive and from which each will begin to
develop his own anthology.)

The review of books and ideas which is part of the collage-
type lecture is accompanied not only by an indication of
what has been ordered by the bookstore but by a mimeographed bibliography. Often I share with students something
about each book—where the author stands on key issues and
some biographical information on the author as a person.

Students are also told about, and encouraged to undertake,
what I usually refer to as the "naive learner" project. The
only rules are that they must learn something new and that it
must be something they want to learn. Their learning may be
an effort to be creative or original, or it may be more purely
social creativity—an empathic or altruistic project. What they
choose and how they proceed to learn is up to them. Some—
when offered *carte blanche*—move toward aesthetic and intellectual creativity. They prefer to paint, write a book, sculpt,
play an instrument, build a brick planter, design a dress, fly
an airplane, or make a movie. Others choose altruistic or
empathic routes—to make friends with enemies, help "bat-
tered" children, or befriend deserted old people. Each is free
to solve the human problems, both the urgent and the va-
grantly delightful, his own and those of his society. Some will
find and expand the inner self, will feel deeply and show it,
will learn to love. A few "strong souls" may even begin to
master what Sorokin called the "Therapy of Overwhelming

Kindness"; to see, as Jesus did, that "love is the highest affirmation of life." And, as an ultimate, there will be a reaching toward enlightenment and new realms of being.

Students must understand, of course, that saying and being are not the same. Nor is intending enough: They may find, as did Linus in the *Peanuts* cartoon: "I love humanity, it's just people I can't stand."

Through these experiences and occasionally by direct exhortation, students are reminded that acquiring knowledge—however exciting the process—is not as important as making friends and finding personal tranquility. Often they can begin the quest of finding the core of their being by making a project of themselves. To do this they must discover what they value and enjoy, but such knowledge must accompany a profound sense of "not knowing." They must be aware that they will, at best, consciously know only a little of what might be known about themselves. Always they will know more than they know they know, as Polanyi has made clear in *The Tacit Dimension*. They must understand with Thoreau that "nothing is what you take it to be."

Gradually most students, except for the neurotically rigid, become comfortable with the ambiguous and the half-known. In fact most seem to welcome a theory of creative development that allows for loose ends and unfinished business. They particularly enjoy Donald MacKinnon's observation that the most creative artists, writers, scientists, and mathematicians have "messy desks." They come to accept that nothing is perfect or known for sure. A few may be ready to move forward to what the sages have called wisdom, knowing that one does not know.

Much of the learning which this new definition embraces not only goes beyond the hard boundaries of facts but also extends to more territory than the intellectual: "There is more in heaven and earth than is dreamt of in your philosophy" (*Hamlet*). Students are told that they should not only evaluate themselves, but watch their development as they go

along a number of paths—intellectual, aesthetic, and altruistic. The length of the walk and the kind of terrain is the
student's own choice.

Aesthetic and altruistic learning, as is true with all genuine
intellectual insights, is a personal experience. One cannot be
original by "coloring inside the lines." Each has to develop
taste in his own way. Each must find his own integrity and
uniqueness. Although the art of others will broaden one's
perspective (certainly part of education is to experience
beauty), none of this can tell an individual what path to take.

Seeing something is not the same as doing it. And in the
doing there is the point where the painting or the poem or
the musical composition takes over and leads the artist. Or
conversely the artist becomes part of what he paints or writes
or composes. Creativity, in its inner aspects, can never be
described. What people say is only a projection, a ghost, of
what they know and feel. Each of us has to rediscover the
process of an art. Otherwise we cannot really know it. And it
is only by knowing these ways that we come to love and
appreciate what we do.

The converse is also true: If we love what we do, the better
able we are to understand it. Research shows that we are
more able to be creative and to do something worthwhile in
an area or a pursuit in which we can abandon ourselves.

It is the same with learning to care about others. The first
step is to become involved and spend time. The research of
the sociologist Robert Blood indicates that the more conversation there is in a marriage, the better the marriage. This
is the process of taming, of making and caring for friends, to
which the fox refers in Saint-Exupéry's *The Little Prince:* "It
is the time you have wasted for your rose that makes your
rose so important." If you have a conference or a conversation with a student and make an effort to listen to him,
you will be more able to accept and like him than if he
continues to be a stranger to you. As Gordon Allport has
said: "It's hard to be down on someone you're up on."

Responsiveness is of many kinds: visual and oral, tactile and auditory. The warm smile, the nod, the encouraging word, the hand on the shoulder, and above all, listening to what is being said. "Give each one your undivided attention," Frank Laubach, the apostle to the illiterates*, writes. "Treat each one like a Rajah." All of the above are forms of love, particularly listening. Your capacity to love another is shown by how you listen when they speak. As someone once said: "What more could we ask than to be utterly attended by a person of good will?" As a teacher you need an unusual power to listen, an ability to empty yourself and be a vessel-in-waiting, to sit quietly and miss neither word nor nuance. Your expression as a listener should be gentle, and yet alert and eager. How do you do this? Certainly not by pretense or forcing. But there are ways that you can help yourself change if you want to become a different kind of teacher. Socrates, it is said, trained himself through meditation to be a gentle, receptive, and loving listener.

Naturalness and enthusiasm are desirable as is a sincere and personal manner which communicates—"I hadn't thought of it that way before," "I am on your side," "I often feel that way too." Such nonverbal communication paves the way to easier relations, just as a display of authority, and aloofness, the hint of being a bully or *grande dame* inhibits response and destroys dialogue. Words, too, can destroy. High-handed sarcasm wilts most young people. In fact any kind of verbal violence can destroy rapport, but good humor, relaxing and supportive, can still make the point tellingly.

There is an illuminating short essay written by John Fischer (an editor of *Harper's*) which contrasts the Japanese gardener with the Italian. The Italian, one might say, gardens according to Euclid, shoving nature around in predetermined and geometrical forms. The Japanese would be horrified at

---

*Frank Laubach is credited with developing methods and providing the leadership for teaching 60 million illiterates. His approach has been for "each one to teach one."

this since he wants to make his garden look natural and encourage plants to take their own special shapes. Each species is planted where soil, light, and water will be best for it. True, the gardener may move a rock, change the course of a stream, train a branch to grow more gracefully. But he does not trim an evergreen into a topiary shape. "In each case," as Fischer says, "he is striving, not to make the rock or the pine tree into something different, but to make the most of its own essential nature."

In these "naive learner" projects, the product is not evaluated (although some are very good). Students have made excellent films, written and illustrated charming books, composed and played music that must surely have had merit. But from the beginning they understood that the important thing to share with the class was the process of learning—how it feels, the frustrations when things go wrong, the joy of being utterly absorbed, and—for a lucky few—what it feels like when a skill or a bit of knowledge really becomes part of oneself.

For the most part students remain rank amateurs in the learning they undertake. Only a few find they are "naturals" and show great talent from the beginning. Many discover, however, that they truly enjoy the new activity and keep on—sometimes continuing to write and revise the book they started, or modify the canvas they are painting. With Paul Valéry, they see that a work of art is never finished, only abandoned. And for those who choose to get to know another person, it is understood that a true friendship cannot be severed or completed. One may take time out, but one keeps one's friends in mind or at heart. "You become responsible forever," said the fox, as he gazed at the Little Prince, "for what you have tamed."

Among those who plan to be or are teachers there will be, in almost every class, one or more near-geniuses. Many have been misshapen by their psychological experiences in the schools and in life, and they all but cry out for someone to talk to, someone who will not only understand but inspire, and, perhaps, become a friend. Paul sat back with his six-foot-two frame and his long legs stretched out like an unfriendly bar at a crossing. The first day of developmental reading class (required by the state board for all who want to teach in the high schools) Paul made clear his dislike of college and schools and the classroom he was in at that moment. He really had learned nothing in all these years of assignments and test-taking except what he had taught himself, and the schools had slowed that process down. He was being forced to jump over stupid hurdles, and he couldn't wait to rid himself of what he termed the rat race.

It became quickly apparent that he had read widely on all manner of topics and that he remembered what he read. Without lifting more than the finger that turned the pages in the books he read, Paul was the best-informed student in the class. It seemed to me that it would be a waste of energy to respond with hostility to his surliness and to the gratuitous insults he hurled broadcast at college teachers. The strained expression and the occasional contortions that marred his basic good looks showed that cruelty had been tried before. No one learns well under the crunch of the bludgeon or emerges as a better human being when the razor's edge of sarcasm and irony is applied. And the gifted die inside a little more each time the teacher treats them in such demeaning ways. There was only one avenue to take. I had to swallow my pride and remember that what I wanted most was to be a good teacher, not to bring Paul to heel. My pride would be built on a shaky structure, indeed, if I could not extend the same caring to a young man who snarled as I did to a little boy who cried.

I consciously took Paul with me into my mind and carried him about for hours at a time, replaying the class scenes and relistening to what he had to say. It was well worth reflecting upon. I came to lean upon his knowledge in class discussions. He had read so widely that there were few areas about which he was uninformed. He was a well, a fountain of information.

And gradually he began to mellow as he became aware of my very real need for him as a resource person and the respectful valuing given him by the class. He sat up straighter and moved his chair nearer to room center.

But however much you try to reach all students, you may fail at times. Some may have to be taken by the hand by others who teach in different ways and some may be fully confirmed *prima donnas* and misanthropes who do not want to be taught. Occasionally a student has heard of your approach to teaching in advance and enters class ready to challenge you on every point. Others may find the emphasis on love so "unrealistic" and so at odds with "The Way Its Spozed to Be" (as James Herndon wrote) that they will go to great lengths to bring a deviant professor back into the fold.

Ronnie was one who announced such a purpose at the first class meeting. Soon after I had told the class that I would be teaching the "required" course differently than they might expect, but that there were other sections for those who preferred the conventional interpretation, Ronnie demurred. In clear tones he announced to the class that he had heard about the way that I deviated from what had become custom and he, for one, considered it an abrogation of his rights to be asked to go to a teacher's home. I told him and the class about my desire to establish an atmosphere that was more serene and more relaxing than what would be easily possible in the rather dirty and shabby third-floor room to which we had been assigned for our weekly meetings, 7:00 to 10:00 P.M. on Thursdays. I admitted that it is possible to rise above the grime and the roar of traffic and the fact that your shoes stick to the floor in the gummy residue of what was once a puddle of Coca-Cola. An inspired teacher and an eager class can disregard such environmental disarray, and I knew of one truly great woman, Danish in descent, who swept out her classroom and arranged it with care for the evening meeting—giving up her dinner hour. But my point was that I lived only five minutes from the campus, and I had a large living room that I had built just for students with a deep carpet, davenports, comfortable chairs, cushions for floor lounging, and coffee facilities. Would they like to be my guests?

After the initial class session Ronnie's first act was to go to the dean with the printed class announcement and demand that the class be held in the room in which it was scheduled. Fears of monetary reprisal if Ronnie took his case successfully to the president caused the dean to ask for a census of class opinion about the location and kind of class meetings. Fortunately for me and the cause of informal meetings, field trips and potlucks, the students—most of whom were already teaching—overwhelmed the dean with assurances that they wanted to break bread together and become friends with their fellow students. Perhaps one of the main allures was the appeal of comfortable surroundings after a day of the often grim austerity and discomfort of a typical classroom. Refreshments (coffee and whatever the ingenious food committee decided upon) also helped to relax tensions that had built up during the day. But nothing was as important as the atmosphere of mutual concern.

In the large informal room, students too may be natural. They wear comfortable clothes, leaving their shoes—Japanese style—at the entrance, and they sit where and how they like. Occasionally someone tries the full lotus position on a single floor cushion, while others seem to prefer reclining, Turkish or Roman fashion, on several pillows. Others curl up on a davenport or lounge on the carpeted steps leading to the cantilevered mezzanine itself—looking downward at their classmates or outward into the trees and ferns. Many, of course, sit in chairs which I hope are somewhat more comfortable than those in the usual college classroom. At least they were chosen with that in mind.

These teachers (mostly young, but some quite mature) were eager to make friends and to recapture a personal identity. Many had almost forgotten about their former selves—once green and young but now submerged under the patina of teacher activities. The person inside was shut out by

the external life of fielding questions and caring for others'
needs in the classroom. There was no time left for the
reflection and introspection one needs to come in touch with
the self again. If they had indeed become "traffic managers
and timekeepers," few wanted to be this. It is a rare teacher
who would not gladly relinquish the Three Deadly Duties—
Noon, Hall, and Playground. As I get to know them they tell
me that they had become teachers because they liked and
wanted to help children and young people—and I see no
reason to doubt their good faith. The best of them like
people of all ages and are gentle and warmly expansive. Not a
few show a natural nobility and generosity of spirit.

As has been pointed out, teachers are often more the
victims than the perpetrators of the system. They may fall
into the rigid, formal behavior demanded of them, but those
who are becoming artists at teaching break away from this
more and more as they become secure. The Creative Intellectuals often rebel openly and soon. Some stage successful
revolutions, but many do not. The ones whom the system
bests either leave teaching or remain—warped and bitter. The
professional teacher usually approaches the problem more
obliquely. Not a few of the true teachers among these find
ways to deal with children directly and personally without
open conflict with the system.

As in all colleges and universities that offer an education
major, the students come from widely different backgrounds.
However many are from homes where funds are limited and
where there has never been more than a scant interest in
intellectual matters. Even those who began college in the 60's
(by 1970 almost half of the American high school graduates
were in college) were often the first of their families to
attend. Many of the students whom I have come to know, to
enjoy, and to admire emerged from this aggregate. They
certainly cannot be described as having been pampered by a
permissive and affluent society, although a few—especially
among the young wives who came back to school with a
rarely concealed joy—have had fine liberal arts educations.

Mainly, as I have said, I teach teachers or novitiates. I find that these students, like all healthy human beings, enjoy friendly, relaxed gatherings. They vastly prefer these to the kind of behavior demanded on factory assembly lines or in military training, where the human being is expected to become a thing or an interchangeable part, and the real self must be submerged in a predetermined role. Fortunately few are ever so overwhelmed or misshapen that they lose all capacity to respond to a happy human group, or to continue the never-ending search for meaning and identity.

This eagerness for self-discovery and fellowship is so near the surface that it continually asks for expression. I was aware of the needs, but not sure how I could even begin to meet them. It was my view that people respond differently when they are in the midst of beauty, tranquility, and nature than in the usual classroom.

Maslow told me in an interview about an experiment using beautified and uglified environments with college students:

> My wife and daughter get sick in nonaesthetic surroundings. Houses just don't have the kind of intrinsic beauty required by my wife. She has to rebuild them.

> She helped me with an experiment in which we tested the effect of a beautified and an uglified room. Many students could not work in crummy surroundings and others behaved in loose, coarse fashions. Still others became curt, abrupt, and harsh. My wife greeted the students in both rooms, but they saw her differently.

> In the uglified room, which was narrow and long and with a single high window, and everything not only filthy but with the walls painted a poisonous green, they saw things very differently than in the beautiful room.

One of the best ways of reaching the higher moments, the peaks, of being, is through experiencing beauty—a sunset, an autumn tree in full blaze, a flower just emerging from the green folds of the bud. What I am speaking of lies below the surface of conscious thought and spoken words. It can be called preverbal or nonverbal; certainly it is intuitive and aesthetic. For most it takes on its fullest and richest meaning when it is concrete and personal. Secondhand accounts of how teachers can substitute informal "open classrooms" and "free schools" for the orthodox pattern are not nearly as effective as direct experience with this kind of freedom. To provide the open classroom for the teacher who is herself in school can make such discussions meaningful.

I now teach in a city college, Portland State University, situated within a few blocks of the new heart of the metropolis with its banks, insurance companies, and parking structures, all built in the service of money and machines. Fortunately some of the gracious gestures of the old city remain to modify the sterile, deadening effect of mortar, glass, and brick. The ribbon of green lawn and densely foliaged trees of the park does offer some surcease from the stale air of overused classrooms—but not enough. In the late 1960's over 10,000 students were funneled into a few buildings and the oases for forming friendships (parks, lounges, coffee bars) were too few and much too overcrowded. Since most students worked, and evening students (whom I usually teach) made of college a series of one-night stands, it was hard for anyone to develop a feeling of belonging and a sense of community. Although many new buildings have recently been constructed, the housing of the School of Education continues to be thoroughly inadequate.

With such concern in mind, but at first with only vague ideas about what I could do, I began taking my students out of these uglified rooms and away from the thick soup of city noise, that was assaulting our senses.

My view was that noise and visual ugliness are hazards to hearing and psychological health. Not only do they blunt the senses and the sensibilities, but they literally baffle the psyche, keeping you away from yourself. My hope was to create a new environment in surroundings natural enough and with sufficient space and beauty and physical comfort so that students could begin to search for their imprisoned selves.

It may be true that much of life in America today is mean, dull, and painful, but this is not a necessary state of affairs. Tiny Denmark, with only five million people, has allowed much of nature to remain just that. There are stretches of forest within short distance of all, and parks literally abound in Copenhagen. In every tiny rural crossroads settlement there is a library, a post office, a school, a bakery for fresh (*friske*) bread, and the blomster sign for *friske* flowers. And in the country at large there are at least a hundred spacious and beautifully designed library-cultural centers where children, teenagers, and their parents cluster at all times. Records and paintings in great variety can be checked out along with books.

I did not have Denmark in mind, since I did not live there until the year of 1970–71, but I had a feeling that the situation could be different than it was in the classroom to which I was assigned in "Old Main." There had been much more beauty in the one-room school where I taught during the Depression. There were the pleasant sounds of nature, and with no money, we managed to have a rock garden without and flower arrangements within. Surely, even with limited funds, I could find a way to give my students a better environment in the aesthetic and psychological senses than they now had.

To accomplish this I asked a designer, James Morrow, whose work I have come to admire greatly, to plan a learning center seventy feet in length, literally a downward extension of my home. Not a new wing, but a lower level that reached further into the ravine than the house proper which was at street level. The large classroom-living area is approximately 30' X 40' with the rest divided into smaller rooms. Outside, a straight-rail balcony, similar to those that encircle the ancient Japanese temples, extends for the length of the house. This is attached to the exterior wall just below the large windows which allow an interplay between interior and landscape. From both balcony and windows one can hear the tall maples moving in the wind overhead, or catch a glimpse of the flashing blue of the Steller's jay, or of the small stream which trickles down from the tiny patch of lawn some twenty feet below street level.

The interior has been kept as simple as possible, to harmonize with the out-of-doors. It has a moss green carpet and natural woods, with stark white walls extending ten feet above the shoulder-high old stone wall that braces the vertical side of the ravine above the small lawn, and continues through all of the rooms. The effort is to cooperate with nature—not to create an environment, but to join one. For the harmony without, as Plato stressed, contributes to the harmony within.

XVIII • The Retreat

In such an environment as was described in the last chapter, or at such times as the class decides to go to the mountains or seashore, most students find the day or the weekend of retreat with other class members a revitalizing experience. They develop warm feelings about themselves and their classmates more quickly and surely this way than in any directed efforts that I might orchestrate, such as sensitivity or encounter sessions. The retreat committee plans the venture with practically no guidance from me—only the minimal suggestions that this is a way for students to get to know one another on a human level and for each to do things he might not ordinarily have time for or even feel competent to do. Invariably these experiences have been as rewarding for the planning committee as for their fellow students who come to relax, enjoy, understand themselves, and make friends.

Even at this stage, a number of years after my first off-campus venture, it is hard for me to believe—although each new class brings confirming evidence—that students can indeed organize and provide a series of experiences that their classmates will find delightful and rewarding. But they can. And when I see the deep seriousness, the gaiety and humor, the extended love and spontaneous originality that emerge from every group in the simplest of settings with the most minimal of directions, I chide myself.

Certainly no one factor makes retreats successful and rewarding, but in discussing this with students who have been in more than one of my classes and have gone on several retreats (could the retreat be a major lure for taking another class?), their conclusion was that one of the principal causes was *expectancy*. What the students hope for when they come probably makes the difference. What they are told—whether by me or one of their classmates—runs something like this:

> You are to spend the day finding yourself and finding friends. Developing the "instinct for communion" of which Buber has spoken—trusting, accepting, yes, even loving. You are to relax, simply to be, to communicate—if you wish—with parts of yourself from which you are estranged, to find ways of being which you have never known. Sit still and let yourself grow. Be, if not your best self, then one of your better selves. Escape, if you can, from your old roles. Forget your teacherisms and your atavisms. You will find that much of this is easier where people do not know you so well that they know only a part of you, know you as a stereotype. "Good old dependable Mary." You may surprise yourself by turning cartwheels the length of the room as one of my charming and reserved young teachers did. It may well be, as Fromm has said, that "[it is] only in the love of those who do not serve a purpose, /that/ love begins to unfold."

What I have come to feel, although I have no properly collected data—only my repeated observations and the comments of hundreds of students—is that the talent for creative expression and for warm, extensive behavior is in everyone. I agree with Charles Silberman, "If placed in an atmosphere of freedom and trust, that is to say, if treated as professionals and as people of worth, teachers behave like the caring, concerned people they would like to be."

Not far below the surface almost all persons have a rich storehouse of talent—particularly if we are willing to expand the definition of talent to include what Dylan Thomas called "My Five and Country Senses." Aesthetic experiencing is important, nature soothes and revitalizes, beauty is balm to the soul. "Climb the mountains," said John Muir, "and get their good tidings. Nature's peace will flow into you as sunshine flows into the trees." The environment can contribute much toward making this aesthetic experiencing possible. It should be one from which the students may, as Plato said, "Drink in good from every quarter." My goal, though, is both the Platonic one of drawing the students toward "the light of reason" and also that of supplying the life-giving force of love. I am convinced, with Wordsworth, that the simple human affections will rise in most groups where the atmosphere is free and accepting.

But how to shape such an environment? How to communicate to people that they are free and trusted—and loved? There can be no falseness and no forcing. The touch must be deft and sure, but it must remain a touch—never a gesture of force or a show of power. The environment as well as the teacher must speak in muted tones. And planning must not obtrude. Technique is most beneficial when it is least obvious. There is no set of facts, no logical paradigm, no mechanics manual that can guide you. Only your intuition, the sensing that this is right and good and the way to go. For this reason the guidance of the retreat should be in the hands of healthy people. As Maslow points out the psychologically healthy know not only what is best for themselves, but also what is best for others. And on those golden days when everything works out for the best, we will understand with Plato that we are all being led out of the cave.

Lois Lawson, who directed one of the retreats, proved to be not only an artist of no small ability, but also an artist teacher. She arranged through the audio-visual department for a film, *Rain Showers,* to be shown just as the groups of friends (no longer simply students or classmates) were finishing a delicious lunch that the food committee had planned and all had helped to provide. This film was a pastoral poem showing animals and children, the awakening of birds, the sudden and dramatic changes in nature and the weather. It was a film with no commentary—only music and sounds from nature. After absorbing this and having earlier experienced walks on the balcony above the ravine, each wrote one or more poems in the seventeen-syllable, Japanese haiku style.

The next activity Lois had planned took place on the upper level in the carport. She and her committee arranged folding metal tables upon which they placed rubber brayers (rollers) and glass rectangles, each encrusted with a properly tacky but clear-toned layer of oil paint. On a nature walk into the ravine following *Rain Showers,* students collected a wide variety of leaves. These were placed on the paint-covered glass, and over both pigment and embedded leaves a rectangle of colored tissue paper was pressed firmly with the roller. From these efforts attractive, often lyrical, designs emerged in great variety and many colors. Many of the resulting leaf prints were fine examples of decorative art, expressing as they did a feeling for an abstract relationship of form and color.

After the prints were made Lois showed the students how the decorated tissue might be elegantly mounted on colored construction paper. Two sheets of this formed the cover for a book which held the haiku poetry compositions of the class. Martha Grinquist, a top-flight secretary as well as a committee member, did the typing and made a trip to the city center for thirty Xerox copies—all within little more than an hour. My booklet is in tones of yellow, orange, and muted green; and I keep it proudly among the poetry on my coffee table, flanking Blake's *Songs of Innocence,* Whitman's *Leaves of Grass,* and other fragments from the poetry of cosmic consciousness and transcendentalism.

Beverly Anderson was another star among teachers. Her typical mood was one of exuberance and joy. As a first-year teacher in an experimental high school (half black, half white, and "open") she was that great rarity, a success: with students, with fellow teachers, and with the administration.

Her planning of the retreat was characteristically deft. It was her idea that each class member should bring to the retreat his or her most meaningful possession, a "favorite thing." The showing of these and the talk that rose and circled with each presentation brought people together who had scarcely nodded to one another before. Jean showed an old Presbyterian hymnal from eighteenth-century Scotland that her children in the school in rural Scotland had given her two years before. As she showed this she told about the plans that she and her husband, a young minister, had made for a new form of religious education.

Valentina, who sat near Jean in the circle of students, brought an enormous bottle of perfume labeled "My Sin." Earlier in the fall a young girl, a hard-working honors student, and her boyfriend had come to her in a state of near breakdown. The girl was sure she was pregnant. She could not talk to her parents, nor could her friend talk to his. Valentina listened and quietly helped. There was a family doctor who was also a friend. There were days of uncertainty and turmoil, but the fourteen-year-old found she was not pregnant after all. Sheepishly, and not without a sense of the implications, the young teenagers worked overtime to buy their favorite counselor the large bottle labeled "My Sin."

David Owen was a broad-shouldered, outspoken coach and counselor who worked with the teamsters at the brewery in the mornings and came to my class in the late afternoons one summer. His face characteristically glistened with perspiration and his shoulders were relaxed and a little weary. He was neither an artist nor a philosopher. In fact reading anything more than the sports page or headlines was not his custom, although he did have a taste for, and some talent, in the art of argument. But his forte did not appear until the day of the retreat.

Having heard about sharing favorite possessions from students who had been in earlier classes, David asked the class to bring theirs. After arriving at 9:00 A.M. the group of thirty divided into five small groups, which moved to self-selected areas. One met on the deck which looked north toward the mountain. A second chose the green lawn far below street level which looked down upon the Lilliputian stream and the wood ferns which dominate it in much the same way that trees arch across rivers. Another sat in a sunny area in the south end of the center, several of these on a jewel-tone, thick pile Finnish Rya carpet. Both of the two groups remaining were in the classroom, one in the teaching end and the other due north of them, partially under the cantilevered mezzanine.

Sharing of things quickly shifted to intimate conversations. An hour went by and then another. Despite the pungent aromas from the casseroles which the food committee had placed on the long tables on the mezzanine it proved to be difficult to get an admittedly hungry group to take time out to fill their plates. The trust walk soon after lunch simply extended and deepened these feelings. Students grouped together for this in their cars and drove to the Bird Sanctuary, a natural area with trails wide enough only for walking. This is in another mountain area ten minutes away.

Birds were everywhere about the lake, and in and above the marshy areas. But in the deeply forested part of the Sanctuary all was dark and quiet as pairs of students—one blindfolded and dependent, the other guiding—picked their ways over the rough terrain. One did the leading out, the other the leading in. And people learned new things about themselves. Ron, a young athlete, said, "I had always seen myself as surefooted before, but suddenly I sensed how precarious my relationship to earth really is and how precious friendships are. There I was, clumsy and half-scared, and finally understanding how those awkward freshmen that come out for football in the fall must feel."

A tall blonde Diana-of-the-Hunt standing next to him said,

> Masako was my partner and she was amazing. There she was, not much larger than a song sparrow, and by the gentlest of guidance she told me through her fingers how and where to go. I never

stumbled once, although I was even more terrified than Ron
when our walk began.

Other classes have achieved rapport through such avenues
as wit and high humor (which, I must admit, dips into low at
times). At least this is the way the creative, improvisational
dramas strike me. Often clusters of students who decide they
will band together, along with a few draftees, are given a
Goodwill-type collection of odds and ends, and told that
within a half hour they must produce a play based on the
inspired use of the oddments. One such collection contained
a sequined red garter, a large map of Arlington and the
Pentagon, a British bounder's hat, three beer steins, a riding
crop, and some fake money from a Monopoly game. The
ensuing drama, done in a loose-tongued, rubber-jointed
"boys in the backroom" style, almost brought the encircled
class to the floor.

The star was Clem, a round-faced, mild-mannered man in
his mid-thirties who had formerly managed the appliance
section at Montgomery Ward's and was newly a teacher in the
junior high school. He was an innocent Bob Newhart and a
sophisticated Herb Shriner all in one, ad libbing his way
through a complex dialogue that brought to life before our
eyes the pudding-faced Colonel Blimp he was playing. He was
the complete bloater, stuffy and over-stuffed, what the
British call a "pompous ass," flashing his family fortune
before the girls in the Red Dog Saloon. Giving long-legged
Nell, the girl with the gratuitous gams and the high-placed red
garter the benefit of his hot gaze, he told her that he wanted
to buy an estate for his horses. She quickly conferred with
her satellites-of-the-bar and together, raising steins high, the
conspirators showed their captive Colonel the lay of some
likely land. Arlington Meadows would be ideal for the horses!
The stable? Five-sided, or course. The Colonel, as he turned
over his fortune, exulted, "Jolly good for my groom. My last
one went crazy, you know. The stable was round, and he lost
his bloody wits trying to corner a colt."

Retreats and discussion groups are often at their best when the group is caught up in humor or snared by whimsy. Obviously one cannot tell a class to be spontaneous. Yet it is one of the surest ingredients of the good mix needed for successful learning. Anyone who speaks (before large audiences or small) knows the importance of what precedes the lecture. An audience that is happy and relaxed, that has just sung a rousing song that almost everyone knows is much more receptive than one that has heard an hour or more of droning intonations.

Creativity is closely linked with whimsy, fantasy, the pleasantly "crazy"—and in some of its most dramatic moments, the frankly mad. (The reader is by now aware that I try to modify violence and rechannel "acting out." From my years of practice as a clinical psychologist I have learned to step lightly in the areas where a misstep could ruin a life.) Humor has a quality that can heal a rift in a discussion that is ready to break through the dam of civility. This is where a ready repertoire of stories, poems, and jokes can stem the flood tide. If the teacher makes humor a viable alternative and is at times a model, talented students will use the deft, humorous asides and sometimes the broadsides needed to break the deadlocks and confrontations. This talent for humor is everywhere. The most unlikely may show gifts of mimicry, and almost all will respond. It is a rare group that cannot relax and enjoy, be at ease, get out of gear, tolerate the human error, feel free to be themselves—idiosyncratic, even peculiar.

XIX • Self-Study and Self-Evaluation

Students will invariably gain insight and satisfaction from the study of a subject on which they are very well informed— themselves. One of the simplest ways to begin this is to ask them to write an autobiographical account of how they learn or prefer to learn, how they began reading, how they feel about reading, what they enjoy. Later on students will study themselves as they carry out the "naive learner" project. As we have seen there are no restrictions on these creative projects, save that each should learn something new, learning freshly as a child does. No written paper is required, only the purpose of self-study should be fulfilled.

The child's world is again invoked at the last class session—often extended to six hours (Saturday morning through lunch, or a late afternoon-dinner-evening meeting). This is "Show and Tell" time. Whether the product, perhaps refinishing a chest or losing twenty pounds, is successful is not important. What each learns about his own learning is the point. This is the process that is to be studied and reported. Experiences are harrowing (one of the young men had weekly meetings for dinner in Skid Row restaurants with a paroled murderer); hilarious (an overweight young woman who wasn't on a diet told about her problems in finding a pilot who weighed no more than a jockey to teach her flying since the total weight the plane could carry was limited); as well as exalting (a lovely young Chinese girl taught an old uncle who had become aphasic through a stroke to speak again).

These projects nearly always include false starts, the inability to find a teacher or teaching manual, the dislike of the teacher's manner or the manual's technique, the misunderstanding or misreading of directions, and plain, unvarnished, awkward ineptness. Surely the naive learner, who makes a serious effort to learn something because he wants to know it, will better understand everyone's problems in learning—those of his classmates as well as those of the young students whom he teaches or will teach.

Each student's report of his growth is also included in an evaluation, usually part of his anthology.* I am not only interested in the critical and creative comments upon articles but I also learn much from their self-evaluations of growth or progress throughout the term. Some prefer to keep diaries on a daily basis, others do retrospective reports. Many report on a wide range of reading, extensive discussion with friends, and a general delight in new ideas. Some prefer to evaluate their emotional and social growth—self-confidence and self-reliance, empathy and altruism—while others tell about cultural explorations and the awakening of new talents and interests.

Finally, on the basis of their work students grade themselves. They often decide at the beginning of the term the grade they need and work for this mark. As graduate stu-

---

*These anthologies are turned in a week before the end of the term, at which time I read them through quickly. Later, after the grade slips go in, I read them again. The total process of reading and reflecting almost always requires two or more hours for each student. This means that with fifty students at least two weeks of my time is involved.

dents, grades desired are A's or B's. Some choose to take "Incompletes" and continue to read and write for a longer period of time than the term has allowed.

EXCERPTS FROM STUDENT SELF-EVALUATIONS

I found for the first time, during the retreat, that teachers were human. All last year—my first year of teaching—I thought about other teachers the way I had when I was in school. I thought, I guess, that they were what the kids say—machines. You can imagine my surprise when I found that I liked everyone I talked to at the retreat and, wonder of wonders, nearly all of them turned out to be teachers.

I used to come to class dead tired. We often have curriculum meetings late Thursday afternoon. I'd barely have time to eat and then the thought of facing three hours of class in Old Main, dirty floors, uncomfortable chairs, the whole bit—it was too much. When you said that we could come to your house for our meetings and put three meetings together for a full-day retreat, some of the class shook their heads as if you were daft but I went right along with it. Even if we didn't learn anything we'd have comfortable chairs and some refreshments to revive us. To my surprise I've never learned so much. Maybe because we talked about so many ideas I hadn't thought about before.

I guess the thing that really impressed me was about loving what you teach and refusing to teach those things you don't care about and don't understand. Now that's something that my principal would *never understand.* He expects us to go step by step and give him a lesson-plan outline with all the horrible details. To cover everything even if we kill it for the kids as we go. What am I supposed to do—defy him and get fired? Close my door and do my own thing? Blow my brains out?

I've never liked to read but I found that the interview with
Margaret Mead was not like the usual reading. In fact I didn't
put it down until I had finished it—all fifty pages. At first I
was overwhelmed with all that stuff the editors gave us. I felt
like a centipede on his back, all wasted motion. So many
pages to turn, so many ways to go. But I kept on reading and
since there were many exciting ideas—things I hadn't thought
about, ideas I didn't agree with, points that I didn't quite
understand—I talked to one of the fellows I taught with. It
got so we'd read something and have a discussion over lunch
every day. Maybe he learned more than I did, who knows?

I must say that when you said, "There are only two points
to keep in mind in Developmental Reading: (1) You develop,
and (2) You read," I thought you were crazy. No machines?
No time tests? No eye-movement exercises? And then you
said, "I'd rather have you read less and think more. Read
slowly and argue with the author. Remember books are
written by people and they make errors, deliberate and
otherwise!" It was too much. Who was I to question B. F.
Skinner? After all, hadn't he trained pigeons to play Ping-
Pong?

I've really begun to think about what a good teacher is and
what teaching is all about. When you said we could read
anything that would help us learn about ourselves and our
students or about learning, I took you at your word. I
decided I'd leave all those books on your shelf at the
bookstore until later and strike out on my own. I found
Gilbert Highet's *The Art of Teaching*—the editors had given
us some excerpts from it—and have really studied it. In fact I
have taken a whole notebook full of notes.

All through school I've been what you'd call the good
student. No matter what the teacher assigned I did it and I'd
practically be in tears if I got marked down or got a low

grade. Now I'm beginning to realize that as a senior I never read anything for myself. I wouldn't even know how to choose anything. I haven't read a book (except the ones that were assigned) since I was twelve. I guess the Nancy Drew series was the last reading for pleasure I did. But all this is changing. I'm finding I like to read, but only certain things. From now on—as much as possible—I'm going to be in charge of my reading. With the third graders I teach I've adopted a new policy. They get to choose their own books too, and I tell them if they don't like things, not to read them. Maybe they'll change later. But after all, each is different, so why should they all like the same things?

I feel more sure of myself and less sure about what I know. When I teach, or even at home with my wife, it's easier for me to admit I don't know. It's a wonderful feeling to realize there's great mystery in the universe and that we won't ever know it all. Of course from time to time we may get a glimpse of what it's all about. But these moments when everything is clear and all is certain are brief. I feel comfortable this way and feel this is how it should be.

I can't claim I've had a peak experience. In fact I'm not even sure what *that* is, but I did relax for the first time in months. And at the same time I was elated. There was a flow of energy that I tapped. It was a great feeling after the grind of six classes a day. I'm afraid whoever said, "Teachers are more apt to be automatons or sleepwalkers than dreamers of dreams," was right.

I thought when you didn't tell Lynn how to make a critical evaluation you were making things too hard and confusing. You're the teacher. You're supposed to know. Yet you answer questions by asking them. Frankly, it bothers me.

I know now that I've always drawn a circle around myself. I just don't want people to touch me or get near to me psychologically. It's still like that with me but I'm beginning to see that it should be different. Maybe some day I'll take a student by the hand and say, "Let's do it together."

It was great to get back to nature. Back to the simple things! All these have been complicated by change. When I watch TV or the jet planes overhead I feel like I'm strapped to a roller coaster with kaleidoscopic goggles in my helmet, careening through heaven-knows-what to heaven-knows-where.

I thought no one cared, that people were ships passing in the night. I realize that "concern for" or love helps us—I read this somewhere—not only to perceive potentialities but to actualize them. As I think about it I realize that when I am around certain people (and this includes some teachers) I literally feel ten feet tall. Children grow in marvelous ways in certain classrooms. Could it be where the teacher has a green thumb? Right before your eyes the children become more creative and gifted.

I found a whole new way of looking at life. Before I felt I was flotsam and jetsam, helpless and tossed about by fate. Now, after reading Frankl, that part in *Man's Search for Meaning* where he says that we can decide our fates ourselves, we are in charge; I feel differently. Living or dying is in our hands. Being happy or sad. We can see beauty in the world and reflect upon it with joy. Or we can see the world as a savage, tattered place that even God has deserted.

I'm part Indian, you know, and I ask—when are we going to practice democracy in school? There were only three articles the editors chose that I liked. I spent my time reading about something worthwhile, though—how the blacks have been treated in this lousy society. As far as the self-evaluation goes, I didn't do one. I don't believe in "telling all." It's an invasion of privacy for a professor to even ask.

Whatever we do it should be relevant to the world we live in, to the issues and problems all of us face. Learning "What percentage of Negroes attended integrated public schools in 1960" or answering "Rousseau's plan for teaching geometry was inductive: 'true or false'," does not help me to understand the world about me. But when I was encouraged to read and examine and come to my own conclusion about the theories and philosophies of Carl Rogers, Abraham Maslow, and Sidney Jourard I felt I was learning. Here were great minds at work. There is still hope for mankind in a world full of power-hungry, political activists, and greedy, tricky, dishonest used-car dealers.

The class directed me toward authors like Fromm, Allport, Glasser, Maslow, and other humanists who value people more than the system. It helped me to discover the intellectual authorities that justified my belief that the individual is the important unit, and that something is terribly wrong when an "ideal system" is set up and the individuals are manufactured to support it. Personally I gained immeasurably from the experience of sharing ideas and insights with a diverse group of people whose excitement with discovery-experiential education approximated my own. Quite frankly it was exhilarating to participate in a group where others felt an enthusiasm toward education. Perhaps the genuine warm friendships generated within the class group say more than anything else what the class was about. Within the class the ideal situation was created, at first without the participants being at all aware of it. There was friendliness, openness, absence of competition, comfort, and free rein to pursue one's own personal or professional interests in an open exchange of ideas. We were guided gently toward a common goal—Becoming.

Months after the fact I have realized what you were trying to do in your class. Your design has become clear to me, finally, although it made little sense to me at the time. I don't think I'm stupider than most, so will take a face-saving approach and admit that I just wasn't tuned in, and was certainly over-extended in the things needing my time. The material you handed out was incomprehensible. So I put it aside for awhile and instead got all the books you had listed at the co-op—a happy decision—and read them before looking at the first material. Then it made sense. Boy, did it make sense.

So, in a way, this is a thank-you note, my first to an instructor, besides being a lame explanation of what happened. Humanistic, third force, existential psychology was something new to me and the results of my reading so far cannot be known; although I do know that I am fascinated. I'm starting now to follow up in the bibliographies, so there is much to consider. The result so far is rather more personal than practical in that I have become aware of how little I know myself and am taking steps to increase my self-knowledge.

The outside activities of a cultural nature were "my dish," my indulgence. An "assignment" (which I made myself) is a marvelous excuse to do what I wanted to do anyway. Go to museums, plays, the ballet. I really went "huckeldy-buck" and saw the ballet two evenings. I only wish I had seen all four performances. And, as soon as the term was over, I spent three days at Ashland with Shakespeare. Chuck and I also went to the Contemporary Arts Gallery. And I now make it a point of touring the White Gallery whenever they change exhibits.

I've never read so much in my life. I feel inundated, soaked in. For the first time the classes I'm taking this summer have made me want to know about something besides the areas I teach—physical education and health. I never thought, and neither did any of my friends, that I could get so involved.

This course was unusual, to say the least. It really helped me to see again. In high school I considered myself mature and very open-minded. But since then I gradually closed in on myself. I became narrow minded. I was becoming more hypocritical. This is not to say that I am no longer this way, but at least I've done some critical thinking. The best part of this course is getting to know new people. I am terrible with words but I want you to know how much I appreciated this opportunity. There were many people in the class that I did not agree with, but I still *liked* them and enjoyed hearing their viewpoint. I think I am beginning to *listen.*

XX • Beginning

*I have always been regretting that I was not as wise as the
day I was born.*

HENRY DAVID THOREAU

I often wonder if the theory I have developed allows me to
justify what I already do, or whether the ways I have taught
were carefully and thoughtfully based on well-defined ideas.
However this may be, I did find that by the mid-50's I had
consciously formulated some educational principles. The requirements imposed by a Ph.D. thesis and by writing research
proposals may have made me try to put order into my
thought processes, which I must admit I enjoyed most when
they were in their natural unpruned state. I liked and encouraged the juxtaposition of ideas that were strange bedfel-
lows. But in support of Emerson's view that we may be
"wiser than we know," as I searched for the premises which
underlay my teaching, I found there actually were some
rather clear themes which kept repeating themselves. Many of
these, as I look back, were already apparent during my first

days of "keeping school" when I took over the teaching, sweeping, woodcutting, and fire-building tasks in a one-room country schoolhouse in a rural community called Eldorado. This was during the Depression or the New Deal, depending on your frame of reference.

Without supervision, without wires for anyone to tap or even the Big Brother admonitions of a public-address system, I was free to design my own program. "Cost accounting" was not a problem since my salary of eight hundred dollars a year was the only cost. There were piles of textbooks, many of them much-thumbed and often water-soaked (Oregon is justly famous for rain), and there were a dozen or so children ranging from ages five to sixteen to be taught. My immediate reaction was that these books were more apt to be impediments than to serve as inspiration. But since there were to be county and state examinations on the contents, they must be studied. My suggestion, to which the children agreed, was that we finish these as rapidly as possible and then plan for more interesting activities. As I remember it everyone was through with the year's prescribed textbooks by Christmas.

We then embarked on a more lively education. Every month we worked toward the production of a festival which usually focused on the study of a foreign country. During the month we would read at random from a box of books which I ordered in advance from the state library. One month our study was on Russia, another on China, another on Ireland. The culmination, the crowning event, of all of this was a monthly program. This included, as all rural Americans knew, a play, recitations, music, and perhaps dancing.

Our first efforts were gauche and primitive; but we improved, as they say, with time and effort. Even at our most awkward moments, however, we enjoyed ourselves. There were days on end when I can remember being at the heights. In those times of joyful frenzy before "opening night" I could, and sometimes did, work for three or four days and nights—no sleep, and no amphetamines.

All of us wore costumes, of course, and make-up. (My two years of teacher training had included several terms of play production.) For each production the schoolhouse, a big open space which we could decorate at will, was literally transformed. Before I opened school my first day my father and brothers had helped me pull up the center rows of double desks and swing them by ropes over the rafters in the woodshed. People told me they hung there for years. We could then, with the newly acquired space, have center-of-the-room theater or feasts with our festivals. On one occasion we celebrated spring and the April birthdays of everyone in the community.

The production itself—the planning, the doing, and the final performance—was almost exclusively handled by children and youth. Before they walked home in the afternoons, many of the high school students would stop by to lend a hand at the schoolhouse, which happened to be at the end of the line on their ten-mile bus trip. Although their farm and household chores were demanding, they gave a great deal of their spare time to make these productions successful. Usually the hard-working parents were only bystanders, glad to enjoy but with no time to participate. This meant that I, at eighteen, and my brother and a friend, both under twenty, were the oldest of the festival participants and producers. My mother, though, stood by in a more active way—advising on plays, encouraging the writing of poetry (because we could rarely find the "right" recitation, these had to be created as were many of the short dramatic skits), and helping with the design and manufacture of costumes. For period plays we were able to borrow dresses which some of Oregon's pioneers had worn in the post-Civil War period.

This was the beginning of what, twenty years later, I called a "redefinition of education," but which at the time seemed simply the thing to do. Curriculum was broadly defined to include a wide range of experiences in the arts, drama, creative writing, physical activities (including a softball team—in those years I played "shortstop"), and even the construction of a rock garden. We used our senses, our imaginations, and our muscles.

Everyone was welcomed at the schoolhouse, not just enrollees. All ages worked together. We were both informal and integrated, as well as ecumenical. The old families were German Evangelical-Lutheran, but a few years before a Catholic and a Jewish family had moved into the community. My family had moved there when I was eleven. Saturday nights we all went together to church, if I may use the term loosely, in the schoolhouse. Here the young minister did little exhorting—I do not remember that any of us felt burdened by original sin or in need of salvation—but instead he joined us in our simple festivities. We often sang country and western songs along with the usual hymns.

Education, at least in my mind, was continuous and integral with living. Perhaps religion was too. It never occurred to me to ask the parents what they thought about how school was kept. But since they saw me almost daily as I walked the two miles to school and home again, and since we all worked together in the berry fields in the summer, they could voice complaints easily. Either they were unaware or it did not matter that subject-matter boundaries, as these were defined by textbooks, were down. It seemed quite natural in this small community to view all knowledge as an "open system" since everything could easily be related to everything else. As far as I can remember it did not occur to anyone to suggest that we limit education to training or indoctrination. Probably no one would have tolerated anything so dull.

Being without "funds" for books or materials from the district, we earned our own way instead. To do this we charged small fees for our festive programs. Fortunately in those days when farmers had no money for moviegoing, and TV had not yet encroached upon family and community life, the home-grown production was still popular. (Much of that time we read our books by kerosene lamps, ironed with heavy metal sadirons heated on the wood stove in the kitchen, and made our own bread from the potato yeast that sat over the water reservoir away from the direct heat of the fuel box.) People from neighboring communities, perhaps intrigued by our artlessness or audacity, began to come to these programs.

As teenagers who often played adult roles, we finally had the courage to compete in an adult drama contest at the Clackamas County Fair and, just as we expected, we won. All of this success brought prosperity to the barren school. We bought a radio (incorporating music, drama, and news in our ever-evolving curriculum), a piano (which several students could play), curtains both for the raised platform that was our stage and for the windows, and the necessary equipment for softball. Students brought their own jumping ropes and marbles and we were able to borrow books in profusion and variety from the state library.

Although I would never have claimed that we were engaged in sensory education or psychotherapy—I'm not sure I knew the terms—many of these forms were there in embryo. Lifetime learning and general education seemed the only sensible approaches. But at the same time we all found ourselves called upon to be specialists. My father was a cabinetmaker and designer, a machinist and inventor, while I was inclined toward the decorative arts. If a neighbor needed a haircut and had no money, I did my best with scissors, a comb, and hand clippers. My mother, who had taken elocution lessons, helped with dramatic flourishes. Having studied the classics and memorized long epic poems, she had a talent for polishing the metres in the poetry and ballads we wrote. She was also an expert dressmaker who could not only create original designs but knew how to fit a stubborn sleeve into an armhole, how to make a skirt out of men's trousers, or a tube dress out of a yard of wool jersey.

After two years at Eldorado (which I have described—as Thoreau did his two years at Walden—as one) I went on to the university to continue my studies in art. There it was my great good fortune to meet Elizabeth Montgomery and to be asked to be her assistant in the psycho-educational clinic. She seemed to understand from the outset what I needed but did not know how to ask for. From that first fall she subscribed to *The Nation* and *Harper's* for me and seemed as pleased as I was when any one of my poems was chosen as "Today's Poem" by the *Oregonian's* poetry editor. She asked me to share her small office, was patient and forgiving when my typing remained erratic, gave me her books to read, invited me to come to her doctoral seminars when I was still a junior, and trained me to give individual intelligence tests and conduct interviews with children and their parents. Clinical psychology was only beginning to take form, but in this early center I learned a little of the art and some of the science by firsthand experiences, and often joint exploration, with a great teacher and a magnificent human being.

The clinic had no narrow definition of learning or of my tasks as the assistant to the director. I was allowed—even encouraged—to collect the children's stories, do interviews, and generally search for news and to publish a newspaper (cutting stencils on a primer typewriter and illustrating it with children's drawings and my own) and to do flower arrangements for the offices, halls, and classrooms. After I worked for five summers with seventy-five children, twenty-five teachers, and three supervisors, there was no question that my consciousness was expanded.

Added to these years of clinical work were those (between 1944 and 1949) when I worked as a clinical psychologist at the University of Michigan Psychological Clinic. Here was an opportunity to meet a number of dedicated clinicians, not a few with lively minds. I continued in my studies of behavioristic psychology (never with enthusiasm) and was exposed to Freud and to psychoanalytic thinking. But it was not until a doctoral candidate of Carl Rogers introduced me to his writings that I found a psychology which appealed. During the 50's I continued to explore and be inspired by his works and those of Gordon Allport and, with the publication of *Motivation and Personality* in 1954, of Abraham Maslow.

Both my own experiences and my reading brought me to the ever-firmer realization that self-awareness, coupled as Marie Jahoda said, with self-acceptance and self-confidence, were all important in what—despite the formidable piles of research—remains a mystery: the teaching-learning process. For the schoolchild, the youth, and even for adults (such as teachers), education must answer those most intimate of questions "Who am I?" and "What can I become?" Not only must all of us try to understand ourselves, but we must realize that the simple discovery of the self, as one is now, is never enough. We have to try to develop into our best possible selves. Fortunately we can shape our own lives and move in the direction of our dreams. But first we must have the dream. The vision, however, does not all come from within. Gradually both from our experience and our intuition we learn that self-knowledge emerges through our human contacts. It is by talking to others and being with friends and companions, with teachers and parents, that we discover ourselves. Good friends and wise counselors help us all to find out who we are and what we might become. And beyond this, to understand as much as possible about the world and how to live one's life, we must seek what Polanyi calls "superior knowledge." This is the record of the most enlightened men and women which, as Thoreau said, is contained in "those books which circulate around the world . . . the only oracles which are not decayed."

My early teaching, as is all too apparent, was more spontaneous than designed. I covered the required curriculum (was faithful in my fashion) and then felt free to explore a variety of tangents with my students. Both their interests and mine suggested where these might lead. When I taught a seventh grade with as many as forty incumbents, in an Oregon sawmill town (few reading above bare literacy level), we were active with building and doing. Discarding the texts they couldn't read, a few volunteers and I took weekly trips on the bus to bring back armloads of books from a city library. Each student ordered what he wanted. Fritz, the biggest and most confirmed of the nonreaders, assured me he could only read on his stomach under the tree in front of the building and below the classroom windows. I accepted his conditions and gradually he learned—though neither he nor I ever knew quite how.

Gerald learned to read by helping to build a marionette stage, airplane controls, and by fashioning his own alter ego—a swashbuckling, oversized marionette, the ill-fated giant in "Jack, the Giant Killer." Velma, mousy and undernourished, took on a new personality at the intermissions of the "play," when her slender, rubber-limbed marionette in the sky-blue pants and red shirt roller-skated to a high-flying, acrobatic fame of which soft-spoken Velma must have only dreamed. With a movable stage and an eager crew and players, we took to the road. How else to get art equipment where school budgets provided for none? Certainly self-direction and perhaps some self-discovery were involved. Teaching others is also a way of building confidence, I later discovered, and these boys (the class had three times as many boys as girls) seemed to revel in teaching their teacher. As a berry-picking girl from the dirt and gravel roads and trails of the foothills of the Cascades (we could see five snow-caps from our bedroom windows in the house that my father built on high ground after the fire), I had never ridden a bicycle or roller-skated. Both were on the Curriculum for Teacher as were numerous picnics and skating parties in an endless variety of planned and unplanned versions.

A year later I was living in Peking and teaching children (fifth and sixth graders) and high school students of all nationalities. At least half, however, were Oriental. My own curiosity and the admitted ignorance of my ten and eleven year olds led me to teach Chinese history (our text was *The Pageant of Chinese History*). Perhaps for the Chinese children this supplied a sense of source and origin, a chance to discover and enlarge the concept of identity. But, in retrospect, I must admit that these very gifted youngsters seemed to have a self-assurance that was rarely found among those I

had taught who came from poverty-stricken homes and who
had "reading" problems. More than one Chinese student who
came to study English mastered it to the point of writing
poetry and charming essays within a year. Could it be that
after Chinese all other languages are a lark?

As my own education deepened and my experience broad-
ened, I came to the conclusion that the conventional school,
the conventional curriculum, and the conventional teacher
cannot give the students what they need to develop their
potentialities. New techniques, new content, new relationships are required. These convictions led me to initiate some
specific programs which were designed as radical changes.
The results of two of these are described in the pair of
chapters which follow; while Chapter XXIII introduces a
third plan, more comprehensive than the former, which I
believe to be both practicable and desirable.

These three programs can be thought of together as a series
of concentric circles. In the first a new curriculum with a
different teaching method was provided within a conventional city school for a selected group of academically
superior students. In the second a group of students was
chosen at random from a rural area to participate in an
experiment of learning in a new school of their own making.
In the third an entire section of a large city—embracing all
ages, talents, and tastes—is seen as a New Community where
all people learn whatever they enjoy doing and at the same
time contribute to the well-being of others. A sense of
community, a spirit of mutual help and zest for learning,
makes of an aggregate of strangers who inhabit a city mall an
open corridor of learning.

XXI • Being and Becoming

At Walden, Thoreau "learned this, at least ... that if one advances confidently in the direction of his dreams, and endeavors to live the life which he has imagined, he will meet with success unexpected in the common hours ..."

Innovation is not as difficult as we imagine and it is possible to live far better lives than we now do. A desire to change and the dreams of how this might be done are all we need: "Money is not required to buy one necessary of the soul" (Thoreau, *Walden*). Education, and the schools we design, can lead us to the New Age the day we decide that this should happen. In an enriched and carefully planned environment, young people can be allowed a home in the world and to feel that they belong. As Dewey said, "The child is the starting point, the center and the end." It is his development, his growth and self-realization, that is the ideal and furnishes the standard.

However, as Maslow has shown us, relatively few people can be said to be in that state of grace called self-actualization although this is the universal human potential.

All of us have great capacity to be ourselves and to think creatively about ways to grow. But the schools have too rarely developed programs where this can happen. In fact the demands of the typical school curriculum seem to keep this from occurring. As John Gardner has said, there is no education offered which is concerned with the fulfillment of the individual. Nor are George B. Leonard's exhortations that there be ecstasy in education, or Charles Silberman's pleas for joy in the classroom, generally heeded. "To possess all the world of knowledge and lose one's own self," Dewey observed, "is as awful a fate in education as in religion."

To set the stage and provide the time for this to happen, we must recognize a fundamental fact that teaching cannot proceed from the outside in. Ultimately, no one can be accountable for learning but the student. It must proceed from within. The function of the materials, the curriculum, and the teacher is to allow this to happen. The student who wants to search the byroads, the underground tunnels, and the celestial highways must be free to do so. The teacher must accept and honor all as creatures of transcendent worth. If he is accomplished, he will have a talent for empathy. And he, as well as his students, will not play roles but instead be open, vulnerable, and self-revealing.

School programs—or whatever form education takes—should do something more than provide freedom and acceptance. They must also be responsive and evocative. How can we help students as they undertake the tasks of self-actualization—what Maslow defines as "the makings of plans, the discovery of self, the selection of potentialities to develop, the construction of a life-outlook"?

My own work as a psychologist and teacher has convinced me that students of all ages have great potential for creative learning. Many, perhaps most, of the potentially gifted and creative are never identified and none use more than a small fraction of their talents. It is all too common for teachers and the public in general to accept the view that a child is already ruined by a bad environment if he were unfortunate enough to have one before he entered school.

People are amazed that we discovered in a very average Midwestern city so many young people with great talent and one of genius level.

The first time I met Mike Grost was at an evening seminar. A group of graduate students and I had been studying human potentiality, creativity, and intellectual giftedness. At the same time I had received calls from Mike's principal, his teacher, and finally his mother*, asking if I could not offer him a better educational plan. He was beginning to daydream and show a marked lack of interest in school tasks that everyone admitted were meaningless for him. In contrast, strangely enough, some of the school psychologists and social workers thought he was not markedly different.

Suddenly it occurred to me that we might work out a mutually helpful plan. Mike could come to class and tell what and how he enjoyed learning and perhaps together we could devise a better school program. I suggested that he talk about anything that interested him. His choice was the duodecimal system. After he had explained this "system of twelves" perhaps three times, most of the graduate students began to understand. Mike proved to be an extremely good teacher— lucid and matter-of-fact. At the break one of my students who taught at the community college asked Mike if any major culture had ever used this as its basic number system. Mike said he thought not. The student—with an "Aha, I have you" tone—asked, "What about the Babylonians?"

Mike countered, "I think if you would investigate the Babylonians you would find that only the astrologers used the system of twelves. They divided the day into twelve hours and the year into twelve months and they had a name for everything."

I asked, "Where did they get so many names?"

*See her book, *Genius in Residence, op. cit.,* Chapters X-XIV, for an account of these discussions and developments.

"Oh," he said, "they named them for the stars."

"But so many."

"They just took the seven planets and kept repeating them," Mike replied.

"But isn't that awfully confusing?"

"Well, you see, if you're an astrologer you get paid more if you're confusing."

At this point class resumed.

Although some teachers resent children who know more than they do, many do not. There are teachers who reach out to, and welcome, the young artists and philosophers, as well as the children who are slow to learn. Surprisingly I found that it was often the teacher who had feeling for one group who also had empathy for the other. As I mentioned earlier the finest of teachers were those who could empathize with all kinds of children. Good teachers, I discovered in some of my early research, automatically adapted their language to the pattern of those they taught whether these were intellectually gifted or slow to learn. For example from the discussion transcripts of slow learners we determined how many difficult words were used and what the average sentence length was; we tried to understand something about the complexities of thought and the amount and degree of abstract thinking. But none of this is necessary for a sensitive teacher. Without any of this technical analysis we found teachers using a simpler language with the slow. Not all teachers, but the good ones do. Possibly there are some teachers who never turn on their hearing aids for two-way communication.

The more gifted and creative teachers, the Creative Intellectuals, tended to like all children and young people. They were able to see the particular genius that certain children had and to recognize talent where no one had seen it before. These teachers were not apt to be jealous or incensed when the young saw things in ways that they had not. Nor were they thrown off balance when it became clear that some youngster had read books and thought through issues that the teacher had not explored. In fact many teachers not only recognize these gifted children but try to find ways to get special help for them.

It is obvious that the teacher who makes the greatest difference is the one who is on the side of the students. I think this is why physical education teachers are sometimes so effective. I've asked coaches about this and they will say, "Of course we want the students to win." Sadly this is not always true in the regular classroom. Students try to play the game but teachers make the rules and call the shots. All too often no one wins—almost never the slow learners. At least this was the way that it was in the 60's. But certainly not with the good teachers. "The best of them," as Lawrence Frank once said, "act as attorneys for youth."

With the needs of the students in mind I worked together with a group of teachers over a period of years—their names and faces changed from time to time—to develop experimental programs in the public schools. For those children who found school difficult and were often called reading problems or slow learners as a result of their inadequate skills, we tried particularly to establish self-confidence. In the research vernacular of the late 50's and early 60's we sought to "improve the self-concept." There was little doubt in my mind that a child who felt himself to be a social failure, a cipher—partly because he was an educational failure—must have his personal needs met. He must be successful and be recognized. Someone has to know his name.

In developing programs for children who had difficulty in school I found that when there were warm and pleasant environments and the "therapy of overwhelming kindness" of which Sorokin speaks, the slow emerged as more confident. They felt that they had a place in the world and that they had friends. Teachers could and did extend themselves for these young people who were so often isolates in groups of their age mates. There was no demand that students read when they could not, no forcing them to stumble on and then suffer the repeated humiliations of corrections. Knowing, instead, that reading makes sense only when young people have something they want to find out about, students were given many opportunities to talk about things in which they were interested. Talking helped them, as it does all people, discover what they thought. They began to acquire ideas that stayed with them—since all of us remember best what we ourselves say, what we put into dialogue. Of course the most skillful of teachers use Socratic questioning and help students discover what they already know, but in working with those who have learning problems one must be very careful about the style of questioning. There must not be a trace of scorn, sarcasm, or belittling. Instead, to help meet their basic needs, a community of affection must be established.

The provision of special programs for adolescents with learning problems made a great deal of difference in how they felt about themselves. But so far the programs we had designed for the gifted seemed to offer little beyond the ordinary. Although they enjoyed the free seminars we could get no "hard" evidence that the program was effective. We had used the American Council on Education *Critical Thinking Test* developed by Paul Dressel and his co-workers at Michigan State University as a pre- and post-test measure but over the years had not been able to show that our experimental groups did better critical thinking (the test asked for evaluative and scientific kinds of thought) than control groups. This surprised us because we felt we knew what we wanted and in our initial efforts we had been helped by Dr. Dressel.

Our problem lay in discovering how to teach in a way that would change the students' thinking processes. Of course there appeared to be tangential benefits from the seminars. Certainly the students were being themselves and were reveling in it. But were we doing our part? Were we supplying the kinds of encounters with people and books needed if young people were to envision what they might become? Or to recognize, as Wordsworth did in his "recollections of early childhood," what they had once been but no longer were? As far as school learning and critical thinking were concerned, they would apparently have been as well off if they had stayed home.

Accordingly we set out to devise a program that would make a difference. We had little disagreement about the higher values and topics—excitement about learning, a willingness to be creative, an ability to think critically, an openness and flexibility of mind, and a concern for others. It was later, when we were choosing issues and articles to illustrate them, that our preferences came through in their full range of diversity. But first we had to lay our general plans.

It seemed to me that we needed to move forward on all fronts at once: to provide work that was diverse enough to appeal to everyone, and to have the messages restated so frequently that they might become as much second nature to the students as they were to their teachers and to me. This might be called teaching by inundation, much as Gardner Murphy once said that creative people needed to "soak themselves" in their subjects. The once-over-lightly approaches, as well as many which require memorizing facts ("sausage stuffing"), tend to have little hold on the mind.

With gifted students self-confidence was well enough developed so that they could be challenged to grow in more independent ways—through intellectual, aesthetic, and moral channels. These students were ready for the higher reaches of being and becoming, for thinking and reading critically and creatively, and for discussions of ethical principles. Some might, if invited, join a "Community of Scholars." Perhaps all could move along the route to self-actualization and start doing things that were socially useful and significant.

Both in our surveys and when we talked with the students, over half of those usually described as academically talented said they wanted to discuss philosophy, to search for new dimensions of experience, to discover more about the world, and to find better ways to live. They particularly enjoyed creative experiences, projects, and opportunities to make of life a work of art. Bored by memorizing, they were stimulated by discussion. They liked to bring things together instead of separating them in what they felt were false dichotomies. They refused to set reason against fantasy and imagination, the subjective against the objective, the inner against the outer, feeling against thought, mind against body. Rather, they preferred synthesis and unity. Lecturing by a teacher who would merely tell them what he already knew repelled them, for their delight was in suggestions about what was not known. Like Thoreau, they reveled in mystery: "How sweet is the perception of a new natural fact! suggesting what worlds remained to be unveiled."

Could we unveil these worlds? With funds from a Federal research grant we started making new materials—an open-ended anthology and a series of films. The idea of both was to encourage free and student-centered discussions on important issues. We found space for this in the curriculum by replacing a ninth-grade course on careers—whose conventional content interested neither the students nor those who were conscripted to teach it. There were few objections to the new plans. In fact the teacher-counselors who had previously taught the careers course helped to develop the new program. As is always true with good teachers—and these were good ones—their contribution was crucial. Along with several others they gave dozens of hours of their time to developing and testing materials. Students also helped with advice at every point.

Work on the anthology began in the first year of the project. At this time we had students make scrapbooks of the things they were interested in, their own views of the world. But these were not too satisfactory. Some of the boys made books of a world on the brink of collision—all jets and missiles. Girls more often retreated to a simpler world, a peaceable kingdom of gentle animals, particularly of horses and dogs. Neither approach was what we had in mind. The boys had shut out almost everything but technology and the girls showed a great lack of interest, perhaps understandably, in "Modern Times." We wanted students to develop their own worlds, it is true, but not without riffling through a cosmological index to get at least a glimpse of the possibilities. We hoped their worlds, and their lives as well, could have that quality which Thoreau prized so much, "a wide margin." Now I don't know how most people feel about the world. The optimist is said to think that this is the best of all possible worlds, while the pessimist is afraid the optimist is right. But no matter which view is right it would seem necessary for young people to be aware of both problems and prospects, threats and promises. Before they choose their life focus, they must have some idea of what may be possible.

With this in mind a group of us spent two years reading current magazines, many of which were not familiar to the students—*Harper's* and *The Atlantic, Saturday Review, Scientific American,* the *American Scientist,* the newsmagazines, and at least twenty more. We all selected the articles that we liked best and felt should go into the book. In preparing these materials we hoped to escape the tunnel-vision of textbooks, of the single point of view and the bland outlook. For each of the broad topics we searched for and usually found many shades of opinion. With a number of minds screening each entry only the most attractive and compelling, the universal in appeal, survived.

Of course we did not agree. Each of us defended our own choices and all involved, articles and people, had to stand up under a bombardment. After a while we narrowed down the choices to one huge boxful. But even this was too much and too complex. So we made further selections from these small digests or excerpts. Then in order to make the contents more manageable and intelligible, we subdivided the whole into four worlds that would relate to the areas of knowledge with which students would be most familiar—the natural, technological, aesthetic, and human.

In the natural world—to use this as an example—we included reviews of Rachel Carson's *Silent Spring,* and the rebuttal by the insecticide companies; Stewart Udall's ideas on "conservation"; and flashbacks to Gifford Pinchot, Theodore Roosevelt, and finally, Thoreau. This world was introduced with Francis Thompson's lovely lines from "The Mistress of Vision":

> *Thou canst not stir a flower*
> *Without troubling of a star.*

This was an introduction to ecology. The purpose was to help young people understand what happens when there is taking and exploiting without giving and understanding. The place of the human species in the universe, as well as our supreme obligations for conserving, maintaining, and improving, were considered. Students discussed the judgment of Aldous Huxley: "We shall be permitted to live on this planet only for as long as we treat all nature with compassion and intelligence." They became familiar with the names, ideas, and often the faces of such naturalists, scientists, and nature-lovers as Joseph Wood Krutch, Edna St. Vincent Millay, John Muir, Wordsworth, Thoreau, Rachel Carson, and William O. Douglas.

Many of the boys rejected the ideas in the natural and the aesthetic worlds. They found the technological world which was presented next most to their liking. However the young Creative Intellectuals, boys and girls alike, were already far along in their ecological thinking.

The materials on each world were held together loosely in ring binders, subject to change at any time. This was a flexible textbook in which students could do their own censoring and deletions, make their own additions and revision. To help them we brought in piles of magazines. We had called a local news agency and asked, "What do you do with the old magazines you don't sell?" They told us they gave them to Jackson Prison. So we said, "Could we have those that Jackson Prison doesn't want?" As a result there was always a supply of very good quality magazines available in the classroom. The students could easily clip or simply browse. They could write critical commentaries, which many did. Some wrote their own poetry and their own articles; others made cartoons or drew pictures.

Not every student, however, was enthusiastic at the outset. Saying that this course was made by "arty" people, some boys put all the aesthetic material in their brown envelopes which we had provided for discards. For a time they referred to it as the "anaesthetic world" or the "pathetic world." But gradually most of them were converted and came to enjoy the program in at least some of its aspects.

In trying to provide for a wide range of interests, back-grounds, and learning styles, the book had something of the flavor of the *Saturday Review*. Its contents included, besides the short articles and reviews, illustrations, cartoons, and poetry. Here again, as the students looked at the format, the stereotyped thinking and prejudgment of many was apparent. They were apt to say: "This isn't the way a textbook should look. Poetry and pictures don't belong." But after a while most of them realized they could make it as exciting and interesting as they wanted to, that the book could become truly their own. After two months of making their changes and additions, they too faced the battle of the bulge. Some books became enormous. At this point their teachers would say: "Now you will need to make some kind of sense out of it; it will have to be edited."

It was important to our purpose that the collection of materials which served to illustrate each of the four worlds should not be confined to events and happenings. The focus was also placed on outstanding persons who had made a significant contribution through action, the arts, or scholar-ship. Consequently in treating the Natural World, as was mentioned earlier, we emphasized along with others the work of Rachel Carson; in the Human World, Eleanor Roosevelt; in the Aesthetic, Carl Sandburg; in the Technological, Vannevar Bush.

But this was not enough. Short biographical sketches could not provide the kind of identification models that were needed if young people were going to develop a philosophy to live by. If they were going to be helped to find their identity, to discover ways to enlarge themselves and their worlds, they should be introduced to real people who had given these questions serious thought. We wanted students to see that a person could live by what she or he believed, that a philosophy of life was necessary for everyone and should be taken seriously—not reserved for occasional reference. It should be used daily in all decisions, even that most important decision of how to spend one's time and live one's life.

To supply models for emulation and to stimulate thinking about values, goals, and purposes, I proceeded (with funds from a Federal research grant) to make a series of ten films planned in conjunction with the Four Worlds anthology and entitled *Being and Becoming.* Their aim was to set before the students some living examples of outstanding persons who were not only creative and scholarly but showed a deep social concern. For this purpose we produced thirty-minute style-of-life films of four women and four men,* shown in the course of their daily activities, as well as an introductory and a final film.

Douglas Knowlton, who was both cameraman and film editor, decided what was notable—and filmable—in the lives they led, how the camera could give a warm and personal view. He followed the models into their working habitat or as they explored the natural world—wherever the individual personality could best be crystallized. The margin for error was precarious with the budget (films were made for $3,000 dollars each) allowing for re-takes only on the first few films. Finally the subject viewed the film, adding a free-flowing commentary based on preselected themes. What the viewer saw and heard was a mature, many-sided man or woman whose life was meaningful because of a sense of direction, an

*Eugene Petersen, historian and museum director; Mary Coleman, probate and juvenile judge; Robert von Neumann, artist and university professor; Barbara Radmore, physician and radiologist; Kay Britten, singer and active in politics; Loren Eiseley, poet and paleontologist; Harold Taylor, philosopher and educator; Anne Roe, psychologist and university professor.

awareness of higher values, a social concern, and a joy in creating.

For example, Loren Eiseley, whom the students had already met in the Natural World, brought them into his mind so that they saw the horizons, both near and far, through his eyes—tree branches forming dark patterns against light, dew suspended on moist leaves, a white caterpillar in its halting progress up a twisted wire "like confused man, moving toward an unknown future." Each student had a mimeographed copy of the film voice track and used it as a basis for reflection and discussion. With Eiseley they experienced the conflict between man and his machines. "Where," he asked, "is all of this taking us? Are we masters here? Or have these, our creations, escaped us and taken on life of their own?" And the students began to see more clearly how man's potential for growth—even for transcendence—was always present although there is much that seems to deny this. Eiseley, poet and paleontologist, reflected on man's evolution:

> Out of those worlds, along with all the brutality which existed then and still exists today, there was still that strange sensitivity, that tenderness, that direction toward the future which so characterizes man at his highest moments.

These films were deliberately different in tone and message from the typical career documentaries. Occupational brochures and films at that time were generally written in what was called an objective and value-free style. They gave the working conditions, the educational requirements, the probable salary, and/or the suggested lifetime earning; but they did not inquire "Achievement for What?" The truth was, though, that while pretending to be noncommittal these scripts, in fact, were deeply committed to materialistic values. They did not raise the question of whether an individual should do work that supported the destruction of other human beings or of the environment or the maldistribution of the national wealth. Thus there was tacit agreement that what existed was good enough and even exemplary. Getting a job and being a success were more important considerations than the route one took or even one's destination. In other words in the career training which America provided after World War II the aim was to help Dick and Jane (or more particularly, Dick) master the rudiments of literacy and "make good"—a synonym for "making money." Was there not more to education and much more to life, than this?

The films, then, were based upon an explicit assumption. When young people are just at the point of discovering themselves and beginning to think about what they might do in the world, they will find that reading philosophy and discussing their values and beliefs are more central to their lives than the economics and practical aspects of career choice. They will be more inspired by Maslow's message that a new vision of the possibilities of man and his destiny is emerging than by the common view that "people are no damn good." If more of us saw humanity as naturally good and perhaps transcendent, might not the world take a turn for the better? Perhaps it is our institutions which corrupt us, as Rousseau suggested. And if social conditions are the result of the way we think, of human attitudes, of what we value and spend our time doing, can we somehow change the world within our heads? Can young people acquire new attitudes and values, spend their time in different ways?

The results of this program suggest an affirmative answer to these questions. There was a definite and measurable change of attitudes. Not only did we keep a record of student reactions to the program throughout the semester, but we tested them at the end of the program on the same measures of attitudes, interests, and values as they had taken at the beginning. For purposes of comparison we conducted identical tests with a control group of ninth graders with similar abilities who had not been in the experimental program. After the completion of the program those who had taken part tested at a level equivalent to that of college sophomores on scales which were designed to measure theoretical and philosophical attitudes, originality, interest in creative life styles, and critical thinking. In addition the girls in the study showed a marked increase in aesthetic awareness and social concern, as well as an acceptance of themselves as women and of their self-actualizing capacities. None of these changes was registered in the control group.

The students told us repeatedly that they were glad grownups had at last decided "teenagers were worth wasting important ideas on." They were impressed (but certainly not always immediately convinced) with the existentialist view that human beings must be responsible for their actions. This last point was indeed the nub of the program. It awoke those who had been unaware of it to the realization that whatever happens is the result of deliberate human action or inaction and that personal responsibility cannot be evaded.

Whether the world is miserable, unjust, and inhumane or whether it becomes serene, peaceful, and just, is up to us. Everything rests upon how we think and feel, and how we treat the land, the plants, the animals, and our fellow humans.

Practically no one will hold that it's better to destroy than to nurture, to hate than to love. The higher values are transparently clear if we stop to think about them. But applying them to our lives is quite another matter. So very few have been willing, like Thoreau, to save at the low levels and live at the high; to pay a minimum of attention to getting and spending and a maximum to being and becoming. In fact our society has become dominated by getting (production) and spending (consumption). For most the careers into which they are funneled or climb of their own volition involve meaningless routines and slavery to the time clock and the wage scale. For a few the vicious circle becomes an equally— or even more—vicious spiral, the never-ending round of a gradient, competitive climbing into the higher circles—up the status ladders to the room at the top with its uninterrupted view of the smog.

"Getting rich" is the one definition of success. Of course we have made some progress. We have moved from the chicken every Sunday to filet mignon, and from the Model T to the "his" and "hers" Cadillacs. But little that the young see or hear, certainly not the career pamphlets, suggests that there is another way to grow. We have antiheroes in abundance. Moral turpitude is headlined daily; moral rectitude, rarely. By contrast there are all too few people, heroes, or ideals with which to identify. Even the artists concentrate on telling us that something is wrong but not how to set it right. Thus artistic creation is, all too often, as Joseph Wood Krutch has said,

> bitter, despairing, contemptuous, and destructive. With rare
> exceptions, the works most, and most justly, admired by
> intellectuals are counsels of despair. We produce parodies,
> denunciations, and nightmares . . . our best artists are engaged in
> disrupting patterns, smashing forms, and deliberately cultivating
> dissonances in painting and music, as well as in poetry, fiction,
> and drama.*

In short we have two dominant patterns: man as "success" or money-grabber, and man as a moral derelict—and the two images seem to converge. Television and the newspapers offer endless pictures of the corruption of big business and its leaders, of government and its officials, of the military and its generals. Not to mention the evil that is perpetrated in dramas of a smaller scale by the petty shysters in business and the Crums and Calleys in the military. *La dolce vita* proclaiming that "goods are good" goes hand in hand with the intonation that "might is right."

Can we expect any change if we continue to train for careers that are usurped by such a system? The militants in the New Left say we must destroy the system. History shows

---

*Joseph Wood Krutch, "The Creative Dilemma: It Is from the Artist That Society Gains Its Loftier Images of Itself," *Saturday Review* (February 8, 1964), pp. 14-17, 58.

all too clearly, however, that evil means invariably lead to evil ends. Those who destroy are themselves destroyed.

Better than to destroy is to change our attitudes and move to the next level. If we want to, we can take another turn up the spiral into the New Age. We have more power to choose and to act, as well as more knowledge of what the consequences of wise or stupid action can be, than ever before in human history. Moreover, we know, better than we ever did, that we are responsible for what we do. We influence everything we touch and are affected by everything that touches us. We can let ourselves be conditioned into condoning violence and cruelty, squalor and inequity. We can learn to be exploiters and squanderers and killers. But we can also refuse to be controlled. We can become self-aware, raise our consciousness, and know what we are about. We can stop sleepwalking, wake up, and take command. The Inner Light may help us find our way. Perhaps we will converge with others on The Way and transform ourselves and the world about us. The New Age will not come to us by itself; we must move toward it.

The most lasting changes are those that occur by ethical conversion. Buddha and Jesus have had greater effect toward far more desirable ends than Caesar and Napoleon. The theorists of communism, Marx and Lenin, supplied reasons and plans for bringing down the system. It was, however, the utopian anarchists, the Christian communitarians, who had ideas for building a new society and a better life. Perhaps the Quakers have seen most clearly and most consistently how this could be done—through the Inner Light and the doctrine of Right Livelihood.

XXII • Fernwood, a Free School

Fernwood was a free school differing fundamentally from other schools.* There was no schedule for the twenty-four adolescent boys and girls who were randomly selected for the experiment from grades 7, 8, and 9 at the Colton Consolidated School (Colton, Oregon). All but four of those selected chose to participate throughout, *i.e.*, September through December, 1966.

At the beginning of the school year the large room was almost empty—just chairs and tables and these in no set order. The two young men, Roger Bishop and Bill Monroe, who were to be the teacher-counselors set the stage very simply the first day of school. They announced to the young people as they sat in the bare classroom that the students could make this the kind of school they wanted. They could find out what was important to them and then work on what was important. Both teachers and students would learn together.

*This chapter was published earlier as an article in the *Journal of Humanistic Psychology* (Fall, 1968), pp. 113-123.

The way the room was to be organized, what the room was to contain, and how the furniture would be used and added to was up to the youngsters. Since it was early fall the out-of-school environment—including the extensive school grounds, the wooded areas and a large pond twenty minutes away—proved irresistible. When it at last became clear to the students that they were free to choose, they reveled in their liberty. At these early stages the teachers prepared what they felt to be, as they put it, "their usual dynamic presentations," only to find that, after teacher talk was underway, the students would begin to disappear. Realizing that they could, in truth, come and go as they pleased, only one or two students would ever sit through even a better-than-ordinary lesson or lecture.

The Colton area where the children lived is one of great natural beauty, although the houses are often shabby and many of the residents somewhat impoverished. Wild flowers, ferns and shrubs, dozens of bird species, wild animals, and towering Douglas firs invite budding botanists and biologists, naturalists, and ecologists to look and listen carefully and sometimes study in depth. (In the run-of-the-week activities most Colton young people did none of this. They knew little or nothing of nature, watched TV instead of birds, and seemed generally unaware of the intellectual and aesthetic possibilities in the natural world around them.) Houses are generally set apart from one another, often small, and privacy is at a premium or nonexistent. Many of the young people have little space to claim as their own beyond a spot in bed. Thus it seemed only natural in the free environment of Fernwood that as days passed they sought out personal refuges, sometimes in groups, but often singly. A boy or girl would lay claim to a corner or a nook and "nest" there.

These claims to space and privacy—inside and out-of-doors—seemed to give security and peace of mind just as did the long, deep, personal conversations. One boy made daily trips to the pond where he stretched out on a raft he had put together. Another who sought solitude, one of the most confirmed low achievers and general misfits, was a boy of sixteen—a nonreader with a tested IQ that placed him in the moron category. Generally belligerent, he was mean to younger students and had been thrown out of school repeatedly and bounced back, always—more inured each time against learning. In the course of these abrasive confrontations he had become a habitual truant, but at Fernwood his attendance record became perfect. At first he laid claim to the merry-go-round where he would lie for hours watching the clouds or waving at the occasional confused taxpayer who drove by. Gradually he gained peace of mind and overcame his aversion to school to the extent that he could cross the threshold and enter the classroom. By dint of alchemy or miracle (and perhaps with the aid of a stack of 200± comic books) he learned to read. His next venture was to become social. As a beginning he learned to play chess, occasionally beat his teachers at the game they taught him, and finally became an excellent conversationalist who could speak on war and peace as well as on the vagaries of the weather. A year after the program ended, he spent half of each day helping mentally retarded children in a special room. He was known for his gentleness and loving ways.

From early September until the Christmas recess the young inhabitants of Fernwood and the often bewildered teacher-counselors lived together from 8:00 A.M. when the school bus arrived until 3:00 P.M. when the bus came again and redistributed the children throughout the wooded slopes and the meadows where their homes were. The foundation of the program was love—love which came to mean a delight in mutual discovery, and a sense of well-being and pleasure in finding out about themselves. There was time to look for Indian artifacts and to visit the old settler who had been hunting arrowheads since he was a boy and now had them mounted in picture frames and sorted in mason jars. There were hours to listen to music, to build things, to plan trips—and go on them—and to read books. And most importantly there was time to form relationships that were natural and meaningful.

Few of these children had ever found a time or a place to

make friends. They lived miles away from potential friends
and often there was much work—endless chores—to be done.
When in school at Colton there had been the relentless bells
dictating when the mind was to be turned on and off and
what words the eyes were to focus upon. The curriculum in
this consolidated school was text-centered and fact-oriented.
Talk, other than recitation, was generally thought to be idle
chatter—discouraged in the classrooms and forbidden in the
halls. Fernwood freed the students from onerous rules and
arbitrary judgments, allowing them to discover and accept
themselves. There was time for each to dream and envision
what he might be and become. And time, as well, to talk for
the hours on end that made friendships possible.

The teacher-counselors played an important role in this
new relationship which allowed the young to bridge generation gaps. The warmth and trust expressed by the teachers,
and the integrity which they demonstrated by not coercing
the students when they had promised freedom, finally won
over the more reluctant students. The teachers set the stage
and then merged with the setting.

However it gradually became clear that gentle teachers
with unobtrusive ways could become models for many of the
students. Both men were leaders in the community, had
taught in the area for a decade, were well educated and with
rich personal resources. They were hopeful, joyful at times,
and quietly confident—committed to serving youth. How
they served was often improvisational but rarely unrewarding
for either them or their students. Mr. Monroe reports:

> I'd stalk groups of youngsters like I might stalk coveys of quail.
> I'd follow along on the trail as though I was out nature-hunting
> on my own and stay within distance so I could see them out of
> the corner of my eye. After several days I could get close enough
> so I could actually hear them talking. This was very exciting. I
> can imagine that anthropologists who go to some strange culture
> might have the same feeling that I had—perhaps someone
> studying animals. I thought of that girl who studied the
> chimpanzees in Africa.

Gradually I was allowed to come into one of these groups—to walk right along with them and not have them scatter and run or leave me. Later they allowed me to say something—now and then. To say something without their turning and walking away. And one day I was even allowed to change the subject. And they listened—and they asked me questions—and I was part of the group—and I felt exhilarated that finally I had become part of the group.

Other groups were formed the same way and Roger and I became friends of the students. Then the conversation really began to roll. In the classroom on rainy days we'd sit around and talk by the hour—talk about books, war, peace, birth—talk about dying—talk about anything. People listened—people shared and the relationships between individuals grew deeper than any relationships I have ever known.

Equally as important as the attitudes of love and helpfulness was the vision of the future that the teachers expressed. Mr. Bishop read J. R. Platt's article, "Diversity,"* and discussed it with the students and put down his own feelings about the new image of man as follows:

Template for Non-Technological Terrestrians

Third Force psychologists, many theologians and philosophers, some educators, and even Marxist theoreticians are defining a new image of man and saying he can choose, strive for, and achieve this image in an evolutionary step with tools he has in his possession today.

The "new" man will become a transcendent version of himself.

Man, not coping with a future that happened accidentally but consciously creating—planning and achieving—the world in which he wants to live.

Man, not passing hostility and fear from generation to generation but helping satisfy in his children, neighbors, and colleagues the basic needs of love, respect, trust, and safety, filling the physiological needs; and starting a cycle of growth as infinite as the universe. Growth motivated by human capabilities insisting on fulfillment.

Man, not trapped and bound by his culture, but able to examine himself and his society with undistorted perceptions; aware of

*John R. Platt, "Diversity," *Science* (December 2, 1966), pp. 1132-1139.

intercultural Truth; able to respect and value an ecology of the universe.

Man, not afraid to be sensitive to his feelings, but aware; cultivating the awareness of emotions, of Being, of Beauty, of living in the "here and now."

Man, not lost in apathy or living in meditation but functioning in and contributing to his world; knowing his capabilities and committing them to his convictions. An exciting man.

Man, honest with himself and others. A self-directed man satisfying himself and transcending himself—altruistic.

Man, with the courage to venture; the courage to stand, alone if necessary, for a principle he believes to be unalterable.

Man, filled with an understanding—trustful, compassionate, accepting, nonjudging, open. A valuing-loving-spirit that permits the communication of his values and allows him to be the paradox that is self-actualizing man.

Fernwood was an effort by two dedicated teachers to translate concepts that were important to them and to me (and that were basic as well to theories of self-actualization and intrinsic learning) into educational practice. Prior to beginning the venture I talked for many hours with these teachers and then spent several weeks reading Third Force psychological literature to develop a statement of aims entitled "Beyond Curriculum."* The major points in some of the lessons we learned at Fernwood follow:

Each individual is different. The range of these differences extend far beyond the reach of textbook levels and the intelligence derived from testing. Each is unique as to rate, style, tempo, and pattern of learning. Each chooses his own values and interests and develops personal tastes. By honoring these directions of growth and allowing them to flourish naturally, we found that students could master what had been difficult topics and material and do this easily. As we have seen, a nonreader began to read without the pressure of applied methods and scheduled class periods. Students who

*Elizabeth Monroe Drews, "Beyond Curriculum," *Journal of Humanistic Psychology* (Fall, 1968), pp. 97-113.

habitually failed English found they could speak fluently and well when they could talk about something of interest rather than on an assigned topic. Just as the school came to a close a boy who had been an indifferent mathematics student did four months' work in three days and ended up six weeks ahead of his former classmates.

Only a fraction of the potential of each is developed and used. This is true in life at large as well as in the conventional classroom. School learning is narrowly cognitive (usually lower-order, *i.e.,* facts). Socialization processes often force constriction of interests and conformity. However when there is a climate of mutual trust and freedom, democratic processes tend to emerge in natural and effective ways. A group of boys decided they wanted to transform the wood-shed into an industrial art center. They had begun to level the floor for pouring concrete when they became aware of inter-lopers in one end, separated only by a thin partition. These turned out to be a group of four girls who had located a study center in the eight-by-twelve space and equipped it with shelves and books. In the ensuing melee the boys threw dirt and rocks against the wall and did their best to dislodge the girls and their artifacts. Words of color ranging into deep blue were exchanged and the Fernwood version of a town meeting was called by someone who rang the bell. The boys claimed that the decision had been made in an earlier meeting that they were to have the entire woodshed for their indus-trial arts center and the girls claimed that no such decision had been made. The boys called for a reading of prior notes by the secretary only to be informed that the group had neglected to elect a secretary. The denouement was that the meeting was stopped then and there to elect a secretary, one of the most literate among the twenty four. But the boys were not able to effectively oust the girls from their quick claim.

Affective, aesthetic, altruistic, and ethical growth is rarely encouraged or even allowed in our schools. As one boy commented when the first snow fell in December and the students raced outdoors to revel in it, "You know what is so wonderful? There is no teacher to say—now sit down and get to work—you've all seen snow before!" The students came to see changes in themselves and toward the end of the term commented that they had not destroyed property at Fernwood—not even those who had habitually scraped and gouged their ways through the Colton corridors. As one of the most hardened of the former marauders commented, "I was not closed in at Fernwood. I wasn't in a cage or a cell, so I didn't need to destroy." One of the last meetings centered on a book that inadvertently had been dropped in a mud puddle. The consensus was that it was not the fault of the boy who dropped it but that all should share in the cost of the replacement of the book. (When the book finally was returned, no fine was levied.)

Young people want to learn and become competent. Natural directions of growth became apparent when students were encouraged to choose activities that appealed to them and to learn in their own ways. Parents, however, were often quite unsure that their offspring could be learning anything important if allowed to make their own choices. At one parent meeting a father commented, "My son isn't learning anything."

The teachers encouraged him to talk and then asked, "What isn't he learning?"

"For one thing, math."

"Do you think he has a desire to learn this?"

Both father and mother said they were sure he did. The teachers reflected that they were glad this was the case. However the parents' complaints continued.

"Six weeks have gone by and he doesn't have a math book. Why can't he have one if he wants one?"

"We are happy to know that he wants a book," Mr. Monroe replied. "It may be that the one he wants is not on the shelf with the other math books. But if he will tell us what he wants, we will get it for him right away. We drive to the library in Oregon City (twenty miles away) every Friday."

As the dialogue continued it became clear to everyone that only the parents, not the son, were interested in a mathematics book. The teachers gently explained that, as Montaigne made clear centuries ago, learning under compulsion has little hold on the mind. Fortunately this boy did find a need for mathematics soon—as he worked on plans to convert the woodshed into an industrial arts center—and he raced through sections of several books in record time and with high comprehension and recall.

One of the areas where much growth was apparent at Fernwood was in the ability shown by boys and girls to present ideas orally. It became obvious, as days passed, that young people learn to talk by talking and they learn what they read and where they stand by making these thoughts and stances first conscious and then public. A free situation peels away the traditional school culture—leaving no protocol to hide behind, no excuse of "overdue homework" to prevent one from facing oneself or coming to terms with a situation. Reality is no longer disguised by daily routines.

Lacking cloaks and masks the students had no recourse but to examine themselves and think about the basic issues and relationships. Who am I? What is the world all about? How can I live the kind of life I want to live and be the self I want to be in this world? (Some began to talk about the "openness" that places in Alaska still offered and to mourn the loss of the frontier.) Competence, in the most basic sense, is a matter of learning to live one's own life, joyfully and zestfully; and these feelings can only come when there is a prior feeling of independence and autonomy—of being in charge of one's own life.

As the boys and girls came to understand how they felt and thought, acceptance of their physical selves—their teenage, out-of-hand awkwardness—grew. And gradually the young people began to accept each other, including even gauche, foot-in-mouth clumsiness, and to accept adults. Their verbal talents and poise advanced to such a level that by spring when this experimental group was asked to speak to a graduate seminar at Portland State University, almost all came eagerly, although this meant giving up free time after school. The level of self-confidence and the sure-footedness of these adolescents in talking to the university students was such that the professor spontaneously remarked that he wished his graduate students could do so well.

An area of competence important to school authorities was the fact that these students did not "lose ground" by being out of the regular school program for almost four months. All but two did better work and received higher grades upon return to school than they had done prior to the free experience.

Young people want to help one another and to share. They easily invent and readily engage in altruistic and empathic projects where there is freedom and time to get to know each other and to discover what needs to be done. Not only did we observe many examples of helpful and responsible behavior at Fernwood, but parents also reported changes.

Parent meetings were a part of Fernwood from the beginning. A father or a mother (or both) of almost every family participated on a weekly or biweekly basis. Many of the adults felt they gained much in a personal sense from the group sharing. However there were apprehensions about the program. Surely a program so much enjoyed by children could not involve real learning. At first some felt that if students chose what to learn they would only select the trivial and unimportant and there was a feeling among parents that discovering friends was not a "matter of consequence." Gradually new perceptions emerged.

At one such meeting an arthritic father whose misanthropy had set him apart from his neighbors for years rose to confess, "I've told my children when to learn, when to work, and what to do all their lives. When they didn't jump, I used a belt. And now I realize that I've been wrong. If they have freedom and love, they choose what to do better than I can tell them."

Other parents attested to newly expressed helpfulness on the part of their children. Front yards lost their litter and rooms became neat. Squabbles with siblings diminished. Parents, some of whom had been school dropouts, began to see the point. At first the statements came in the guise of faint praise and were personal in nature. "Anything you'd do is bound to be better than what they did to us in school." Later applications were more universal. "The world is in such a mess that anything you can do to teach love is for the good."

Students learned to live together in such ways that hostilities and hurt feelings diminished, sharp elbows became round and smooth and proverbial long toes (the *sine qua non* of hurt feelings) were shortened. And upon return to the regular school Fernwood youngsters often explained the inconsistencies of teacher behavior and the need for the young to be tolerant of their elders to students who had not experienced Fernwood.

Young people have an intrinsic sense of beauty and appropriateness. This will emerge as aesthetic judgment and taste if they are at liberty to make things and to express themselves. By such participation they come to appreciate not only the products but also the efforts of others. And if given encouragement to express themselves they find a gift of language.

One boy reflected on the beauty he had experienced the week before:

> I particularly enjoyed the feel of things, kicking the sand and letting it fan out and slide down, feeling the grass crinkle under my feet. And that day we were on the trip I looked at the river slowly going on its way, then rushing over the rocks, and smoothing off again into a pool. At night I watched the stars fall, burning up before they hit earth. And I listened as the trees whispered words into my ear.

Young people are eager to become more aware of themselves and to find a philosophy to live by. This striving gradually merged into efforts by the Fernwood students to become their best possible selves, to find something important to live by and for, and to commit themselves to. As Louis Raths comments "When a self is recognized values can develop."* This happened in the free program. As we have seen the young people found words to express themselves and found they had thoughts worth expressing. Gradually they became free to wonder about the mystery that surrounded them—the secret of life itself. And they began to talk about this and many other things that were important to them. No one laughed at these concerns. Awe became natural and human nature could reveal itself.

Self-discovery and philosophical conjecturing were never forced, but the young people generally chose talking at length with each other and their teachers over more obvious delights such as taking trips. (Two Volkswagen buses and a school bus were available for this aspect of the program.) These choices might have been quite different if the teachers had been different people. Some teachers do not, by their very outlook on life, invite philosophical discussions. Some do not inspire. And some are so lacking in self-confidence and self-control that when they allow their students freedom, bedlam results. Nor can all teachers be effective as counselors. Here the personal equation is all important. The counselor must enjoy being with people, be interested in them for their own sakes, and he must wish them well. Beyond this he should know what he values and what he is willing to dedicate himself to.

The Fernwood teachers were mature in these ways and thus able to help the boys and girls make some order out of this confused and confusing world. As for the young people, they had all the time they needed—hours, days, or weeks—to consider various alternatives, to speculate about the ethics of each situation, and to weigh the immediate and long-term consequences of choices. Most importantly they were free to select the alternatives that truly appealed. (It is obvious that

*Raths, Louis, *et al.*, *Values and Teaching* (Columbus, Ohio: Chas. E. Merrill, 1966).

children who are punished or coerced by grades or group opinion are not free to choose.) Thus interests and feelings were tried out and acted upon and those that remained cherished after close examination came to take on the stature of values.

Individual differences and unrealized potential dictated self-selection and individualized learning. The freedom in Fernwood was such that students could learn in their own ways about things they wanted to know. Most of the suggestions about things to do came from the children, although the teachers did encourage them to visit the Portland Art Museum, the airport, and the zoo. Books were always available and new ones could be obtained on the weekly trips to the library. Some became so addicted to reading that parents complained. The mother of one of the girls was a chronic complainer: a woman of easy virtue who welcomed a variety of men into her home, but felt her daughter's love of books showed an inability to focus on important matters.

As the young people became practised in decision making they learned to center their interests: A boy learned much about history by studying the strategies of Napoleon and Caesar and reenacting battles in a sand pile at home; and to widen their horizons: Four girls decided to go to England and read the daily papers diligently searching for jobs for fourteen-year-olds. When they could not find work, they decided to become columnists and began writing a teenage column which they sold to the local paper. Later a publisher of a Northwest teenage paper "discovered" their talent and one was asked to become his editor.

Individual differences and unrealized potential dictated that we expand the learning environment. This new educational setting incorporated a larger environment—reached out to home and community and beyond to the state and to the world. More of knowledge and more of life were admissible as curriculum. Since we held that students could learn from anything and from any of the worlds—natural, aesthetic, technological, and human—they must be freed to do so. They could learn what they needed and when they needed to without waiting for a unit in curriculum or "to be taught."

The learning environment—what it was permissible to learn from and about—was virtually unlimited. Students learned to shingle roofs by assisting their fathers and neighbors; they learned about southern Oregon by planning and taking a five-day trip to historic Jacksonville and Crater Lake National Park; they learned about animals by assisting the Portland Zoo veterinarian as he went about his daily tasks; and about flying and planes by spending whole days (not taking an hour's tour) at the airport. Thus they came to experience themselves and the world. The end came suddenly and unexpectedly (we had planned originally for a year's program) when we received word the first week in December that the grant was canceled and our infant program was not to survive. At this time, ever more funds were being appropriated for the Vietnam War. The children were disconsolate and one of them wrote a letter which reflected how we all felt.

> Dear Mr. President Johnson,
>
> I am in a school class for 7th, 8th, and 9th graders. It is an experimental class where we have full freedom. We have our own government consisting of one chairman, one assistant chairman, one secretary, and one treasurer. This class works on the idea that students will want to learn. We are very concerned about our next funding period. It may be cut off by the Northwest Regional Educational Research Laboratory. This may happen because their funds were cut in two. Dr. Elizabeth Drews who is responsible for our project is in Washington, D.C., looking for other sources of money and talking to her friends about our class, hoping to influence them. Would you please talk to someone too?
>
> Sincerely,
>
> A Fernwood Student

XXIII • The New Community

There is no longer any doubt that we are living in a time of dramatic change—perhaps cataclysmic, perhaps transcendental. The schools, as we know them, do not educate the whole child nor do their programs foster self-actualization. The home seldom offers inspiration or succor. Too often the family warps, while the society—sick unto death—alienates. What we inhabit are merely local jurisdictions, not genuine communities. Today, particularly in the modern city, it is difficult to find one's self or one's place in the family of mankind. The "ship of fools" drifts without helm or rudder.

But there is a way out of this spiritual malaise. Reforms are being attempted on all fronts. Not all the voices which come to us are destructive or negative. We hear—and who would disagree?—that we should humanize and individualize, that we should transform and transcend ourselves. Into living and learning alike, we should bring joy. We know that we must engage again in the human dialogue. Irrespective of age, social class, professional status, or occupational skill, all of us must learn how to live and work as inhabitants of the world, in community and communion.

We can supply the models and visions of something better—perhaps the "significant other" of sociologists, but certainly not the "Wholly Other" of the old religions. The revolution that surrounds and at times engulfs us is religious as well as political. But it is not being conducted by the old church, the traditional God, and clerical hierarchy which control from above. Instead the new spirit is both immanent and all-pervasive. It is within us and without. Heaven is no longer a lifetime away and "up there," but rather, if we will it, here and now.

What I have in mind is to create a New Community planned with a definite purpose in view. Its aim is to encourage the growth of the whole individual and of the whole society in a synergic relation to one another. The core of this New Community is a Learning Mall. From this node facilities and activities will be provided for every interest and for all age groups. To staff the Learning Mall a Learning Center has been organized so as to educate a small nucleus of persons animated by the spirit of humanitarian altruism.

Underlying these suggestions are the concepts of humanistic psychology and education whose various threads have run through this book. Potential is not lost in childhood, like some odd bit of clothing, nor is it divested when we leave youth behind. People of all ages retain great and undiscovered talents. It is their human heritage. This potential of each will be most apt to awaken and flower if the conditions are right for growth. Before we are born our genetic templates are already laid out, and for each of us the roulette wheel of heredity stops at a different number. Beyond these (that is, among the broad assortment of potentialities with which nature endows each person) endlessly different environments trigger the growth of these varying capacities in unique and unknown ways. Most of the talents in most people lie dormant, and none are fully awakened. Hence it is very important to plan an environment which is more likely to nourish growth of many kinds. Particularly needed for an

age that is undergoing a social and spiritual crisis is the calling
forth and cultivation of the higher values.

Every individual is clearly unique. Nobody now living ever
had an exact counterpart in any previous age, nor will one
appear in the future. Even identical twins are markedly
different. If people are to become what they might be,
instead of pale shadows, all must be encouraged to grow in
their own idiosyncratic and extraordinary ways.

But paradoxical though this may sound, the individuality
of each cannot develop to maturity except in community
with others. Each person is in constant need of others, not as
trainers and certainly not as coercers, but as friends and
counselors, as recognizers and encouragers.

Nothing short of rediscovering community and bringing all
together as fellow learners will answer this great need. Only
such an innovation can breathe life into the constrictive,
automaton-like schools or the even harder commercialism of
the city centers. The walls must become permeable, the
machine must be transformed into an organism. A life force
must find its way into the formal shells of what are now
concrete blocks and faceless dwellings.

The New Community will not be merely a new system. It
will have a quality of organic growth. There will be significant change in both the individual details and the overall
design of the lives of those who enter it. Barriers, once
labeled "inside" and "outside," will be removed. There will
be fusion and mutual enhancement rather than friction and
hostility; reciprocity rather than "oppositeness." And since
the ultimate goals are wisdom and compassion, reason and
love, each individual's growth will reinforce that of all others.
Each will find a part of the self in the common humanity of
all, in what anthropologists have called the psychic unity of
mankind and what Emerson spoke of as Universal Mind. And
each will become progressively self-actualizing by having
gained insight into his own style.

The Learning Mall will be grounded on the proposition

that all learning is a process of sharing. What any single person discovers and experiences (of wisdom or goodness or beauty) increases the common stock. It adds to rather than detracts. Learning, as it is understood in the New Community, is integral and continuous with life. When we stop learning, we stop growing; when we stop growing, we begin dying. The Learning Mall is intended, therefore, to help people grow for as long as is humanly possible. Everybody has something to teach; and everybody has an infinite amount to learn.

The New Community will become a reality when larger numbers of people feel a growing sense of oneness and seek each other's company for shared activities. It is human to want to be wanted, to yearn to be liked. Love, as Maslow has said, actualizes potentialities. When empathy, concern, and caring are extended and received, the bonds of community are formed, and within such a context it is possible to practise a truly democratic system of participation and self-government. This will contrast with the democracies which have existed hitherto, since their achievement, even at their best, has been devoted to liberty and equality, but has neglected fraternity.

The New Community will be founded on Rousseau's faith that men are basically good, but that many of us become corrupted and grow up warped because of bad institutions: the unhappy family, the poor school, the Corporate State. To live a better and more human life, everyone must find a community, make friends, and have a sense of belonging. All must have workfellows and playfellows. And as both work and play become more truly rewarding, as each person develops a sense of vocation—that point where working and playing become indistinguishable—life will take on a meaning that it has never had before. Feelings of separateness, loneliness, and alienation will fall away like discarded husks when our daily life is lived among friends and family, and when we also love the work we do. These are truly the essential things in life and involve, as Buber knew so well, what is basic for all—"at one and the same time a giving and a receiving."

What is necessary is not the constraint and the domination nor the heavy hand of authority that is now being tried. This does not and cannot produce better human beings. Neither can the individual who runs free and wild grow properly. Only through experiencing cooperation and reciprocity—the loving family (Fromm), the good agency (Sorokin), the enlightened teacher-counselor—can each begin to find himself, and move toward what the Quakers call the Inner Light. For there is no therapy like that of "overwhelming kindness."

We shall need, then, to devise an environment of another pattern than those around us—one which will invite and welcome, which will be open and free, diverse and flexible, innovative and fluid. Since creativity is soaring flight, the possibilities are indeed infinite. They are as boundless as our powers to imagine and invent.

In all this there is nothing which should be considered impractical, esoteric, or "far-out." Neither the New Community, nor the Learning Mall which will give it form, is a distant dream or remote Utopia. They can be realized very soon, for they lie, in fact, latent within everybody's neighborhood. For purposes of concreteness I shall illustrate this in the following pages from the area which I know best, the neighborhood where I live. All of us can find the seeds of community under our feet, dormant in the very ground where we are standing now.

What I shall sketch out is a composite. Much of this has actually happened, is happening, or could happen. It draws from and incorporates many features of small communities, both past and present, with which history and travel have made us familiar. There are touches here of Thoreau's Walden and a Japanese garden, of the Athenian agora and a medieval piazza, of Grundtvig's Folk High School and Copenhagen's Tivoli, of the workshop and the scholar's study, as well as open classrooms, free schools, adventure playgrounds, and the work of the teachers and philosophers and the architects and landscape gardeners who envision a new society. What is important in the New Community is that it can be a comprehensive whole, and can combine the best of all worlds.

If the various elements I shall describe sound overly optimistic, this is because the experiments of this kind which we know best are those which have succeeded. But the reason for their success is self-evident. It is because they have responded to genuine human needs. That is also why, if we proceed with a New Community in the same spirit, there are valid grounds for hope.

The process of forming the New Community will be a slow one. It will begin at the Learning Center which will allow young people from the community itself, who would like to take an active role in making it a New Community and seem ready for this, to experience a new kind of education—learning to live. This will involve living with others—in cooperation, communion, and communication—as well as discovering oneself and one's own capacities. The community itself becomes the curriculum; instead of textbooks we study the culture that is created as people freely associate in the area where they live. The first steps the students will take lead both inward toward themselves and outward toward their community.

Visions of what might be will be offered in philosophy seminars. These will bring students into contact with many life styles, but particularly those that stress social concern, empathy, kindness, and affection, and will encourage the students to extract meaning from their own experience.

Students from the public schools and the university will work together with a counselor guide, a resource coordinator, and at times philosopher-generalists to initiate community activities that will be mutually enhancing. The members of the Learning Center will be limited to less than fifty, about forty of whom are officially designated as students. Half of these will be from junior and senior high schools in the area and the other half will be undergraduates and graduates. The schools will have agreed, as will the university professors involved in the project, to excuse the students from traditional subjects and required class attendance. They will then be free to do the reading, talking, and thinking necessary for the development of a personal philosophy. Also they will have time for the community projects which they will design and carry through.

The learning experiences which will evolve are primarily of two types: thoughtful, inward studies focusing on self-development and leading almost always to conversations and discussions; and other projects in which they develop their already considerable talents in understanding and helping people. In the Learning Center itself much of the focus will be on each student's subjective growth—the self-actualization process. Students will read Aldous Huxley's *Island*, for example. They will puzzle over his saying that Wisdom has no place for enmity and his belief, with Darwin, "in the possibility of a new kind of Wisdom for everybody . . . prophetically glimpsed in Zen and Taoism and Tantra . . ." They will explore the meaning of Emerson's "We are wiser than we know" and relate this to Michael Polanyi's concept that we know more than we know we know. They will reflect on Laing's statement:

> . . . what we think is less than we know;
> what we know is less than what we love;
> what we love is so much less than what there is.
> And to that precise extent we are so much less than what we are.*

And is it really true, as Thoreau so often contended, that ideas, if you keep them in mind, have a habit of getting realized?

Out of the reading and sharing with one another and the vision presented by the philosophers, poets, and artists who

---

*Ronald D. Laing, *The Politics of Experience and the Bird of Paradise* (Middlesex, England: Penguin, 1967), p. 26.

come to participate in the seminars, students will increase in awareness. They will keep their minds open and growing while their hearts, in Wordsworth's terms, "wait and receive." They will understand that a vital part of self-affirmation comes through helping others. The world does not need to be a desert—bleak and barren and inhospitable; with our own creative power we can change it. If we want a New Community based upon love and trust we can set about immediately to help establish it.

But how do we form a community?

Together the community planners and the members of the Learning Center will begin building the New Community in one section of a large city. Later, other people may be inspired to do the same in other areas. The total environment must be planned with coherence but yet allow for openness at every point. A survey of the area will show which of the existing buildings can be used for new purposes. A record will also be kept of open plots not in use or of space that may become available (when buildings are demolished) for vest-pocket parks, playgrounds, and other special uses.

To plan the land space for human use all kinds of specialists will be consulted: city planners, architects (particularly landscape architects), playground and recreation specialists, teachers and psychologists, park managers, health consultants, social workers. Their mission will be to understand not only the contours and needs of the land (the knowledge that comes from the old style as well as the new sociological geographers) but also the contours and needs of people—the ways of the young and the aged, the values of both unity and diversity. In such a view of learning and living the entire landscape as well as the social matrices become a matter for study and understanding, for invention and construction. Small, tentative steps will be taken to renew old relationships which have been lost and to create unities which had never before existed. Hopefully the people who live in the area which is to become the New Community will not only respond to the suggestions of the planning group and of the students but will begin to take responsibility for their own rebirth. As soon as small clusters start thinking about creative growth and mutual aid, ideas will flow with astonishing rapidity—and some of the students will serve as the catalysts.

Maria, for example, who is a university sophomore, has always delighted in the dance, interpreting it as a language and an art form. Given freedom to choose any part of the community, she unhesitatingly joins a dance group whose studio is near the new Municipal Auditorium and the university. She agrees wholeheartedly with their view that dance, including yoga, should become a more important part of life, that it can lead people to new kinds of awareness, to new parts of themselves, to new kinship with others. Talking with the dancers Maria discovers that they would like to become more integral with the community, which, she reflects, can only enhance everyone involved.

She helps the dancers present small vignettes before various groups. Help also comes from the editor of the New Community newspaper which a fellow student from the Learning Center has chosen as his way of working toward community. He publishes a series of articles on the dance in addition to featuring announcements of performances. The dance group offers to work with a physical therapist to help disabled children and adults, introducing them to new and better ways to move.

Another student, Bob—when asked to choose his own way of helping others—finds that his memories draw him to a group of old people in a retirement home. He sees in his mind, again and again, his once burly grandfather clinging to him wistfully whenever Bob is ready to leave after one of his infrequent visits. It is as if his grandfather were resisting, none too effectively, a great loneliness. A number of visits in the space of a week lead to the development of a studio workroom from what had previously been storage space. All kinds of activities proliferate. Bob enjoys the musical efforts and, he cannot explain how, finds himself as the much-in-demand accompanist for a male quartet which has resuscitated the songs of the 20's. His grandfather, a skilled carpenter, has organized a small group who make playhouses—complete with tables, benches, and doll cradles—for the vest-pocket parks.

Literally these students-at-large in the New Community are living in and acting upon it in a manner which has a special appeal to them. Not only are they being socially creative but their experiences are more intense than before. The thesis underlying this approach to education is that only by such action can one begin serious learning.

What form will the New Community take? What will be its general design and overall pattern?

The concept of a New Community can perhaps best be understood by seeing how a particular section of the city can be transformed. Work and play, leisure and education will all be reconsidered by the planning group and the Learning Center members. Active assistance will come from all the schools in the area, including the community college, the specialized schools, and the university. These will be invited to participate to the extent that students, parents, teachers, and administrators desire. But there will be no exclusiveness. Suggestions and contributions from any institutions, organizations or businesses in the area will be welcomed. Similarly all residents in the section will be offered the use of developing facilities and asked to contribute in ways that they would enjoy. All will be equal as members of a community. Instead of any being the objects of instruction, all will be learners and all will teach themselves and others. By being voluntary members of a cooperating society and being infused with the spirit of mutual aid, all can become the agents of their own growth. The assumption is that everything can educate everyone: nature, the shops, the educational institutions—but, above all, other people. Walking in the springtime might be seen as more educational than reading or telling about it. And, for the efficiency-minded, one can point out what John Ciardi has said: "It takes longer to speak a springtime than to see one."

Within the approximately 200 acres designated as the New Community, certain steps will be taken. Cars will be separated from people. Except where through-traffic arteries are involved, cars, buses, and trucks will be redirected, channeled, and controlled. To make the area better for human beings a series of malls will be established. The young and the old will particularly profit from such an action, but any public-spirited citizen will breathe a sigh of relief—and without inhaling exhaust fumes! Many, perhaps most, of those who make use of the New Community will live within its boundaries.

The area is approximately ten miles long and two miles wide and includes dwellings, (apartments and private residences), shops, schools, parks, and public buildings (museums, libraries, and a state university). Regular and frequent bus transportation will be provided for the ten-mile length from the river greenway to the western hills, (the hills where the nature and wilderness parks and zoo are located), as well as two or three main streets which cross the New Community. Within the malled areas ramps will be constructed. Since the rainy season is a long one, there will be many cloistered walks with frequent benches. The only wheeled vehicles allowed will be slow electric delivery trucks, small electric cars for the handicapped and the elderly, white bicycles for all to use (Amsterdam's Provo-style), as well as baby carriages, strollers, wheelchairs, and shopping carts. These gaily and distinctively decorated shopping carts can be borrowed as needed. The handicapped, the poor, the elderly, and the young will be given or can purchase for minimal amounts season's tickets on the shuttle buses.

One of the most popular of the sauntering and sitting areas will be the mile-long strolling street (somewhat on the order of Copenhagen's Strøget) which begins at the park blocks (one block nearer to town than the museums) and extends upward to the library and over the throughway—shops continue on the bridge as do those on the Ponte Vecchio over the Arno in Florence. There will be boutique and handicraft outlets, art studios, and coffee shops that will line this bridge on both sides. The roofs overhang to shield shoppers from rain. The center has islands of shade trees and benches alternated with clusters of tables and chairs outdoor-cafe style when the weather permits. Local business will help with the development of the strolling area and the shops. This is on the northern edge of the mall and borders the downtown shopping area. Everyone is welcome: tourists, shoppers from the suburbs—whoever may come.

The over-all plan of the New Community will provide in the Learning Mall activities for every group and areas for every activity. I shall start with some suggestions for the infants and the children—for the two reasons that this is the time when all of us start to become social and the young are the most underdeveloped in our contemporary society.

Children will begin in the nursery schools and the small playgrounds—learning to move from a dependence on home and mother to the independence of life in the world at large. Here they will learn the give-and-take of sharing, participating in experiences as rich and complex as they desire. Their mothers and fathers will be encouraged to participate with the children whenever possible. There will also be trained teachers, foster (or real) aunts, uncles, or grandparents, aides, older friends or brothers and sisters, and age mates.

Each nursery school will have only a small number of children (8-10), a small and attractive play area, protected yet open, with a sandbox and a sheltered deck for wheel toys and tricycles. These will be built in every area where there is the need.

Wherever there are children, play space is a necessity. Every three or four blocks in the areas where families live there will be a small play-park. Here will be swings, wooden climbing apparatus with a slide, a small playhouse or two as well as a patch of green lawn with pots or boxes of attractive flowers, benches and a table for mothers, shoppers, or kibbitzers, and a patio sheltered from the rain. Often these will serve as waiting stations for buses.

At three locations will be the larger play-parks, each with an enclosed adventure area. The latter will be built in the style that was originally developed outside Copenhagen by the famous landscape architect. C.Th. Sørenson, and was later adopted by other Scandinavian countries, the Swiss, and the English. Professor Sørenson had previously found that formally designed playgrounds often bored the children, that "installed" equipment did not let their bodies move enough or their minds soar, and that they needed protection from prying and directive adults so that they could learn freely.*

Each of the three large playgrounds in the New Community will differ from the others because all are continually in a process of development. Here is where the children will create their own environment out of old bricks and planks, ropes and tarps. They will work with real tools and try out the elements—experiencing earth, fire, air, and water. Here will be private places for youngsters to create their own worlds, where ramshackle dens can be built from used lumber draped with a tarp to keep out rain and more substantial clubhouses can be erected with the help of the play-park leader or some of his university or high school student aides. As William Jennings Bryan once said about voters: "People have a right to make their own mistakes." Children should be given enough rope, not enough to hang themselves, but certainly to hang *from*!

But young people will not be the only concern of the New Community—adults can also discover or develop something for every taste and need. The goal will be to foster a spirit of mutual helpfulness and a joy in learning among all groups—races, classes, men and women, rich and poor, young and old, the Social Leaders and the Creative Intellectuals. Shops, homes, museums, and the streets themselves will become arenas for learning and for establishing the bonds of friend-

---

*The best book I have ever read on playgrounds is Lady Marjorie Allen's *Planning for Play* (Cambridge, Massachusetts: MIT Press, 1969). All who read this will understand the humanizing role which adventure playgrounds can have in the lives of children.

ship. Arts will range from the alfresco street theater and wandering minstrels to the finished products of a craft center, a repertory theater, a conservatory, and a studio.

The arts can be practised in a cluster of shops and centers available for that purpose or they may be learned in the time-honored way: a young protegé working in an artist's studio, a child learning to quilt as her surrogate grandmother shows her how to cut and stitch the patches. A fine but small art museum, an excellent museum art school, the art department of a university, and the facilities of the public schools all offer other opportunities. Senior citizens, the handicapped, practising artists and craftsmen, and young people will all be involved in an infinite range of creative expression. Materials will be as natural as the forests, the sea, the rock outcroppings or, in contrast, they may be the products of the chemist's flask and cauldron—Styrofoam or spun copper. Block printing might be as intricately refined as the Japanese processes developed during the Edo period or as simple and direct as potato prints on farmers' feed sacks.

Leather tooling, batik printing, clay molding, silk screening—all will be available. Studying can proceed at the elbow of a friend or mentor, on the production line of a small shop, in a classroom, or by one's self with a book for guidance or nothing at all but one's wits. Critics will be one's age mates, one's seniors, or nonexistent—if the hypersensitive tyro so desires.

Nearby, what some would call the practical arts will find outlets for creative expression. The baker who specializes in French pastry may, if the youngest apprentice insists, try his hand at gingerbread sculpture. No one is surprised when a group of gourmet cooks take over the lower floor of a large house off the alley and gradually install modern stainless steel equipment at the same time as they collect nineteenth-century cooking utensils, molds, and trivets. Down the street there are looms of many sizes and levels of complexity and yarn colors which span the rainbow. A fabric shop next door serves as outlet for weaving, needlepoint, and embroidery and has the air of a comely hybrid—half Scotch House and half Scandinavian homecraft shop. The knitters prefer to be on their own with a circle of comfortable chairs and a program of reading to discuss. Often they are inspired to give a series of book reviews which nonknitters—seamstresses or even thumb-twiddlers—can attend. But the seamstresses and the tailoring buffs more frequently stay close to their bobbins and fitting forms. Costume design is a demanding art and especially so for those who work with the civic players. In fact the costumers often have more in common with the carpenters—particularly those who design stage sets.

Woodworkers stand somewhat between these arts and the skills of those who ply the mechanics' trade. The boys and men, and the rare young women (who inhabit the communal garage and tear down and build up cars)—during their mechanic's apprenticeship—often seem to have little time for anything else. They are encouraged, though, as are all in the community, to experiment with many forms of work and play. The inventors who often lock themselves in their solitary cells also have to be urged at times to try out and explore alternative activities. And occasionally even an overzealous hobbyist prefers seclusion. In contrast the denizens of the Rube Goldberg Center are a breed apart. Extrovertive and playful they vie for the public's attention.

For those who are devotees of what the English call the "fun of the fair" and who revel in the stunts and hilarity of the amusement park, there will be many of the offerings of a Tivoli. Games of chance, rides that leave one breathless, tests of one's skill and strength—darts, horseshoes, Indian wrestling, or Judo—all will have their place. A pantomime theater will have performances every summer evening; and here one will also find Punch and Judy, the Magic Man, and the dog and pony acts. There will be opportunities both for those who want "to get into the act" and for those who prefer to watch from an amused distance.

The noisier, flashier activities will be located in the zoo area, not near enough, of course, to disturb the animals—

although it will be remembered that some of the apes may enjoy the pratfalls of the Laurel-and-Hardy-type comedies and the "shoot-outs" of the Wild West shows. (Research has found that apes show a preference for Westerns when given a choice of TV programs although some also enjoy the majesty of nature—viz., Jane Goodall's report of the old ape who missed his evening snack because he was watching a sunset.) People who seek the more tranquil areas, the secluded alcoves, and the nature trails will also be shielded from the noise of the crowd. For them the roar of the lions and the whistle of the small zoo train (which can be heard in the distance when the wind is right) will be less disconcerting than the human carnival.

Many of the younger children will prefer the animals at the Walk-In Animal Park to the larger and more savage varieties which are viewed safely across a moat. However not all large animals are segregated. Many children enjoy riding the friendly elephant and the well-trained camel. At the Walk-In Park there is a Shetland pony for the less daring and a number of animals that children can help feed, and if they are so inclined, pet and cuddle.

Some of the smaller animals that enjoy this sort of thing can be adopted out for periods of time if the child and his parents, friends, or a teacher can arrange for a good temporary foster home. Aldous Huxley wrote in *Island* about MAC, the Mutual Adoption Corporation, which allowed children to go to live with parents' friends when tensions at home rose too high. This is an animal MAC which can test a child's readiness (or a parent's tolerance) for a pet. These young friends of the small animals may be the same ones who a few years later ask to be apprenticed to the zoo veterinarian and want to help with the baby animals and their mothers.

In contrast to the budding naturalists and ethologists the young physical scientists and engineers may prefer the Museum of Science and Industry and the planetarium. Here they can gain insights into the universe, the planet Earth, the evolution of species, and man's history as a toolmaker.

Ecologists and nature lovers have unlimited choices. There are many small gardens in backyards of the private sector where homeowners share choice blooms, rare herbs, and plant lore with apartment-dwellers who in turn help with the weeding, pruning, and digging. For those who prefer, there is the public domain—the borders along the malls, the beds and pots of flowers in the courtyards and squares or simply at street corners. Professional gardeners and the Green Thumb Crew will supply guidance, but most children and many adults will gladly adopt, as their own, projects which they will design and nourish. All will be encouraged to cooperate by working with a neighborhood group on plans for their own block or perhaps even with the New Community planners on a master design. At the same time everyone will be free to innovate in the area of their special interest—from tubs of petunias to hanging baskets of tuberous begonias.

Some will want to study the forms of Japanese gardens. A group may decide to design a Zen garden, complete with meditation platform and a pool with several spectacularly colored carp, perhaps direct descendants of those which swim in the pools of the Imperial Palace grounds in Tokyo. This will be a quiet, serene area for those who like the privacy of their thoughts and prefer to wander above the city noise. For others who so choose, there will be opportunities to study Japanese flower arrangement and, if they desire, to seek to understand its relation to Zen and to the tea ceremonies.

The Wilderness Club will also attract many of those who prefer to be far from the crowds. But more physical than metaphysical, they may wish to learn mountain climbing rather than to meditate. Others of a quiet disposition (neither the potential mystics of Katmandu nor those who carry an Everest in their knapsacks) will find abundant nature trails. Here plant species will be labeled by the neophyte botanists. Some of these will be content to participate in the labeling, but others will begin introducing new kinds of flora—if they find those that can be smoothly transplanted without disturbing the ecological balance.

There will be elements of mystery as well as guileless transparencies; light and shadow; tranquility and excitement. As a city school superintendent I worked with once said, the environment should "agitate the comfortable and comfort the agitated." For the resigned and world-weary middle-aged children who are still largely locked into the system of the schools, there will be whole new galaxies to discover in their free hours and on weekends and holidays. And gradually those hours called school time will change. Instead of adults telling them what is known, they will discover at the Museum of Science and Industry, at the planetarium, and on the nature trails what is unknown, what is intriguing and tangential, puzzling and problematical. But when the young people need to, they may always retreat into the comfort of the familiar, into the "old shoes" of established relationships.

They can visit their "faithful" friend the St. Bernard, stationed at the Rest Center and Student Sanctuary near the Park Blocks or the clusters of friendly goats in the children's Walk-In Animal Park. Others may return again and again to appreciate the mallards and the swans in the small lake below the Rose Garden, the racoons that live near the Log Cabin Conference Center at the beginning of the Wilderness Trail, and the peacocks that preen on the lawns of the old Masters Estate (open to visitors every afternoon). Some may prefer to visit their favorite nook in the library, the place where hassocks vary in height and upholstered platforms are arranged under cantilevered overhangs (maximum security when one reads a mystery), or their favorite tree where they can stretch out, dappled by sun and shade. Those whose main satisfactions are of a physical nature will be able to circle a racetrack on their bicycles at any one of the three major play-parks any hour of the day. And the more social will seek out a special friend who, even at eighty-six, always has time to listen to woes and share joys.

There is another kind of retreat besides that to the familiar and the known. This is the retreat that offers solitude and a chance to discover oneself. The inward and contemplative need private places where they can be alone and seek out new parts of themselves and come near, at times, to the core of their beings. New forms of relationships, new communities, new worlds can be dreamed about in recesses within many of the private and public gardens or in the shelter of small enclosures or gazebos. These, like other havens or activity areas, can be spoken for in advance. The young and their elders can be "scheduled in." Through analysis of the use of locations and areas (the computer specialists can tell us how) we will more adequately understand what appeals to young and old and those of varying temperaments. It is to be expected, however, that there will be many changes in preference as all come to know themselves better, as new possibilities are introduced, and as growth in character proceeds.

A child who has never had a room of his own, never lived below the third floor in an apartment building, never seen his mother put flowers in a vase, may not be aware of how much he enjoys plants until he goes on tours of the gardens and plays among the mazes built from planter boxes that are burgeoning with flowers in the malls. One day when the florist and his wife talk about their work, he realizes that he loves them and the beautiful, fragile, exciting blossoms with which they work.

A small girl, just seven, lived with her parents and grand-mother in a turn-of-the-century mansion near Washington Park. But she could do nothing for herself, and she had never been really dirty. She could not even comfort herself by turning to books since she could not read. Intelligent enough, she was hopelessly constrained by the fear of making mistakes. Within weeks after entering the learning community both she and her grandmother became converts to "creative art." They raced through finger paints and papier-mâché into pottery which they coiled and "threw" with gusto. At this point the child felt secure enought to take leave of her grandmother and degenerated (or was uplifted) into digging and burrowing with the sandpile crowd, a stage she had never gone through. Grandmother was relieved and found herself drawn to ever more detailed studies of clays and glazes. A natural scholar, but thwarted by years of social duties—entertainment in the grand style—she could at last let her mind follow its own lead.

Increasingly we see that more of the private sector becomes public domain. A New Community will be created by building bridges across what once were social chasms. Generations will come together in the spirit of mutual aid. All will gain. The older couple in the large house with the gracious gardens and the fine library will find that by sharing their premises (always on their own terms and with those who also respect books and flowers) they have made new friends—usually not of their generation or of their class—who are quick to offer help when they are ill. Messages are carried, the temperamental collie gets her daily walks, the telephone is answered, a hot meal is brought in each evening.

Children, too, benefit from closing the gap. Some may find an endless source of inspiration in books as did Dolci when he discovered reading (at age 15) and through this met his "kin"—Plato, Shakespeare, Goethe, Ibsen, the Buddha, Dante, Tolstoy. Others, looking for their kin, may find a great talent. Brian was a quiet recluse of a child, apparently always in search of something. As a small boy he was continually underfoot and in the way. He seemed to be lost but no one could ascertain from what. Only when he listened to music—and he had begun keeping time with his rattle before he could sit up—did he seem content, to find that for which he searched.

When he entered school he was already reading and now made his quests more apparent by posing unanswerable questions to his parents and teachers. Finally he asked his mother the supreme question, "Who are my parents?" She stumbled and gulped, "What do you mean?" He replied that he knew that she and his father couldn't be—it wasn't that they weren't nice people, it was just that he had so little in common with them. His father, after all, preferred baseball games to symphonies and neither of his parents had ever bothered to acquire a record collection.

Taken off guard, Brian's mother informed him he was adopted and when pressed, added that his mother was a local barmaid. Nothing would do but that Brian meet her. The result was bitterly disappointing. Brian, slender, sensitive, and pale with flaming red hair, had nothing in common with the well-upholstered, plainspoken woman who preferred listening to the truckers play the one-armed bandits to hearing Toscanini or even Mantovani. She confessed that she had no idea who Brian's father was. After this encounter the boy was more lost in the world than ever.

When he was ten, however, and was already playing the piano creditably by ear, Michael (a young music major in the university who was also at the Learning Center) noticed him as they both listened to Brahms with rapt attention. The music was being played by a string quartet which performed every other day in a small pavilion in the gardens of the library. Michael had never seen a child so engrossed: Brian stayed for both performances and seemed unaware of anyone around him. The friendship blossomed and Michael introduced Brian to professors in the music department. Soon the ten-year-old sat in on the composition classes and turned out promising work from the beginning. By the time Brian was fourteen the junior symphony was playing his compositions.

Eventually Brian found that he had much in common with the young poets who clustered at the paperback bookshop-cum-cafe. They, too, read mythology with insatiable appetites, and asked each other questions about the creative unconscious as well as the darker forces that bar the way to higher humanity. Particularly Brian was drawn to those who discussed Plato's view of Reminiscence—perhaps it was in these memories of what went before that he would find his own origins. In the poetry of cosmic consciousness, first Blake and then Emerson, Thoreau, and Whitman, he found much that pointed to what and who he was.

Nearly all of the young poets and writers, *all* of the serious ones, were reading addicts. Generally they had learned to read early and at some time in their childhood or teens had spent hour upon hour in the library reading in great gulps and often with no sense of discrimination. They too perhaps searched for their kin, as Brian and Dolci had done, and for the answers to all the perennial questions that seem to crowd into the minds of the philosophically inclined. Willingly they let themselves be carried away to the new worlds which every "educated imagination" offers to every other one.

Near the bookshops and the library-cultural center is a small printing shop which turns out two biweekly news-magazines. One of these simply publishes the news of the New Community. Expanding the concept of what is "fit to print" it includes poetry, essays, and impressionistic writing as well as reviews of theater, music, art, and the wide array of other planned and unplanned events. The announcements of model-plane flying tournaments are printed side by side with the feature story on the Wandering Minstrels. Everything, really, as the editor says, that has "relevance and merit and readability" is included.

The other journal belongs to that species of publication which has been called the "adversary press." In the tone of these little newspapers (weeklies, biweeklies, and monthlies) it questions and challenges the culture and the society. But, in keeping with the spirit of the New Community, it is not merely critical. As many essays of advocacy are published as of admonition. Front-page space is given to muckraking exposés but also to the bus driver who plants a garden in the vacant lot at the end of his run and to the one-armed dog catcher, a former logger, who is conducting a crusade for beauty in a seaside town by planting and caring for deserted corners and parking strips.

True, the oil company whose tankers polluted the bay is excoriated; but in the next column is the account of two retired librarians, friends who live together, who make it their mission to learn about every newcomer within a four-block area and to welcome them with coffee and fresh-baked cookies. When needed, they offer to be babysitters, and they introduce the newcomers to the array of possibilities that the New Community offers.

This sketch of the New Community is not intended to be complete. It is no more than an impression of the atmosphere, the purpose, the flavor. Here is a liberating environment, both evocative and responsive. People take part because they feel free to explore and invent, to work and to play. Gradually they learn courage and persistence, tolerance of diversity, as well as self-reliance. The New Community can satisfy the inherent curiosity of each and stimulate learning of all kinds—of the muscles, the senses, the mind, and the spirit.

This concept, then, which is a new ecological design as well as a vision of human growth, unites three of the themes of this book:

That every person has great undiscovered potentialities which need to and can be actualized;

That the highly gifted who are everywhere require special encouragement, since their creative imaginations can lead to higher levels of civilization;

And that humanity has reached a time when our most urgent common need is social creativity.

To develop our best talents in the direction of altruism and mutual aid was never more important than now. In the values revolution which has gained momentum in the last ten years, the evidence multiplies that this truth is increasingly, although not always consciously, recognized. And it is chiefly the young who are searching, as Thoreau did before them, for ways to live out their principles in accordance with a higher ethic. There is a renewed search for self-expression and individuality but within what Ruth Benedict called a synergistic society. The great hope is that everyone can be himself and yet develop a common humanity.

XXIV • Conclusion and Commencement, Requiem and Renewal

If the present age is to be a great creative era—and it must be or we will not survive—creativity must be expressed in the genre appropriate for the age. Athens of the fifth century, B.C. and the Italian Renaissance were times of extraordinary artistic originality, and their art forms have survived as an inspiration for all times. The Age of Science has produced unparalleled insights into the nature of matter and things. But now we have entered a new period which demands social creativity, and the focus is becoming ever clearer. If this age continues without disaster intervening, this will be the era of human transcendence—the rebirth of humanism in a more noble and elevated form.

These new forms must be invented. It is, as we have seen, in fields of diversity (and perhaps adversity) that creativity flowers. Polarities coming together give off creative sparks, as does the connection of positively and negatively charged wires. Opposites attract as well as repel. Transitions and closures occur—at least in creative minds—when all manner of incompatibilities are brought together. Aldous Huxley tells how this happens in music and art. The antiphonies become symphonies. Several themes come together and these differences combine into something new: "The nearest approach to a demonstration of the doctrine of the Trinity [Huxley observed] is a Fugue or a good piece of Counterpoint." This kind of music, rich and intricate, has an allure for the most gifted minds. Mike Grost did not discover music until in his mid-teens, when he was well along in college, he started listening to Wanda Landowska. Somehow the complexity of the fugue, tone upon tone, opened his mind to the splendors of music and he began listening by the hour to the great classics of past centuries.

Painting, too, as Huxley pointed out, can offer, "simultaneity of incompatibilities." A Van Gogh landscape can depict the flowing serenity of undulating hills and olive trees set against tormented brushwork and passionate violence of color. In the landscape art of the Sung dynasty the very essence of the human feeling—deep and mystical—is portrayed as a vivid contrast to the nonhuman otherness and outwardness of the landscape, the hills and clouds in which man can only be seen with a magnifying glass. Similarly the Oriental gardens have always brought together contrasting elements—simplicity and elegance, openness and distance, water tumbling with abandon over rocks or standing still and deep.

The creative insight comes at that moment when the unlike and the unlikely join and become compatible and comely. This happens in an instant, in the "moment of being." It is the intuitive flash, the split second when insight arrives and all is clear, when of a sudden everything fits and makes sense. Polarities join. Divergencies unify. In nature the lion lies down with the lamb. In physics (via the complementarity principle) the particle lies down with the wave. And, as the popular book and film tell the story, the dot falls in love with the line.*

*Norton Juster, *The Dot and the Line* (New York: Random House, 1963).

This creative fusion can only occur in a genuine version at a moment of love. Otherwise it is contrived and mechanical.

Young people who describe themselves as citizens of the world, who see a need for larger unities than the nation states, understand with Kipling (in *Gunga Din*) that "there is neither East nor West, border nor breed nor birth." They read this to mean that armed conflict is archaic, and would probably rewrite Kipling to say that "all men are neighbors, though they come from the ends of the earth."

These unions of differences, these creative junctions, are usually sudden and brief. The insight arrives unheralded; if it is not captured, it often goes again as quickly as it came. These moments have been reported as peak experiences, as oceanic feelings, as a time of cosmic consciousness—when "the doors of perception are cleansed" and a oneness with the infinite is sensed.

But despite the fact that insights come and go, they are also continuous. The new one builds on the old and the result is an ever enlarging whole. The individual adds a new facet, he or she approaches "infinite variety"; and it is this which supplies vitality and excitement, a newness and a freshness much like that offered by Gothic art. Each gargoyle was carved by a different craftsman, as Ruskin tells us in "The Stones of Venice," with the feeling of love and the necessary inexactitude and imperfection which come from a highly personal and creative action.

The very imperfection and unfinished nature of these moments of insight allow for uncertainty, a promise that something lies beyond awaiting new discoveries, and an ever enlarging realm of the known and the unknown. These people who are complex and inconsistent tend to inspire and delight others. In fact they surprise themselves and thus find joy in their own company. Solitude for them, as Wordsworth knew, can be creative. Their hearts "with pleasure fill" and they can warm themselves by their own flame.

Such people love everything, large and small. They prize the complex, the subtle, the new, and the mysterious while, at the same time, they return to the simple, the obvious, and the old. A blade of grass holds an infinity of delight. They come to feel, as Thoreau did, that if the birds and flowers try them by their standard they will not be found wanting. Nothing palls because each experience is fresh. The context is new, the eyes see with continuously renewed vision.

Youth, particularly the Creative Intellectuals among them, understand all of this. There is general agreement that "The time is out of joint"; but, unlike young Hamlet who railed against his fate—"Oh! cursed spite," today's young plunge in with determination to "set it right!"

Bibliography

Addams, Jane, *The Spirit of Youth in the City Streets*. New York, The Macmillan Company, 1909.

Allport, Gordon, *Becoming*. New Haven, Yale University Press, 1955.

Axline, Virginia M., *Dibs in Search of Self*. New York, Ballantine Books, 1964.

Barron, Frank, *Creativity and Personal Freedom*. New York, Van Nostrand, 1968.

Beauvoir, Simone de, *The Second Sex*. New York, Alfred A. Knopf, 1952.

Becker, Ernest, *Beyond Alienation*. New York, Braziller, 1967.

Bruner, Jerome, *On Knowing: Essays for the Left Hand*. Cambridge, Harvard University Press, 1962.

Buber, Martin, From Herbert Read's translation of a lecture which Buber gave on the concept of creativity at Heidelberg in 1925. See Read's *Education Through Art*. London, Faber and Faber Ltd., 1963.

——, *I and Thou*. New York, Charles Scribner's, 1958.

Bucke, Richard, *Cosmic Consciousness*. New York, E. P. Dutton & Co., original copyright 1901, 19th edition, 1959.

Camus, Albert, *Resistance, Rebellion, and Death*. New York, Alfred A. Knopf, 1961.

Cross, Patricia, *Beyond the Open Door.* San Francisco, Jossey-Bass,
    1971. (See especially the chapter, "Women as New Students.")
Dale, Edgar, *How to Read a Newspaper.* New York, Scott-Foresman
    and Company, 1941.
Dewey, John, *Experience in Education.* New York, The Macmillan
    Company, 1953.
——, *Freedom and Culture.* New York, G. P. Putnam's Sons, 1939.
——, *Art As Experience.* New York, Putnam's Capricorn Books, 1958.
Drews, Elizabeth Monroe, *The Creative Intellectual Style in Gifted
    Adolescents.* Vols. I, II, and III. Lansing, Michigan State
    University, 1964, 1965, 1966.
——— and Leslie Lipson, *Values and Humanity.* New York, St. Martin's
    Press, 1971.
Dubos, René, *Torch of Life.* New York, Simon and Schuster, 1962.
Eiseley, Loren, *The Immense Journey.* New York, Random House,
    1957.
——, *The Firmament of Time.* New York, Atheneum, 1960.
——, *Being and Becoming,* (film, produced by Elizabeth Drews), 1962.
Ellis, Julie, *Revolt of the Second Sex.* New York, A Lancer Book,
    1970.
Emerson, Ralph Waldo, *The Complete Essays and Other Writings.*
    Brooks Atkinson ed., New York, Random House, 1940.
Farson, Richard, "Rage of Women," *Look,* December 16, 1969.
Frankl, Viktor, *Man's Search for Meaning.* Boston, Beacon Press, 1963.
Freedman, Mervin, *The College Experience.* San Francisco, Jossey-Bass,
    1967.
Friedan, Betty, *The Feminine Mystique.* New York, W. W. Norton &
    Company, 1963.
Fromm, Erich, *The Art of Loving.* New York, Bantam Books, 1956.
Frye, Northrop, *The Educated Imagination.* Bloomington, Indiana
    University, 1964.
Gabor, Dennis, *Inventing the Future.* New York, Alfred A. Knopf,
    1964.
Gardner, John, *Excellence: Can We Be Equal and Excellent Too?* New
    York, Harper & Row, 1961.
——, *Self-Renewal.* New York, Harper & Row, 1964.
Glasser, William, *Schools Without Failure.* New York, Harper & Row,
    1969.
Goodman, Paul, *Compulsory Miseducation.* New York, Horizon Press,
    1964.
——, "The Present Moment in Education." *New York Review of
    Books,* April 10, 1969. pp. 13-24.

Gross, Ronald and Beatrice, eds., *Radical School Reform*. New York, Simon and Schuster, 1969.

Harman, Willis, "Explorations in Human Potentiality:A Graduate Seminar on Human Potentiality at Stanford University" in Herbert A. Otto, ed., *Explorations in Human Potentiality*. Springfield, Illinois, Charles C. Thomas, 1966.

Robert Havighurst has had a long-time interest in the gifted. Some of his thinking on the adolescent which I have found particularly helpful is in Robert Peck and Robert Havighurst, *The Psychology of Character Development*. New York, John Wiley & Sons, 1960.

Heist, Paul, *The Creative College Student*. San Francisco, Jossey-Bass, 1968.

Helson, Ravenna, "Women Mathematicians and the Creative Personality," *Journal of Consulting and Clinical Psychology*, 1971, Vol. 36, pp. 210-20.

Henry, Jules, *Culture Against Man*. New York, Random House,

Herndon, James, *The Way It Spozed To Be*. New York, Simon and Schuster, 1968.

Hollingworth, Leta, *Gifted Children, Their Nature and Nurture*. New York, The Macmillan Company, 1926.

Holt, John, *How Children Learn*. New York, Pitman Publishing Corp., 1967, and other books.

Huxley, Aldous, *The Perennial Philosophy*. Cleveland, The World Publishing Co., Meridian Books, 1962.

——, *Island*. New York, Harper & Row, 1962.

Jackson, Philip, *Life in Classrooms*. New York, Holt, Rinehart and Winston, 1968.

James, William, *The Energies of Man*. New York, Moffat, Yard, and Co., 1913.

Jersild, Arthur, *In Search of Self*. New York, Bureau of Publications, Teachers College, Columbia University, 1965.

Johnson, Wendell, *People in Quandaries, The Semantics of Adjustment*. New York, Harper & Row, 1946.

Jourard, Sidney, *The Transparent Self*. New York, D. Van Nostrand Company, 1964.

——, *Disclosing Man to Himself*. New York, D. Van Nostrand Company, 1968.

Keller, Helen, *The Story of My Life*. Garden City, New York, Doubleday & Company, 1922.

Kropotkin, Peter, *Mutual Aid, A Factor of Evolution*. New York, Alfred A. Knopf, 1925.

Krutch, Joseph Wood, *Thoreau.* Clifton, N.J., William Sloane
    Associates, 1948.
Laing, Ronald, *The Politics of Experience and the Bird of Paradise.*
    Baltimore, Penguin Books, 1967.
Laubach, Frank, *Teaching the World to Read.* New York, Friendship
    Press, 1949.
Lipson, Leslie, *The Democratic Civilization.* New York, Oxford
    University Press, 1964.
——, *The Great Issues of Politics*, 4th ed. Englewood Cliffs, New
    Jersey, Prentice-Hall, 1970.
Mackinnon, Donald, "The Nature and Nurture of Creative Talent" in
    Dael Wolfle, ed., *The Discovery of Talent*. Cambridge, Mass.,
    Harvard University Press, 1969.
Mannes, Marya, *More in Anger.* Philadelphia, J. B. Lippincott
    Company, 1958.
Maslow, A. H., *Motivation and Personality.* New York, Harper and
    Bros., 1954.
——, *New Knowledge in Human Values.* New York, Harper and Bros.,
    1959.
——, *Toward a Psychology of Being*, 1st ed. New York, D. Van
    Nostrand Company, 1962.
——, *The Psychology of Science.* New York, Harper & Row, 1966.
May, Rollo, *Love and Will.* New York, W. W. Norton & Company,
    1969.
Mead, Margaret, *Continuities in Cultural Evolution.* New Haven, Yale
    University Press, 1966.
Mill, John S., *On Liberty.*
——, *The Subjection of Women.*
Mills, C. Wright, *The Power Elite.* New York, Oxford University Press,
    1956.
——, *The Sociological Imagination.* New York, Oxford University
    Press, 1959.
Montagu, Ashley, *The Human Revolution.* Cleveland, The World
    Publishing Co., 1965.
Montessori, Marie. See biographies: Standing, E. M., *Maria Montessori*,
    London, Hollis & Carter, 1957; and Smaridge, Norah, *The Light
    Within: The Story of Maria Montessori,* New York, Hawthorn
    Books, 1965.
Morgan, Arthur E., *The Small Community.* New York, Harper and
    Bros., 1942.
——, *The Long Road.* Yellow Springs, Ohio, Community Service, Inc.,
    1962.

Neill, A. S., *Summerhill; A Radical Approach to Child Rearing.* New York, Hart Publishing Co., 1960.

Platt, J. R., "The Coming Generation of Genius," *Horizon,* March, 1962. pp. 70-75.

——, *The Step to Man.* New York, John Wiley & Sons, 1966.

Polanyi, Michael, *Personal Knowledge.* Chicago, University of Chicago Press, 1958.

——, *The Tacit Dimension.* New York, Doubleday & Company, 1966.

Priestley, J. B., *Margin Released.* New York, Harper & Row, 1962.

Read, Herbert, *Education Through Art.* London, Faber and Faber Ltd., 1963.

Reich, Charles A., *The Greening of America.* New York, Random House, 1970.

Roberts, Catherine, *The Scientific Conscience.* New York, Braziller, 1967.

Rogers, Carl, *On Becoming a Person.* Boston, Houghton Mifflin Company, 1961.

——, and Barry Stevens, *Person to Person—The Problem of Being Human.* Lafayette, California, Real People Press, 1967.

Rokeach, Milton, *The Open and Closed Mind.* New York, Basic Books, 1960.

Roosevelt, Eleanor, Chairman of the Commission on Human Rights which drafted *The Universal Declaration of Human Rights: A Standard of Achievement,* United Nations, 1958.

Roszak, Theodore, *The Making of a Counter Culture.* New York, Doubleday & Co., Anchor Books, 1969.

Rousseau, Jean Jacques, *Emile.*

——, *Confessions.*

Russell, Bertrand, *The Conquest of Happiness.* New York, Bantam, 1968.

Schweitzer, Albert, *Reverence for Life.* New York, Harper & Row, 1969.

Silberman, Charles, *Crisis in the Classroom.* New York, Random House, 1969.

Sorokin, Pitirim, *The Ways and Power of Love.* Chicago, Henry Regnery Co., Gateway ed., 1967.

Terman, Lewis, *Genetic Studies of Genius,* Vols. I, III, IV, and V. Palo Alto, Stanford University Press, 1926 ff.

Thompson, Watson, *Turning Into Tomorrow.* New York, Philosophical Library, 1966.

Thoreau, Henry David, *Walden and Other Essays.*

Tillich, Paul, *The Courage to Be.* New Haven, Yale University Press, 1965.

Torrance, Paul, *Gifted Children in the Classroom.* New York, The
    Macmillan Company, 1965.
Troyat, Henry, *Tolstoy.* New York, Doubleday, 1967.
"Utopia," *Daedalus,* Vol. 94, Spring, 1965.
Whitehead, Alfred North, *Aims of Education and Other Essays.*
    Glencoe, Illinois, Free Press, 1967.
Whitman, Walt, *Leaves of Grass.*
Wordsworth, William, *The Collected Works.*

Index